# Future Health Organisations and Systems

# Future Health Organisations and Systems

Edited by

**Sandra Dawson**

and

**Charlotte Sausman**

Foreword by John Wyn Owen

First published 2005 by
PALGRAVE MACMILLAN
Houndmills, Basingstoke, Hampshire RG21 6XS and
175 Fifth Avenue, New York, N. Y. 10010
Companies and representatives throughout the world

PALGRAVE MACMILLAN is the global academic imprint of the
Palgrave Macmillan division of St. Martin's Press, LLC and of
Palgrave Macmillan Ltd. Macmillan® is a registered trademark in
the United States, United Kingdom and other countries. Palgrave is
a registered trademark in the European Union and other countries.

ISBN-13: 978–1–4039–1752–2   hardback
ISBN-10: 1–4039–1752–3       hardback

This book is printed on paper suitable for recycling and made
from fully managed and sustained forest sources.

A catalogue record for this book is available from the British Library.

Library of Congress Cataloging-in-Publication Data

Future health organisations and systems / edited by Sandra
Dawson and Charlotte Sausman; foreword by John Wyn Owen.
    p. cm.
    Includes bibliographical references and index.
    ISBN 1–4039–1752–3 (cloth)
    1. Medical care–Great Britain–Forecasting. 2. Health care
reform–Great Britain. 3. National health services–Great Britain.
4. Medical policy–Great Britain. I. Dawson, Sandra. II. Sausman,
Charlotte, 1970–

RA395.G7F88 2005
362.1'0425'0941–dc22                                    2004060613

10   9   8   7   6   5   4   3   2   1
14  13  12  11  10  09  08  07  06  05

Printed and bound in Great Britain by
Antony Rowe Ltd, Chippenham and Eastbourne

# Contents

# Tables

# Figures

# Foreword

This collection of essays provides a significant commentary on the shape of UK health systems, focusing on systems and complexity, on policies and strategies and people and knowledge. It is a companion volume to *The Future Health Workforce*, edited by Celia Davis and published in 2003. Both books have their origin in a conference organised under the auspices of the Policy Futures programme, supported by the Nuffield Trust and held in September 2002 at the Judge Institute of Management at the University of Cambridge. The Policy Futures programme informs ongoing policy discussion at the Nuffield Trust. The work represented in this book is contributing to *Policy Futures Mark 2* which will be published as a pathfinder consultation document in November 2004 and definitively in the early summer of 2005.

The objectives of our policy futures projects are to encourage and develop new ways of thinking about health, to explore influences on UK health and policy implications in terms of where UK health should be in 2020, to scan and anticipate developments in the health environment, and to evaluate current and planned policy developments in the light of the outcome scanning.

The challenge of the period ahead will be the emerging burden of chronic disease as the population ages, rising costs driven by new medical technologies and pharmaceuticals, and a need to focus more on prevention and primary healthcare. Against this background current policy and political imperatives require governments to increase patient choice whilst maintaining equitable access despite increasing pressure on health budgets and rising expectations. Ensuring the sustainability of financing will be a key challenge for government, but equally governments will have to address how health systems can be designed and managed to enable the private sector to play a greater role.

These emerging systems must meet multiple objectives including maximising health gain, equitable distribution and efficient use of resources, improvements in service quality as well as acceptable levels of accountability. Ultimate responsibility for the overall performance of the whole health system lies with government but a new role is emerging – that of overseer and trustee rather than operational manager – what WHO terms 'stewardship'. Stewardship entails setting direction by formulating health policy, defining vision and establishing clear performance indicators in conjunction with consumers and the wider public, exerting influence through regulation and advocacy particularly as decreasing central control requires greater independence, and finally collecting and utilising intelligence by identifying and transferring innovation and good practice across the systems.

This set of essays is a contribution to improving understanding of some of the matters that have to be addressed in and around the vision for future health systems, their operating environment and the assessment of risk. In short, effective health systems in the future will need to be more focused on healthy people and prevention, capable of providing patient choice, able to address inequity, resilient, adaptive, ultimately sustainable and supported by a robust evidence base for decision making to transfer what works intelligently from research to practice.

John Wyn Owen CB
Secretary
Nuffield Trust
July 2004

# Acknowledgements

Grateful thanks are due to many people beyond the writers who have contributed selflessly to secure the completion of this book. Marie Anne Kyne Lilley organised the conference at which these papers were first discussed; she was subsequently joined by Linda Chang, Kay Fieldhouse and Clare Robertson in providing transcription, editorial and research assistance as the chapters were revised several times. We are indebted to the Nuffield Trust under the guidance of two successive chairmen, Sir Maurice Shock and Sir Denis Pereira Gray, and secretary John Wyn Owen for funding, inspiration and guidance in the work. As always family and friends have been generous in their priceless support.

SANDRA DAWSON
Cambridge, August 2004

# The Authors: Contact Details

**Linda Rosenstrøm Chang**, BSc BA MA, is a research assistant at the Judge Institute of Management. Contact details: Judge Institute of Management, Trumpington Street, Cambridge, CB2 1AG, UK; phone: +44 (0)1223 339 649; email: lrc29@cam.ac.uk

**Joan Costa-Font**, PhD, is research fellow at LSE Health and Social Care and reader in Applied Economics at the University of Barcelona. Contact address: LSE Health and Social Care, London School of Economics and Political Science, Houghton Street, London WC2A 2AE; phone: 020 790 6484; fax: 020 7955 6803; email: j.costa-font@lse.ac.uk.

**Penny Dash**, MA, MSc, MBA, MB BS, MRCP is an independent advisor in healthcare, a former head of strategy at the Department of Health, and a senior associate of the Judge Institute of Management, University of Cambridge. Contact details: Judge Institute of Management, Trumpington Street, Cambridge, CB2 1AG, UK; email: pennydash@aol.com.

**Sandra Dawson**, DBE, MACantab, BA, FCGI, CIMgt, DSc (Hon), MFPH (Hon), is director of the Judge Institute of Management, KPMG Professor of Management and Master of Sidney Sussex College, University of Cambridge. Contact details: Judge Institute of Management, Trumpington Street, Cambridge CB2 1AG, UK; phone: +44 (0)1223 339590; fax: 01123 339601; email: s.dawson@jims.cam.ac.uk

**Mark de Rond**, DPhil, Oxon is university lecturer in Strategy at the Judge Institute of Management, University of Cambridge. Contact details: Judge Institute of Management, Trumpington Street, Cambridge, CB2 1AG, UK; phone: +44 (0)1223 764135; fax: +44 (0)1223 339701; email: mejd3@cam.ac.uk

**Ian Greener**, BA, PhD is Lecturer in Management at the University of York. Contact details: Department of Management Studies, University of York, York, YO10 5DD, UK; phone: +44 (0)1904 434651; fax: 01904 433431; email: ig6@york.ac.uk

**Scott L. Greer**, BA, PhD is research fellow at the Constitution Unit, University College London, and leader of the Devolution and Health

Project, supported by the Nuffield and Leverhulme Trusts. Contact details: The Constitution Unit, School of Public Policy, 29/30 Tavistock Square, London WC1H 9QU; phone +44 (0) 207679 4977; email: s.greer@ucl.ac.uk

**Karen Jochelson**, DPhil, Oxon, MBA, London is research fellow in the King's Fund's Health Policy – Public Health Programme. Contact details: The King's Fund, 11–13 Cavendish Square, London, W1G 0AN UK; phone: +44 (0)20 7307 2663; fax: 020 7307 2810; email: kjochelson@kingsfund.org.uk

**Justin Keen**, BSc, MSc, PhD, Professor of Health Politics and Information Management, Nuffield Institute for Health, University of Leeds; phone: +44 (0)113 343 6941; fax: +44 (0)113 343 6348; email: j.keen@leeds.ac.uk

**Graham Lister**, PhD, MSc, BSc is senior associate at The Nuffield Trust and secretary of the UK Partnership for Global Health www.ukglobalhealth.org. Contact details: The Nuffield Trust, 59 New Cavendish Street, London W1G 7LP UK; phone: +44 (0)1753 889201; fax: 01753 889200; email: G_C-Lister@msn.com

**Annabelle L. Mark**, MSc, FHM, FRSM is Professor of Healthcare Organisation at Middlesex University Business School, and research associate at the Oxford Healthcare Management Institute, Templeton College, Oxford. She is the founding academic of the biennial conference Organisational Behaviour in Healthcare. Contact details: Middlesex University Business School, The Burroughs, Hendon NW4 4BT UK; phone: +44 (0)20 8411 5857; fax: 020 8202 1539: email: a.mark@mdx.ac.uk

**Zoë Slote Morris**, BSc(Econ), Diploma, PhD, is the Nuffield Fellow in Health Policy at the Judge Institute of Management, University of Cambridge. Contact details: Judge Institute of Management, Trumpington Street, Cambridge CB2 1AG UK; phone: +44 (0)1223 339 609; email: zsm20@cam.ac.uk

**Elias Mossialos**, PhD, is Brian Abel Smith Professor at the Department of Social Policy at the London School of Economics, and co-director of LSE Health and Social Care. Contacting address: LSE Health and Social Care, London School of Economics and Political Science, Houghton Street, London WC2A 2AE; phone: 020 790 7564; Fax: 020 7955 6803; email: e.a.mossialos@lse.ac.uk

**Calum Paton**, MA (Oxon) MPP (Harvard) DPhil(Oxon) is Professor of Health Policy and director of the Centre for Health Planning and Management at Keele University. He is also Chairman of the University Hospital of North Staffordshire NHS Trust. Contact details: Centre for Health Policy and Management, Keele University, Keele, Staffordshire ST5 5BG UK; phone: +44 (0)1782 517190; email: c.paton@keele.ac.uk

**Michael Rigby**, BA, FSS is reader in the Centre for Health Planning and Management, Keele University. Contact details: Centre for Health Planning and Management, Darwin Building, Keele University, Keele, Staffordshire, ST5 5BG, UK; phone: +44 (0) 1782 583193; fax: +44 (0) 1782 711737; email: m.j.rigby@hpm.keele.ac.uk

**Wendy A. Rogers**, BM.BS, BAHons, PhD, MRCGP, FRACGP is Associate Professor of Medical Ethics and Health Law at Flinders University, Adelaide, Australia. She would like to thank NHMRC for funding support (Fellowship ID 007129). Contact details: Department of Medical Education, Flinders University, GPO Box 2100, Adelaide SA 5001, Australia; phone: +61 (0)8 8204 3132; fax: +61 (0)8 8204 5675; email: wendy.rogers@flinders.edu.au

**Charlotte Sausman** (née Dargie) PhD MA is a senior research associate at the Judge Institute of Management Studies. Contact details: c.Sausman@jims.cam.ac.uk; phone: +44 (0) 1223 870803.

**Jeremy Wyatt**, DM FRCP F(ACMI) deputy director of R&D at the National Institute of Clinical Excellence (NICE) in London. He is also a visiting professor in Medical Informatics at the Academic Medical Centre, University of Amsterdam and also holds a position at the Centre for Evidence Based Medicine in Oxford.

**Derek Yach**, MBChB MPH is Professor of Public Health, Yale University. Contact details: Department of Epidemiology and Public Health, Yale University, New Haven, Connecticut, USA; email: derek.yach@yale.edu

# Abbreviations

A number of abbreviations, which may be unfamiliar, appear regularly in this volume. These include:

CHAI      Commission for Health Audit and Inspection
CHI      Commission for Health Improvement
EHR      Electronic Health Record
EPR      Electronic Patient Record
GP      General Practitioner (medical doctor)
HpfIT      Health Plan for Information Technology
ICT      Information and Communication Technology
NHS      National Health Service
NHSIIMS      National Health Service Information and Information Management Strategy
NICE      National Institute for Clinical Excellence
NSF      National Service Framework
PCT      Primary Care Trust
PFI      Private Finance Initiative
PPP      public–private partnership
SARS      Severe Acute Respiratory Syndrome
SHA      Strategic Health Authority
UN      United Nations
WHO      World Health Organisation

# Introduction

*Sandra Dawson*

The story of UK health systems in the first decade of the 21st century is one of diversity and change. Still dominated by National Health Services, contemporary UK health systems were created in 1946 in the immediate post-war period to provide stability, security and prosperity to the population as part of the welfare state. Today many of the institutions and structures that were established in the post-war period remain in the modern NHS, and yet society has changed. There is greater diversity and strength in public expectations and in expressed and latent needs for health and healthcare services. There is greater diversity and strength in the industrial, scientific and professional circles, which generate at increasing rates opportunities for spending money based on claims to improve health and healthcare. The NHS has to try to meet this multiplicity of demands whilst maintaining its founding principles of universality, and treatment on the basis of need, free at the point of demand.

The purpose of this collection is to examine some of the changes taking place in UK health organisations and systems and to understand how they may impact upon and be interpreted in the future. It also aims to present some new ideas that may be influential in determining future patterns of organisation and performance.

The book is divided into three Parts. Each Part is approached by examining aspects of health and healthcare through a different lens, which highlights particular facets, opportunities and tensions as we look to the future.

The first Part with papers by Sausman and Dawson, Yach, Paton, Lister and Greer examines issues through a lens that scans whole systems and reveals the complexity from which our hopes and fears of the future spring.

1

In Chapter 1 Charlotte Sausman and Sandra Dawson examine the shape of the UK health system through a summary analysis of four dimensions. The first is ownership, which embraces funding, organisation and accountability. The second is scope, with particular questions being raised about appropriate emphasis for investment and spending on different stages in life cycles, between social, welfare and healthcare, and in terms of the balance between sickness and health. The third dimension is the range, interests and influence of clinical, managerial, political and general public stakeholders. The fourth and last dimension to be discussed is dynamics of the health system itself, including the mechanisms and influences which drive the system. These include subjects, which will also be the focus of subsequent chapters, namely: costs, public expectations, political expediency, information systems, industrial structures and values.

In Chapter 2 Derek Yach challenges us to think beyond healthcare to health and provides an international perspective on the UK. Immediately this requires that special attention is paid to tobacco, nutrition and lack of physical activity, since these are vitally important determinants of disease patterns and as such are different to the determinants of individual cases of death and disability.

In the main, risk factors outside the healthcare system determine the incidence of disease, whereas the response of healthcare systems through diagnosis, treatment and care systems as they impact on individuals, explain levels of case fatality and disability.

To tackle a public health agenda at population level requires a massive shift in orientation on the part of many key players. It requires a shift in the way economists value health and the environment, in the way politicians and executives in national political systems and multinational agencies define and prioritise health policy, in the way public servants are prepared to prioritise interdepartmental activities even at the expense of their own special projects, in the way businesses define their strategic goals and arenas for business activity and in the way all of us as citizens seek to lobby and influence for particular patterns of investment and priorities when we vote, as well as when we act as employees, employers and family members.

Yach advocates a huge multi-sectoral, multi-agency agenda in which there are conflicts, trade-offs, and radical changes in policy priorities. But it is an agenda which is realistic for all its ambitions, and one which we fail to acknowledge at our peril, if we really do have a vision for health in 2020 that will deliver a radical improvement in the global and national health status.

In Chapter 3 Calum Paton argues that national health policy is driven more by ideological factors than a rational technical analysis concerned with cost effectiveness and quality in service provision. Consequently he argues that policy implementation is frequently more complex and more likely to face obstacles in implementation than would be the case for conventionally owned organisations. He describes how policy is driven by shifting political agendas, wherein a public commitment to local devolution is undermined by the maintenance of key capital and planning decisions as central functions. Beyond tensions between the political centre and the operational periphery he identifies the primary challenge for the future as achieving reconciliation between the views and perceived interests of the clinical professions, the state and the public. Paton describes the political characterisation of health policy under Margaret Thatcher in the early 1990s, John Major at the turn of the ultimate decade of the 20th century and Tony Blair at the turn of the century. He suggests that Tony Blair's 'New Labour regulatory state', with its emphasis upon audit, inspection and clinical governance, continues to embody chronic tensions between clinicians, patients and the state. The challenge he says is to forge a coherent link between the policy aspirations for local devolution and autonomy, improving national health status and clinical self-management.

Paton concludes with some radical proposals for reshaping the healthcare system in order to address the unresolved and suboptimal tensions which persist in spite of, or maybe because of, the decades of attempts to secure health services reform. He argues for clearer definition of the role of primary care, with encouragement for referral to more specialist care according to agreed criteria; for clearer ownership and status for NHS organisations; a reduction in the number of performance indicators and targets; more symmetry between incentive and values systems and less rigidity and bureaucracy. The key to a more successful future for all parties is, he argues, rebuilding trust between government and the medical profession. This will require developing and communicating areas of consensus, and being open in looking for compromise where consensus is not, at present, possible. This process he says is likely to mean compromise between legitimate political targets and clinical aspirations.

In Chapter 4 Graham Lister scans the system environment of health in order to advance our understanding of the generation of costs within the complex whole. He generates high- and low-cost scenarios based on an evaluation of the likely impact of ten cost drivers: meeting European standards, rising consumer expectations, dramatically increasing public provision of hospice care, increasing investment to secure health promotion, disease prevention and self-care, demographic changes with migration, birth and death rates, medical and pharmaceutical technology, the impact of information and communication technology, changes in pay and remuneration and efficiency gains through work organisation and process redesign. Over a 20-year period Lister forecasts a growth in health expenditure for the UK from 8 per cent to somewhere between 11 per cent and 14 per cent.

In the final chapter (5) in Part 1 with its focus on the whole system, Scott Greer echoes Paton's analysis in Chapter 3 and asks provocatively 'Why do good health politics make bad health policy?' He describes how the very centralisation of the UK state that made the NHS possible makes it vulnerable to incessant reorganisation and micro-management from the centre. These unintended consequences threaten to undermine the NHS through creating chronic problems in morale of the professional and skilled clinical and managerial workforce, and in failing public confidence and trust in the NHS's capacity to deliver high quality services to universal quality standards.

A fundamental problem for the future is how the workings of the healthy democratic system that gives great power to elected governments can be used productively and creatively to avoid slowly destroying the health service which arguably is one of it greater achievements.

Greer argues that the solution lies in greater decentralisation of operational power and more systematic exclusivity so as to incorporate key stakeholders, particularly clinical professionals, but also one might add, patients, in determining operational arrangements.

In the second Part of the book papers by de Rond and Dash, Rodgers, Jochelson and Mark focus on the development and implementation of national policy and organisational strategy.

In Chapter 6 Mark de Rond and Penny Dash describe some of the difficulties faced in the NHS in developing and implementing realistic strategies. With reference to the vast amount of literature on strategic management they describe how strategic choices often reflect emergent, multi-faceted and 'messy' processes embedded in complexity, uncertainty and diversity of interests and objectives. They show how strategy, albeit in many guises, requires pragmatic resolution of questions of priority of focus and effort, of defining the nature of value propositions and of developing appropriate capacity and capability to develop and realise the focus and value propositions which are dominant. They show that an understanding of these requirements often appears lost in the NHS where one can encounter a high level of disconnect between, and ambiguity surrounding, strategic development and implementation, clarity of purpose and appropriate capacity. Add this to the continuous complications arising from the leading involvement of politicians who feel they must justify the performance of a taxation-funded system to sustain the mandate from their constituents, and one easily accounts for the consequent centralist, politically driven approach, which disempowers local managers and which has already been the subject of criticism in this volume by Paton and Greer. Through pairs of comparative case studies, each one of the NHS twinned with a commercial example, the authors suggest that the NHS needs to focus on a future in which leading managers need to be able to define and communicate a clear set of aims for their organisation, to make an analytical assessment of the impact of future trends on their anticipated strategic and operational paths, to seek out and learn from examples of best practice, to innovate, to develop top quality communication skills and to develop management structures aligned to strategic focus.

The authors conclude that if NHS organisations can be encouraged to develop local management capacity, supported by local data collection and analysis and a willingness and capacity to look outside the NHS and outside the UK, they have the potential to build robust plans for a future in which service provision will be dramatically improved.

In Chapter 7 Wendy Rogers discusses the ways ethical values do, may and should inform health policy with particular reference to the UK. She takes three themes in health policy, which are evidenced in most developed economies, and shows how each theme relates to specific ethical values and to assumptions about the ways the values can be protected and promoted.

The first policy-value link is demonstrated in discussion of the need for evidence-based medicine and technology appraisal and its relationship to three values. First the value of beneficence, that is the aim of acting for the good of patients; secondly the value of non-maleficence or the duty to do no harm; thirdly the value of equity of access and the minimisation of regional variations. The second policy is patient-centred care and its relationship to the value of respect for patient autonomy. The third policy area is the commitment to public health and the prevention of disease and its link to the value of harm minimisation and to utilitarian reasoning, which seeks to balance the sum of benefits and harms at population level.

Rogers reveals the complex tensions in health policy development, which arise because the bases of values can often be in conflict. For example, harm reduction at population level can conflict with respect for patient autonomy if individuals wish to dissociate themselves from population programmes. Criticisms, which underlie current interpretations of the identified values in UK health policy, are outlined.

The chapter concludes with a look to the future under two questions. What are the values that might underpin the UK National Health Service in the future and how can these values act together with each other and with policy in a synergistic rather than antagonistic manner? A plea is made for a rethink of the underlying fundamental nature of values in UK health policy and for a greater honesty and realism about what a more coherent system of values would look like. It is suggested that we should encourage a focus on respect for autonomy rather than on open-ended choice. Similarly beneficence in terms of acting for the (health) good of others requires, as Derek Yach suggests in Chapter 2, that we draw attention to social and economic factors which influence health status, and realise that population-based health interventions will not necessarily distribute benefits evenly across the population and may indeed increase inequalities in health.

Rogers is persuasive in her arguments that the facilitation of ethically explicit and realistic discussions of values with strong participation from all key stakeholders will be very important in the future development of health policy. A reformed policy process should be aimed at achieving a decrease in ethical contradictions, greater unity of purpose and thereby improved outcomes from a series of achievable health policy goals.

In Chapter 8 Karen Jochelson examines policies and practices in the publicly funded NHS in England and considers its largely unrealised potential to embrace a real commitment to sustainable development. As an employer of over one million people, a consumer of some 8 per cent of GDP and a utiliser of almost 23 million square metres of floor space, the NHS could seriously advance the future health of the nation if it began to use its resources in ways that were less wasteful and ultimately less costly. In these ways it could reduce the damage it causes to the environment and to public health, and in the long term free up resources to reinvest in better healthcare as well as securing healthier living almost immediately.

Jochelson begins by assessing the resources of the NHS and the potential impact its activities may have on the environment and on health. Government policy on sustainable development is explained. The attitude of NHS organisations in London to environmental and social issues is examined. The article concludes with some examples that suggest the health, environmental and financial benefits of incorporating environmental awareness into the management of the health service. Jochelson proposes that decision makers in the NHS should see the addition of sustainable development principles and goals to daily decision-making as an integral part of modernising and investing in the future.

Sustainable development complements present NHS values in two ways. Firstly, it builds on the idea that the NHS can promote good health. Secondly, a commitment to sustainable development principles builds on the public service ethos of the NHS, which embodies the idea that its activities are driven by concern for the welfare of others and the common good, rather than by profit. Environmental concerns should not be marginalised as 'estates issues', but should inform how the NHS uses its resources, conducts it activities and acts in the community. Jochelson makes an impassioned plea for will and vision in the NHS to show that using public resources in a sustainable way means not just using them to provide a high quality public service, but also means using all its resources – financial, human and material – in ways that build community, protect the environment and safeguard health for the future. That is, the pursuit of aims that are congruent with the founding principles of the NHS.

In Chapter 9 Annabelle Mark examines the importance of acknowledging emotion in every aspect and level of participation in the policy and practice of healthcare in the 21st century. She explains that the NHS was in part founded on an emotional base with its commitment to reduce the fears of illness, infirmity and death, and to enhance premature social cohesion with a comprehensive universal service. However, alongside emotional and value-based arguments, were those appealing to rational economics in terms of efficient provision of services and a healthier, and hence assured, more productive workforce. She suggests that the emotional and the rational have coexisted somewhat uncomfortably for 60 years. Policy makers in the future need more explicitly to acknowledge these tensions and to realise that overly to focus on one side (the technical rational side) at the expense of the other (the emotional and value based) is bound to increase public dissatisfaction with the service.

The concepts of emotional labour and emotional intelligence are used in discussion of future issues for clinical workforce development, with particular implications for education and training, work profiles and organisation design.

Stress is given to the inevitability of emotional involvement of patients and carers, through the emotions of fear, anxiety, joy and hope which are commonly associated with birth, growth, well-being, sickness, infirmity and death, which are after all the very essence of healthcare. Critical issues for a future in which emotional involvement as well as rational analysis are each given emphasis and are in acknowledged and constructive tension include patient involvement in two fundamental modalities. One is in priority setting at national and regional levels in a democratic system, the other is in decision-making about care and treatment in individual cases at individual, family and close community levels.

In the third Part of the book the focus turns to people and knowledge with papers by Greener, Keen and Wyatt, Rigby, and Costa-Font and Mossialos.

In Chapter 10 Ian Greener examines the role of the patient in UK healthcare reform. He unpicks the difference between the role of patient as customer, where health professionals, predominately doctors, make choices on behalf of patients and the role of patient as consumer, in which individual patients make choices within and between health encounters. Immediately one is drawn into consideration of information asymmetries, expert power, trust and rationality within the doctor–patient relationship.

Not only, however, must the role of the patient be considered in relation to the role of the doctor and other health professionals, but also the role and experience of the patient is shown in this chapter to be intimately bound up with the role of the state, which is the subject of earlier Chapters 1, 3 and 4.

In various guises, an internal market for healthcare has been predicated upon, and to some extent encouraged, a notion of patient choice and at least a 'mimic consumerism' in that choice is exercised not by patients, but by their agents, either as GPs or Health Authorities. This analysis builds on that of Wendy Rodgers who in Chapter 7 has already opened discussion of the ways ethical values do, may and should inform health policy with particular reference to the UK.

Enabled by the Internet and direct telephone helpline services like NHS Direct, greater emphasis could be placed theoretically on the choices and independence of expert patients and active welfare participants. In a Giddensian 'third way' (Giddens 1994, 1998, 2002) patients could be involved as much more active and independent agents who create the healthcare system at both macro-institutional and micro-clinical encounter levels as well as experience being the subject of its creation. At present however, Greener finds an unpalatable over-emphasis upon calculative rationality and assertive independence in the shifting sands of incomplete expertise and partial information in the Giddensian analysis.

Having explored theoretical foundations, Greener presents the results of a study of patient approaches to choice, conducted through focus groups and interviews in Bristol, UK. He found reports of very low levels of active choice about registration with GPs or about major treatment interventions. In terms of hospital-based treatments, even in areas where there was demand for patient choice, as in maternity services, patients reported often finding their choices curtailed. In areas where there was neither reported interest nor reported availability of choice of treatment or involvement in treatment decision-making, little active involvement was reported. Indeed he notes that in spite of policies to encourage those with chronic diseases to become 'expert patients' and to be more autonomous in respect of their responsibilities for their own care, such patients often have only partial information drawn from their own experiences and a deep suspicion that the mainspring for policy for their 'involvement' was an objective to cut professional clinical time and therefore costs involved in chronic care rather than to secure real patient empowerment. In contrast he found a strong interest from patients in exercising choice about the timing of treatment, but that this could only really prevail where privately funded treatment was sought.

Greener found great contrast between the active assertive choices made by the same respondents to his health survey when they were questioned as parents exercising choice of schools for their children. The extent of their activity and involvement in questions of school choice was in sharp contrast to the views of the same people when they spoke as passive recipients of healthcare. Choice and rationality in his terms are thus shown to be highly contextual.

Greener's conclusion is that patients are eager and able to be customers acting through professional agents, but are frequently and in some cases holistically, neither eager, nor feel able, to be consumers. The argument follows, therefore, that in looking to the future, health policies need to be situated within a realistic understanding of the dynamics built in relationships between customers and consumers and experts and administrative authorities. There is in this sense no point in rhetorically proclaiming situations which assume a strong basis in trust, power, expertise and information within clinical encounters when the macro-policies focused on national institutions appear to deny these aspects. This mismatch may indeed result in undermining the very relationships and objectives the macro-policies are apparently designed to support.

In Chapter 11 Justin Keen and Jeremy Wyatt provide a link between the involvement of patients and the development of information systems. They compare the rate of diffusion of electronic networks within society broadly construed to the rate found within the more specific area of healthcare systems. They conclude that in the UK, and elsewhere, diffusion in healthcare is far less comprehensive than one might expect. They identify four patterns of diffusion, each representing a lesser degree of wholesale diffusion: extensive and comprehensive as in Internet use; extensive within functional areas of responsibility, as in patient information systems; what Keen and Wyatt call Polynesian with usage in small islands scattered in low density across a large organisational seascape, as in tele-medicine and electronic records; and lastly no diffusion at all with individual developments becoming obsolete at the prototype level. They suggest that the large extent to which healthcare organisations exhibit Polynesian patterns of diffusion can be explained by a widespread immature understanding amongst the key players of the importance of the politics of relationships between supplier, user and representatives of the state.

Keen and Wyatt find that in healthcare organisations this 'supplier–user–funder–owner' relationship is immature, characterised by some mistrust and misunderstanding about ownership and control, even before one adds considerations of patients' rights to information, not only about themselves, but also about publicly funded organisational processes. The changing, somewhat unstable political landscape of relationships allows particular alliances to build involving clinicians, suppliers, civil servants and politicians which then lead to particular and separate IT investments, without necessarily securing benefits of learning from mistakes and successes encountered elsewhere. With greater sharing of this knowledge, a more coherent national strategy, with greater emphasis on clarity of evaluated outcomes, may emerge. However ironically, securing the benefits of this knowledge sharing and learning will depend on more effective information systems being developed. Without careful analysis of objectives and constraints within a context heavily influenced by medical professional norms, ICTs may, against the expectations of policy makers, tend to exaggerate rather than solve problems of fragmentation of service delivery.

Information systems will be significant in their influence on future patterns of healthcare, but their significance is not guaranteed to be positive. The rate, pattern and experienced impact of diffusion will depend on the roles and relationships that develop within and between suppliers, politicians, civil servants and clinicians, in a context in which greater attention will need to be paid to patients, with their rights both to information and to privacy, and to patient and carer representatives and associations.

In a complementary paper Michael Rigby in Chapter 12 takes up the IT (Information Technology) story where Justin Keen and Jeremy Wyatt leave it. Rigby too notes the lack of integration within information systems strategy, architecture and operations, vertically between functions and horizontally between interest groups and organisations.

A distinction is made between two roles for IT. One is as a neutral agent to provide direct support and response to users. Even though this role in many ways is reactionary, nonetheless it requires innovation and development within the parameters of current organisational and human systems if IT systems are not going to stagnate and lose their potential for improving development and delivery of health and healthcare. The second role for IT is as an active innovator in which IT specialists take leadership in identifying potential opportunities, developing applications and carefully thinking through potential and unintended pitfalls. This role should not, Rigby argues, be left to suppliers.

Each of these roles is vital to the future of healthcare. Each requires the selection of, and support for, different skills and working environments within an integrated strategic framework which pays attention to needs and aspirations of users and systems at different functions, levels and at different times within health systems.

Potential for three developments which could transform the future of health policy and practice is discussed: timetabled personal integrated care delivery; resource booking deployment and electronic patient healthcare portfolios. New paradigms for IT-enabled care delivery and new health IT systems are described. Impeding factors in their realisation are identified as sufficient and appropriately directed investment; a natural preference to invest in direct care rather than its support; a lack of a development or 'innovation' culture and experimentation and 'laboratory' type settings, and criteria developed strategically to guide the innovation process. Rigby, like Keen and Wyatt, describes a 'Polynesian' situation in which there are many islands, which are often unconnected, sometimes barren, but occasionally highly fertile. They are at the mercy of oceans where political and immediate resource considerations control the tides more than a strategic sense of how to realise well-founded but challenging hopes, and allay the real fears, which IT in health engenders.

In Chapter 13 Joan Costa-Font and Elias Mossialos consider patient and public involvement in investment choices in terms of a very particular aspect of the future of health and healthcare. They proceed from the assumption that new developments in biotechnology may give rise to more efficient clinical technologies, improved population health status and better value for money in per capita diagnosis and treatment. However, in spite of the promise of substantial health benefits in the future, new developments in biotechnology seem to be associated with low levels of public acceptance. A major challenge for future health policy is thus to secure appropriate communication and knowledge transfer about both opportunities and risks from techno-logical innovation and to invest in securing better understanding of lay reactions to the implications of scientific discovery and technolo-gical application.

Costa-Font and Mossialos examine the informational constraints on public decision-making about biotechnology applications in the context of the UK and the wider European Union. The risk–benefit decision-making framework is re-examined in search of an explana-tion of the rationality of individual behaviour regarding biotechnolo-gy. The role of core values is described as responsible for ambivalence in individuals' attitudes to biotechnology. They argue that when both values and information about risks are influencing decision-making, attitudes might be expected to be 'ambivalent'. Empirical analyses of the Eurobarometer data on attitudes to biotechnology and the deter-minants of ambivalence are examined with a view to identifying how the advantages of well-founded biotechnology may be effectively coordinated into future health policies and practices.

In the final chapter Sandra Dawson, Zoë Morris, Linda Chang and Charlotte Sausman comment on the implications for future health policy of some universal contemporary challenges deriving from ageing populations, growing health inequalities, rising public expectations, competition between seeking improvements in public health and meeting demands for the diagnosis, treatment and cure of individual sickness, and the incessant strength of advancing knowledge in driving costs. They draw together common themes and identify five interrelated issues that, they argue, must feature centrally in health policy makers' agendas for the future. Thus this final chapter on future health organ-isation and systems reminds the reader that whilst health and life sciences are dominated by advances in science and technology, their promise will not be fully realised unless there is parallel engagement with political, ethical, clinical, professional and managerial determination to address issues of values, purpose, democracy, public engagement and relationships of mutual respect. Furthermore that the foundations of realising the potential of new opportunities in harnessing technological developments lie in imaginative change management processes which acknowledge the importance of positive engagement between all the key players: clinicians, managers, policy makers and the general public.

## References

Giddens, A. (1994) *Beyond Left And Right: the Future Of Radical Politics*. Cambridge: Polity Press

Giddens, A. (1998) *The Third Way: the Renewal Of Social Democracy*. Cambridge: Polity Press

Giddens, A. (2002) *What Now for New Labour?* Cambridge: Polity Press

# Part 1
# Systems and Complexity

# 1
# The Shape of UK Health Systems

*Charlotte Sausman* and *Sandra Dawson*, in association with
*Linda Chang*

## Introduction

Variation in national health systems can be characterised in terms of
four key dimensions, namely ownership (how is the system funded,
organised and who accounts to whom for what), scope (the parameters
of the system governing what is included and what excluded), its stakeholders, and the dynamics (the mechanisms and influences that drive
the system). How any one system is profiled on these dimensions gives
it special shape. The shape sets constraints at any one time around what
is feasible for the present and likely for the future. The chapter will
describe the present shape of health systems in the UK, indicate some
key differences with other countries and use this analysis as a basis for
discussing the implications of change in the future.

## Ownership

Who owns the health system – is it publicly or privately owned, or does
it exist in the form of social ownership? Is all or part of the system under
one form of ownership? The ownership of the system shapes its organisation and its accountability. For example, a centrally funded, public
system leads to a centralised hierarchical structure and mechanisms
of accountability. If we, the national electorate, are the owners of our
health system then the systems of organisation and accountability must
be directed to our interests in the same way a public limited company
will have a corporate structure and consequent mechanisms of organisation and accountability in order to meet the interests of shareholders.
Each type of system will have structures or mechanisms in place in
order to represent the interests of its owners – be they members of the
public, shareholders or subscribers.

In this section we describe the features of the UK health system according to the following parameters: funding, organisation and accountability.

## Funding

The National Health Services (NHS) of England, Scotland, Wales and Northern Ireland are publicly funded health systems. As members of the voting public we elect a parliament that has the authority to raise taxes and consume resources on our behalf. Executive authority is given to the government of the day. Ministers, be they members of the House of Commons or the House of Lords, are appointed by the government to oversee the work of government departments. The Secretary of State for Health for England has overall responsibility for the work of the Department of Health, whose remit is to 'improve the health and well-being of the people of England', following devolution (Department of Health, 2003). Funding of the Department of Health is controlled by the Treasury which has the authority to approve resources to spending departments based on accounts they present to Parliament. The Department of Health presents accounts according to estimates of its needs to fulfil its parliamentary duties. From the overall spending allocated to the Department of Health most is distributed to health authorities and primary care trusts which both commission and provide services such as primary care, general dental and pharmaceutical services. Other expenditures include capital advances to trusts, education, training, research and development, centrally managed expenditure on behalf of the NHS and monies to companies providing services or facilities to the NHS.

About three-quarters of NHS funding comes from general taxation. About 13 per cent comes from National Insurance contributions, 7 per cent capital refunds and 2 per cent charges (Department of Health, 2000). About 80 per cent of funding covers England. Funding is distributed on the basis of a population-based funding formula. As a result of this formula the Scottish system receives 25 per cent per capita more funding than England, Wales 18 per cent more and Northern Ireland 5 per cent more, on a per capita basis (Dixon, 1999).

Representation in the UK health system is through the parliamentary system at the national level, with corresponding authorities in Scotland, Wales and Northern Ireland following devolution. Now, the home nations have the opportunity to plan and develop their own health policies on many issues, including control of (regional) NHS, community care and food safety. The way in which governments develop their stewardship role in relation to health and the health system will continue to diverge between the home countries. There is scope for increasing regionalism in health policy terms, including the possibility of new public health functions as part of the remit of elected mayors.

In spite of the strong commitment to a tax-based system, elements of private funding are becoming more evident in the UK health system. A major initiative has been to find ways to attract private sources of capital with which to service the NHS estate – its buildings, namely hospitals, research centres and laboratories, and administrative organisations. Most capital investment in the UK health system is now privately financed or forms part of a public–private partnership (PPP). Under PFI, private consortia bid for private finance contracts, own new buildings and estate and then lease them back to the NHS through long-term contracts. Since Labour came to power in 1997, PFI projects with a combined value of £18 billion have been approved. From 2002–03 to 2004–05 £25.5 billion of new investment is expected through PPP and PFI (HM Treasury, 2002). Whilst the UK Treasury has been the greatest proponent of the use of private finance, it remains controversial and there are ongoing debates about its value for money to the public sector (Dunnigan and Pollock, 2003; Pollock et al., 2002; IPPR, 2001; Health Select Committee, 2002).

In terms of services, most non-clinical services are now provided through a system of competitive tendering, which includes private sector bidders; consequently private sector companies provide services such as laundry, cleaning, catering and maintenance. The health system also relies on companies that provide research, laboratory testing, medical equipment and pharmaceuticals amongst others in order to function. These private organisations hold contracts with the public health system.

In terms of staffing, private contractors now employ many non-clinical support staff and whilst many nurses are employed by NHS organisations, some nursing staff is provided by agencies that are largely private sector companies. For medical staff, the NHS employs doctors in hospitals, but depends to some extent on locum cover through agencies. Consultants have always been able to undertake private practice in addition to their NHS commitments (Gould, 2004). Finally, general practitioners are independent contractors who are reimbursed by the NHS in relation to the number of patients their practice serves. The contractual terms between the NHS and GPs have changed. GPs fear that the new contract will mean that patients are less safe because they will be treated by primary care organisations out of hours rather than by GPs. Some also worry that patients will have trouble getting appointments on time. There is also concern as to the ability for young doctors to establish themselves. It could also mean that GPs earn less (Koralage, 2004). They may also earn more, if they choose to work out-of-hours. The out-of-hours patient needs are being covered by telephone services, nurses, private GP services, specialist recruitment agencies and overseas doctors.

The UK health system has thus already seen shifts in the balance of public and private funding and ownership of its constituent parts taking into account buildings and infrastructure, services, and staff and it is likely that capital investment in health system infrastructure will be financed through private consortia or PPPs in the future. What *would* mark a change in the future would be changes to the funding or provision of *clinical* services.

A complete overhaul of the system of UK health financing from central taxation to an alternative such as social insurance is routinely debated in think-tanks by other policy commentators. The current Labour government commissioned its own international comparison of health systems as part of the Wanless review into UK healthcare funding requirements. The review concluded in its 10-year NHS Plan (2000) that transference to a social insurance system would increase administrative costs and overall costs in the future(Wanless, 2002). However, an insurance-based system might prove more responsive to an increasingly diverse set of health demands amongst the population. Top-up payments for particular services such as 'hotel services' in hospitals may emerge in the future, particularly as such non-clinical services are within the terms of private finance contracts.

The Labour government remains committed to long-term funding of the health system through general taxation. However it has also acknowledged that sustained increases are required to meet long-term expectations of the system and to make up for previous underinvestment. Recently the government increased National Insurance contributions to help pay for increases in health funding.

## Types of organisation

The structure of the English Department of Health itself is somewhat unusual amongst the spending departments of government. The NHS has many of the characteristics of a government agency, although it remains tightly within political accountabilities – the CEO of the NHS reports directly to the Secretary of State for Health and civil servants staff the regions of the NHS. The recent history of the NHS is characterised by reorganisations reflecting counteracting trends to decentralise and centralise (Day and Klein 1997; Paton, Chapter 3, this volume). In October 2000, the posts of NHS chief executive and the Department of Health Permanent Secretary were combined thus breaking any suggestion of a principal–agent relationship between the Department of Health and the senior management of the NHS.

The restructuring of April 2002 shifted commissioning responsibility to smaller organisations, Primary Care Trusts (PCTs) and local authorities. Following a further reorganisation and a big injection of additional funds in 2003 in England, around 300 PCTs receive approximately three-quarters of the NHS budget to plan and commission services locally. They are also responsible for improving the health of the local community. NHS Trusts are the organisations that run hospital services which PCTs commission. New forms of organisation, 'Care Trusts' were also introduced to share responsibility for health and social care at a local level; but few were developed,

A previously strong regional structure for the NHS is now much reduced in size and scope. Local NHS organisations are accountable to one of the 28 Strategic Health Authorities (SHA), which work with local organisations to develop strategies for the local health service.

There is a strong performance monitoring system in place in each of the organisational tiers. PCTs and NHS Trusts are monitored by the SHAs, which are, in turn, performance managed across their locality by one of the four directors of Health and Social Care, which cover four broad geographical areas of England. The NHS has a series of national targets on such issues as waiting times for treatment, which form a key part of this performance monitoring process. Finally the new structure is designed to facilitate the development of networks amongst organisations trying to tackle a public health issue or specialist services such as cancer. Traditionally the departmental structure of the UK public sector, together with ministers who have departmental responsibilities shapes a hierarchical structure where local organisations have a remit and accountability to those at departmental level. That structure remains in place, and is a driving force in the UK health system. However, at the same time the government tries to encourage organisations to work with other departments and other sectors such as the voluntary and private sector, where appropriate, in order to tackle complex social policy issues. However, the strong accountability structure up to central government and parliament does not facilitate this type of joint working or indeed locally initiated developments (Paton, this volume, Chapter 3).

The remaining functions of the Department of Health include: the overall management and accountability of the health system, developing policy, overall regulation and inspection of the NHS, and intervention, if operational problems at a local level are sufficiently concerning to merit it. Successive governments have made use of powers to set up organisations to operate outside the traditional Department of Health bureaucracy. The current government has established national organisations such as the Commission for Healthcare Audit and Inspection (also known as the Healthcare Commission) and the National Institute for Clinical Excellence which retain independence from the Department of Health hierarchy, but are part of the overall NHS. These organisations will promote improvement in the quality of health and healthcare. In addition, the government makes use of 'task forces' and review bodies, made up of non-civil servants to advise on particular issues. More than 50 reviews have been set up by the Department of Health since the current Labour government came to power in 1997 (Ahmed, 2000). Since 1997, 31 watchdogs, advisory bodies, and quangos have been created at national level concerning health with a variety of roles, principally in the area of regulation (Kmietowicz, 2003). These bodies are now themselves under review.

The types of organisation operating in the NHS in Scotland, Wales, and Northern Ireland diverge somewhat from their English counterparts. In Scotland, there is a combination of direct management by boards and professional leadership and management through a variable number of disease-focused multi-disciplinary clinical networks. These networks have started to allocate resources by disease budget heads. Regional committees elected by doctors provide for strong clinical professional presence in resource allocation and policy decisions. In Wales, there is separation of commissioning and provisioning roles in organisations, which operate at a local level. In Northern Ireland, uniquely, healthcare and social care are integrated. The Health and Social Services Trusts are commissioned by the Health and Social Care Groups and the Regional Health and Social Care Boards. Organisation charts for the NHS in England, Scotland, Wales and Northern Ireland are illustrated in Figure 1.1.

## Accountability

Figure 1.1 identifies the lines of accountability in the home nations for systematic accountability through the system to the Secretary of State for Health who is accountable to parliament, and to the electorate. In Wales and Scotland accountability is through the Welsh Assembly

English Department of Health → Strategic Health Authorities (28) →
Primary Care Organisations (303)

Scottish Executive Health Department → Health Boards (15) → various
disease-focused multi-disciplinary Clinical Networks

NHS Wales Department of the National Assembly → Regional Offices (3)
→ Local Health Boards (22)

Health, Social Services and Public Safety of the Northern Ireland
Executive → Health and Social Services Boards (4) → Health and
Social Services Trusts (19) → Health and Social Services Groups (15)

*Figure 1.1*: Accountabilities in the health system for England, Scotland, Wales,
and Northern Ireland

and the Scottish Parliament respectively. In Northern Ireland, the
minister for Health, Social Services and Public Safety answers to the UK
Parliament.

There are several types of accountability in the UK health system and
these are identified in turn. In terms of financial accountability, this
operates nationally through the structures of the NHS and the parliamentary system. The chief executives of each national health service are
the accounting officers for the department and are responsible for the
accounts presented to parliament. At an operational level, local organisations are accountable to the SHA, which is in turn accountable
to the directors of Health and Social Care. If there are matters of failing
performance, there are channels through which the matter will
be dealt. There are other statutory authorities, which also operate on
behalf of the electorate. They include the National Audit Office, which
reports to parliament on the appropriate use of public money through
the Public Accounts Committee; the Audit Commission, which regulates
public finances; and the Health Service Ombudsman who investigates
complaints against the NHS, particularly failures in service and mal-
administration. Patients may make complaints through their local PCT,
to the hospital in question, if relevant, and to representative bodies in
local hospital trusts known as Patient Advice and Liaison Services (PALS).

As a centralised, national system, accountability in the NHS is
through national structures. The chief executive of a local organisation
such as an NHS Trust is the Accounting Officer for the organisation,
responsible for the financial accounts as well as the overall governance

of the organisation. The chief executive reports to a board that is accountable to the Secretary of State for Health. The Commission for Health Improvement, which in 2003 became the Commission for Healthcare Audit and Inspection, inspects each organisation.

Much of the change in recent years to the UK health system has been about the restructuring or reorganisation of the system in order to make the constituent parts act in the interests of the centre. The centre is, in turn, redefining its role in terms of being a target-setting organisation, an inspector of NHS organisations, and responsible for national policy agendas to which NHS organisations must adhere. Some NHS organisations, for example Foundation Trust Hospitals created in 2004, have been given greater managerial freedoms through reform, which is driven by a belief that organisations and management structures that mimic those of the private, corporate sector would improve management of the health service. However reflecting national political involvement and public accountability to parliament and therefore to the electorate with all the political risks entailed, there has also been a sustained increase in inspection, audit and performance monitoring of NHS organisations. The internal regulation of publicly accountable organisations is a requirement of the publicly funded system. One of the tensions created from these countervailing forces is the limits on the ability of senior management of local organisations to set organisational priorities, locally driven priorities, within the overall regulatory framework. There is a balance to be struck in regulating organisations and ensuring they adhere to national policies, whilst at the same time allowing those appointed to manage their organisations.

The creation of 'foundation trusts' in 2004 within the UK health system is an interesting development in the mechanisms of governance and accountability in the UK health system. The intention is that foundation trusts will be somewhat removed from traditional forms of accountability to the Secretary of State for Health and instead will be held to account by a series of arms-length regulators, principally a new Independent Regulator as well as the Commission for Health Inspection and Audit. Reshaping the health system towards a regulatory centre with arms-length agencies would bring it in line with other service sectors in the UK such as the prison service, education and housing.

These tensions and oscillations between central government withdrawing except for their vital part in setting 'the rules of the game', and central government intervening at every stage to manage local operations if there is a hint of a problem were discussed in a former era when the internal market was introduced in 1990 (Winstanley, Sorabji and

Dawson 1995). Foundation trusts may also represent a new type of ownership and representation within the UK health system. Local citizens and employees of the trust are eligible to become members of the trust. The membership will become the owners of the trust electing representatives from the membership to a Board of Governors who will oversee the management board and run the trust. The current government states that:

> NHS Foundation Trusts will herald a new form of social ownership where health services are owned by and accountable to local people rather than to central government. In this way, much stronger connections will be established between providers of NHS services and their stakeholder communities, extending involvement beyond current arrangements for consultation and building on the sense of ownership that many people feel for their local hospitals. (Department of Health, 2002)

## Scope of the system

The UK health system spans our health needs from birth and infancy to death. We are entitled to seek advice and care throughout our lives, from antenatal services to child health services, screening, testing, routine appointments with our general practitioner, surgery, medicine, chronic illness and palliative care. Our health system is inclusive as it covers hospital services, emergency services, primary care, community care and mental health. It also covers public health, health protection and health promotion. The government is charged with responsibility for the nation's health as well as the nation's health services. Of course, as Yach (Chapter 2) displays in an international context, many factors interact in order to produce health outcomes. Here, one of the functions of the health system is to work with other sectors to protect and improve population health.

As individuals, our future health status is often set at birth; being influenced by our genetic inheritance as well as the economic, social and cultural environment in which we are born, which determines our opportunities as well as threats to our health. The 'life course epidemiology' approach has shown how where we are born and subsequently live has an effect on our life chances. The Sure Start programme, for example, aims to reduce child poverty in England over a 10-year period by providing local, integrated services such as childcare, education and healthcare for young children in deprived electoral wards. The policy is administered through the Education Department, but local healthcare organisations are involved. It is an example of organising the health system with other local services in order to target those with poor health outcomes in order to try and overcome some early disadvantages.

The Black report, published in 1980, identified the extent of health inequalities in Britain.(Black et al., 1980) In the twenty years following the Black report large sections of the population have prospered but relative inequalities and poverty have increased (Palmer et al., 2003; Lynch et al., 2000; Goodman and Shephard, 2002; Shephard, 2003). The Acheson Report (1998) again looked at health inequalities and recommended wide-ranging policies to reduce health inequalities, most of which were outside the immediate scope of the health system, in areas such as tax and benefits, education, employment and housing. The main focus for policy in relation to the NHS was on improving the equity of access to NHS services, including a more equitable allocation of NHS resources. The funding of NHS resources pays attention to deprivation and the needs of populations, but Acheson wanted improvements here on the basis that there are inequalities of access.

A recent evaluation of the impact of Acheson's recommendations supported the integration of policies to reduce health inequalities into mainstream health policies and the introduction of performance measures and indicators to track health inequalities (Exworthy et al., 2003).

Given the range of factors that impact on health, the question we might ask in relation to the health system is, how does it contribute to better population health outcomes, and improvements in the health inequalities between different groups? How can the health system work to produce 'better health' and how can that be measured?

It is difficult to assess the impact of the health system on population health outcomes. We lack health outcome data even for specific treatments. For populations, the range of factors impacting on health outcomes makes it difficult to isolate the effects of the health system. However, the World Health Organisation measured the comparative performance of health systems in 2000, ranking the UK 18th in the world – better placed than Italy or Germany, but way behind France which was ranked 1st (WHO, 2000). Although the WHO system was criticised for its methodology and the lack of data upon which it based its conclusions, it sparked a determination in many countries, including the UK 'to do better' and focused more research resources on attempting to ensure methodological improvements in subsequent reviews (Wait, 2004; Wait and Nolte, 2005). Even so, in the WHO 2000 comparison, the UK was found to compare favourably on the equity and access of its health system, principally because through a taxation-based system no one is excluded and there is no consideration of ability to pay. It is also an efficient system in terms of its use of resources. However, the UK system has long waits for elective surgery, poor cancer survival rates, poor quality physical infrastructure, and low levels of professional staffing compared to its European comparators. (For international comparisons see: Anderson, G. et al., 2000; Bindman, A. et al., 2000; Evans, B. et al., 2000; OECD Health Data, 2004; the review concluded in its 10-year NHS Plan that transference to a social insurance system would increase administrative costs and overall costs in the future; Wanless, 2001, 2002, 2004).

Since 1992, the UK has established national indicators to track health improvement (*Health of the Nation* (1992), *Our Healthier Nation* (1998), *Towards a Healthier Scotland* (1999), *Well into 2000* (Northern Ireland 1997), *Better Health, Better Wales* (1998)). *Our Healthier Nation* set national targets for reductions in the nation's major killers – cancer, heart disease, stroke, accidents and mental illness. These are now followed through in terms of a local 'Health Improvement Programme' which local Primary Care Trusts are responsible for delivering.

Beyond the multi-faceted influences on health status, which create an inevitable porosity to the boundaries between those concerns traditionally seen as 'health' and those which relate to nutrition, education, literacy and the physical environment; the other major challenge for the future is determining the relationship between health and social care, within the bounds of what is feasible or desirable. For persons nearing the end of their life, and those caring for them, as well as those suffering from chronic disease, particularly when mental health is involved, the distinction between health and social care is nothing but a source of frustration, with duplication of effort, neglect of certain key concerns and apparently unnecessary demoralisation and disputes around who is to do what to whom which are driven not by restrictive sectional practices but by central regulation. Determining an appropriate scope for the systems in England, Wales and Scotland is a major challenge for policy makers, if resources are to be utilised most efficiently and health status improved.

In terms of overall scope and access the UK health system stacks up well against social or private insurance schemes where the care received relates to contributions made, and to systems where user charges exist for each visit to a professional (Mossialos and Thompson 2001). However the formal structure of the system may serve to hide disparities of access that are only observed through health outcomes statistics. In terms of geography, access to a GP appointment as well as waiting times for elective surgery varies by organisation and by area. It is here that government targets are focused on improving national performance by tackling geographical variations. To view disparities in access another way the National Consumer Council along with other relevant organisations recently highlighted the disparities in exemptions from prescription charges (Laurance, 2003). Those on income support and older people qualify for free prescriptions as well as groups such as children and expectant mothers. Some treatments are also exempt from charges such as diabetes, epilepsy and physical disability. However, chronic conditions such as asthma, cancer and multiple sclerosis are not exempt.

## Stakeholders

The identity of stakeholders in a health system and the nature of their role also shapes the health system. The range of stakeholders, taxpayers, members of the public and patients, and their ability to be represented and influence the health system is dependent on the factors already considered, namely the ownership and scope of the system. We have an involvement in the health system and a right to have interests represented. But how are those interests represented and at what level, by what mechanism and to what effect? At the same time the influence of stakeholders in the health system is part of the historic development of medicine and society, of scientific discovery and the potential to treat illness, and of the professions. In considering the future shape of the UK health system it is important to consider how the role of stakeholders is changing, and here factors such as the increasing influence of the patient and patient choice as well as the development of rights and responsibilities in the future are significant.

### The health workforce

Over a million people are employed in the NHS, which makes it the largest employer in Europe. This workforce includes doctors, nurses, therapists, pharmacists, a range of other health professionals and scientists as well as support staff, managers and administrators. Around three-quarters of the NHS workforce work in hospitals. One of the key issues, as identified in the sister volume to this collection (Davies, 2003), is whether the supply of health workers, and in particular, the professional health workforce will be at a level that will meet future demand, both in terms of the future health needs of the population, and the expectations of the public. We are currently in a position where the overwhelming issue is a shortage in supply in all professions, and yet there is increasing demand, principally to meet reforms being put in place to improve the NHS. Internationally, the UK at present employs fewer doctors and nurses per head of the population than other OECD countries(OECD, 2004). The Wanless report concluded that NHS Plan targets for nursing would meet their future scenarios if they were achieved, but that the planned increase in doctors was 'well short of needs' – by a figure of 25,000 after 20 years (Wanless, 2002:90).

How does one account for the predicted shortfall? Nurses are mostly female and over the last twenty years, women's employment opportunities have increased and nurses' relative earnings in relation to the workforce as a whole have been reduced. These changes can be seen in the ageing nursing workforce, where older groups are not being fully restocked by younger cohorts. Contrary to the nurses, doctors have, over the past twenty years, sustained their relative pay in relation to the workforce as a whole (Wanless, 2001:190).

However, to fill gaps in supply the UK still needs overseas trained doctors, mostly from outside Europe, significantly from India, New Zealand, South-east Asia and Africa. Like the nurses, the medical labour force is ageing and it is a concern that certain cohorts are not being replenished and that more doctors are retiring early. More than half of medical graduates are now female (Young and Leese, 1999) and, in 1998, a third of medical staff in hospitals were women (Dowie and Langman, 1999). The increasing numbers of women GPs is important because it has implications for the future organisation of general practice, as more women are interested in career breaks and part-time work than their male counterparts.

The UK, along with other developed countries, faces supply shortages of doctors and nurses and relies on overseas staff to fill the gaps. In the future as barriers to mobility are reduced, with a single European-wide market within an increasingly 'global' labour market for health professionals, the opportunity to use other countries' resources in times of shortage will have implications for the pay and conditions of all health workforces which will become increasingly resistant to control.

The Wanless review echoed numerous reports from the organisations representing key professions in the provision of healthcare in saying that the UK health system is severely understaffed and that significant improvements in the recruitment and retention of professional staff will be required to meet future expectations of the service. There will also be changes in the way staff are deployed in the future. New services such as NHS Direct and walk-in clinics are already providing new roles. In general, technological developments are likely to continue to shift services out of hospitals, which means staff treating different conditions and learning new skills in the community and primary care.

Current changes to make the health system more focused around the patient's experience may influence the way groups of staff are organised so that teams of people with different skills and expertise work together because they are concerned with a particular patient, or key members of staff will coordinate the care of an individual patient, rather than care being organised in a traditional way around clinical specialties. Current developments, for example, include the expansion of the prescribing rights of nurses and in primary care, nurses taking on roles in screening, health promotion and the management of chronic diseases. In secondary care, nurses are taking on responsibility for coordination of services such as outpatients' clinics and minor injury services (Sausman, 2003).

### Citizens, users, patients

UK citizens have an entitlement to the benefits of the health system, free at the point of demand regardless of ability to pay. This creates a somewhat special relationship between the public and the NHS, which since its inception following the Second World War has become an important institution, a key part of the modern welfare state. Its status as an institution and the status afforded to the medical profession created a dependent relationship with citizens, users and patients, where patients are the grateful recipients of care where it is needed. Its institutions provided an egalitarian setting where all patients were treated to the same service in the same environment. However, society has changed since the welfare state was conceived and rising prosperity and the demands made by citizens and consumers of a modern service industry challenges the principles of equity. People already exercise the choice to pay for more speedy private treatment and better facilities during their stay in hospital. Although the private medical market in the UK remains small there are now cases of patients paying to go abroad for treatment (BBC, 2004; BBC, 2002).

The value that is placed on the concept of a national health service is challenged by increasing complaints and litigation being taken against the health service (complaints were up 50 per cent in April 2003 from April 2002 (BBC, 2003)) as well as survey data which demonstrates the frustrations of patients with delays in treatment and high profile failures in the service (CHI, 2004; Wanless, 2002). Whilst survey data and particularly the evidence of opinion polls can be challenged, people are more expectant and questioning of the service and less deferential to the assertions of professionals and elites within the service when they make decisions such as funding and rationing on their behalf (Coulter, 2002a; Owen, 2002).

Traditionally, members of the public have not extensively engaged with the health system other than when requiring services, and then the relationship is generally characterised as one of recipient rather than an active involvement with the system and its providers. The model of foundation trusts is designed to promote the engagement of people in their local health system. Consideration has also been given to the idea of a 'contract' between the NHS and local communities, where a local Primary Care Trust will account to its 'public' for current spending and consult on future spending plans in ways which are directly and locally accountable. Involving or engaging the public with the health system and a wider notion of public health and health issues is viewed by some as the key to an effective functioning of the health system in the future along with better population health (Detmer et al., 2003; Wanless, 2002; DoH, 1997).

As contracts between practitioners and the service are changing, so too is the relationship between practitioners and patients, and between the service and the public. Angela Coulter describes a model of the informed patient whereby growing consumerism and individualism in society permeate into the health arena, modifying patients' expectations of care and shifting the balance of power in their relationship with healthcare providers (Coulter, 2002b). With the domination of chronic diseases it is more likely in the future that patients will have a longer-term relationship with the health system than was traditionally the case. As practitioners are required to acknowledge the views and experience of the patient, so there are calls for a redefinition of the relationship between the public and the health system. Rodgers, Chapter 7 and Greener, Chapter 10, gives further discussion of these issues in this volume.

The Wanless review into the future of the UK health service recommended 'a more effective partnership … between the twin planks of public and patient rights and responsibilities' which is based on explicit standards that the public can expect from the health service, more information to patients and the public, involving patients in the governance of NHS organisations, and providing the public with information on how local health services are performing (Wanless, 2002:116). In their scenarios for the future of healthcare offered by the Wanless review, in the desirable 'fully engaged' scenario, public engagement makes the most dramatic improvement, health status improves considerably, life expectancy increases and people have confidence in the health service. The health service responds well, with a focus on disease prevention.

## Politicians and policy advisors

As the chapters in this volume by Paton and Greer illustrate, the UK health system is highly politicised. This should be seen from an historical perspective – as the status of the NHS institution grew so did the political stakes in achieving success in the health policy arena. When the NHS was created the responsibility of the Minister for Health was not a cabinet position. Today the Secretary of State for Health is one of the most high-profile positions in government. It seems to be believed in Westminster by many people focused on reelection, that general elections in the last twenty years have been won or lost on promises in relation to the NHS. The prime minister, Tony Blair has stacked his reputation on the success of the NHS Plan, published in 2000. The NHS was a key manifesto commitment for the Labour government elected in 1997, with its pledge to cut waiting lists. The prime minister became personally identified with reform of the NHS when, after a winter of hostility in the media over an alleged crisis in the NHS over bed shortages, he promised in February 2000 to bring UK health spending up to the European average. Following this commitment the Chancellor, Gordon Brown's March 2000 budget announced a substantial increase in NHS funding over the following five years. This commitment launched the NHS Plan; the government promised substantial increases in funding for the health service and in return, the service was to undergo substantial reform in order to achieve government targets. As he reports in his foreword to the plan the prime minister met daily on the issue of health during the formulation of the NHS Plan. It is also significant that it was the prime minister and not the health secretary, Alan Milburn, who presented the plan to parliament in July 2000.

The formulation of the NHS plan illustrates the direct influence that politicians and policy advisors have on the UK health system. The government had already implemented many reforms to the NHS since it came to power in 1997 but during the winter of 1999–2000 the service reached something of a crisis in terms of performance figures on people waiting for treatment, access to emergency services, and the confidence of the staff working in the service. Unlike many significant reform programmes in relation to health systems, the prime minister became involved at a detailed level with the Secretary of State as he authored the

NHS Plan for Health. Together they met with advisory groups involving members of the clincal professions and other interested parties as they formulated the plan.

The resulting analysis was that the service had so far failed to deliver on the public's expectations for the following reasons: under-funding, staff shortages, lack of national standards, demarcations between staff and barriers between services, lack of clear incentives and levers to improve performance and over-centralisation and disempowered patients.

The Plan announced a considerable range of new initiatives, new structures and systems across the service that will meet the criteria. They included: more facilities including hospitals, primary care centres and IT systems; more staff; reform of the relationship between the Department of Health and the NHS in terms of 'subsidiarity' and 'earned autonomy' for local organisations; national standards and inspection of health organisations; a 'streamlined centre'; systems for evaluating drugs and disseminating 'best practice'; new arrangements for commissioning that combine health and social services; changes to medical contracts including new demands on consultants' working patterns; extended roles for staff; increased patient representation through the NHS; and joint working between the public and private sector described as a 'concordat' with private providers.

The Plan has also set out key targets to be achieved in the Department of Health Public Service Agreement. They include targets on national health outcomes such as the reduction of mortality rates from heart disease by 40 per cent in people under 75 by 2010 and service targets such as 100 per cent pre-booking of inpatient and outpatient elective admissions by 2005 and guaranteed access to a primary care doctor within 48 hours by 2004.

The implied causation is that with greater investment and re-organised and re-designed systems the NHS will meet its service targets and improve population health according to national indicators. The government has also set a national target on reducing overall inequalities in health outcomes by 10 per cent by 2010, as measured by infant mortality and life expectancy at birth.

Thus, in the UK system national politicians are able to exert considerable influence on the shape of the health system and recent history shows just how much politicians are able to influence factors such as priorities, spending levels and organisational structures which make up the health system.

The criticism that is often directed at health systems in the UK is that national politicians spend their time managing the NHS rather than meeting their broader obligations in terms of national population health. With a national public health system it might be presumed that resources for improving public health would be easier to secure. However, the majority of health spending is directed to healthcare or illness services, although as mentioned above, there are now national and local health inequalities targets that are the responsibility of the Department of Health.

With devolution to the home nations, politicians in the elected authorities of Scotland, Wales and Northern Ireland are able to diversify from policies relating to the English health system. These countries always had administrative authority in relation to the running of health services, but devolution has brought political freedom. As an illustration the Scottish parliament voted in 2001 to grant free long-term care for older people, which departs from the English policy which grants only free long-term nursing care. The Scottish and Welsh authorities have coalition governments which allows different political priorities and different political interests to emerge in health policy.

### Voluntary and independent healthcare providers

With the domination of the NHS in the UK's health systems it would seem that the voluntary and independent sectors have a small role to play. Unlike other systems, hospitals are publicly owned and publicly run. However, there are several ways in which these sectors are represented in the system.

First, the independent sector provides private medical insurance and runs private hospitals as well as paying for treatment in NHS hospitals, thereby providing a source of income for hospital trusts. The proportion of private health insurance has remained stable over the past two decades at 12 per cent of total health spending in the UK. Moreover, a significant proportion of elective surgery takes place in the private sector (circa 275,000 operations yearly), with individuals making out-of-pocket payments for treatments, sometimes overseas. The government signed a 'Concordat' with the Independent Healthcare Association, which allows commissioning organisations within the NHS (principally PCTs) to commission services from the private and voluntary sectors. Dental and optician treatments are also offered in the private sector.

Second, residential care for older people in England is predominantly provided by the private sector, and increasingly the voluntary sector. The same goes for the provision of residential care for people with disabilities. Therefore, whilst public provision continues to be the norm in the UK health system, in certain sectors there is mixed provision – and in some, such as residential care for older people, other sectors dominate. The role for private providers in the system allows these sectors to be included in national health policy decision-making, indeed the present government has looked to independent providers as good models of healthcare delivery. If an NHS hospital fails to meet government targets, independent sector providers are included in those bidding to take over the running of the organisation.

Third, the private sector contracts for most of the catering, cleaning and laundry services in hospitals following the programme of market testing in the 1990s that ensured that public-sector provision competed against private-sector contractors for non-clinical services. Private staff agencies are also important and the private finance initiative is encouraging private consortia to own and run services for the NHS estate.

Thus the government increasingly looks to the independent and voluntary sectors to assist in the provision of services and to play a role in influencing national policy debates. Even so this is considerably less given the national structure of the health system and the British parliamentary system, than in a locally determined system.

## Industry, the scientific community and pharmaceuticals

The huge variety and enormous scope of medical and technological development is difficult to track exactly. There is growing therapeutic potential, new knowledge about preventive strategies and more technical know-how in health. The role for technology in healthcare is increasing with regards to developing the services and treatment offered and in influencing the settings in which treatment and care take place. New materials, new communication media, new biochemistry, new bioengineering, and rapid advances in understanding genetics open huge possibilities for diagnosis, treatment, prevention, work organisation, and of course for realigning and increasing expenditure (see Chapters 4, 11 and 12 in this volume).

Developments in science and technology increasingly drive developments in the health sector. Many of the discoveries are located within private sector industries or funded from private sector profits. The pharmaceutical industry funds most Research and Development (R&D) in healthcare in the UK. Globalisation is affecting the pharmaceutical sector, which is seeing mergers and consolidation among its biggest companies. The NHS, although a comparatively low spender on drugs when compared to European counterparts, is facing increasing annual pharmaceutical expenditure, which looks set to continue. Figures from the Department of Health show that prescription costs rose by over

10 per cent for both the primary and secondary sectors in 2002–3, with statins (drugs to reduce cholesterol) accounting for 20 per cent of the increase (Health Service Journal, 2003). The Wanless review predicted an increase in annual spending on statins from the current level of £700 million to £2.1 billion in 2010 and this includes the assumption that all statin patents expire by 2010 (Gibson, 2004; Wanless, 2002:23). A significant proportion of worldwide company-financed pharmaceutical R&D is located in the UK and this allows the industry to have a voice both within the health sector and also through the Department for Trade and Industry.

What will affect industry in the future? There are several important developments. The effects of globalisation in terms of increasing cross-border flows of people, goods, services and capital, and the expectation of increasing returns in industry, mean that the successful pharmaceutical base in the UK is not a continuing certainty. Developments in cross-national policy are important, including the role that the European Union takes in regulation. The issue of patents and generic drugs and price controls are key issues, along with the relationships between the various organisations – public and private – involved in human genetic research. Second, the assessment and evaluation of technology in healthcare is becoming increasingly important with the pressures of new discoveries within the context of limited resources in the publicly funded NHS. The role of Health Technology Assessment and the National Institute for Clinical Excellence, which evaluate the economic and clinical value of new technologies and determine the 'added value' and cost-effectiveness of new medicines being introduced within the NHS, are likely to play a key role in matching these twin pressures for the future.

## Dynamics of the system

When considering the dynamics of the health system there are several ways in which the analysis could be focused. We have already talked about financial flows within the health system whereby universal budgets for the NHS are set by parliament and the Department of Health distributes money to local purchasers of services. We could also talk about the patient journey through the system. Patients usually enter the UK health system via a consultation with their general practitioner; citizens have to register with their local GP practice and are free to request appointments, for which there is no direct charge, unless a prescription is issued. Access to the secondary sector of the NHS is made via a referral from a general practitioner, for which patients usually have to wait for an appointment. There is only direct access to the secondary sector via the accident and emergency department. Patients are treated in the hospital to which the general practitioner refers them and they are discharged following treatment, with follow-up care usually provided by general practice. In the future it is envisaged that patients will be able to exercise choice in terms of provider and to have a booked appointment made directly with the hospital via the primary care practice.

In terms of the organisation and delivery of UK health services, as a centrally driven, national organisation, the NHS represents many features of the classical public bureaucracy. The strengths of the bureaucracy include its reliability, its ability to treat users or patients in an equitable way, and its ability to contain costs over time, unlike many other healthcare systems. Its weaknesses include its inability to adapt to the changing needs of its users, to respond to the pressures of a modern healthcare system (such as the adoption of new technologies and therapies), the lack of transparency on internal costs, and the lack of incentives and motivation for highly qualified, dynamic personnel.

In the early 1990s there was extensive reorganisation of the system with the introduction of the internal market, which separated purchasers and providers in healthcare and attempted to create competition for services. A systematic review of the evidence concerning the impact of the internal market produced mixed evidence on grounds of efficiency (a greater improvement in overall efficiency as measured by cost and activity levels than before its introduction), equity (no reduction in equity caused by patient selection), quality (some improvement with GP fund holders and movements up and down on dissatisfaction surveys), choice and responsiveness (no increase in choice) and accountability (no increase for GP fund holders and Trusts and some questions raised). The authors concluded:

> Perhaps the most striking conclusion to arise from this survey of the evidence is how little overall measurable change there seems to have been related to the core structures and mechanisms of the internal market. Indeed, in some areas where significant changes might have been expected, there were none. (Le Grand et al., 1998:129)

The implementation of the internal market does illustrate the direct impact that national policies have on the system – policy makers are able to effect change in the system; in fact, part of the problem of the system is perceived to be the high level of influence that policy makers, principally politicians, have on the service, which means it is politically driven and subject to numerous policy changes which often involve substantial reorganisation. When the current Labour government came to power it identified waiting lists as the key problem with the NHS, setting itself the election pledge of reducing the in-patient waiting list (those waiting for an in-patient appointment after seeing a specialist) by 100,000 (Labour Party General Election Manifesto 1997). Since the election, waiting lists have fallen. With the publication of the NHS Plan, the emphasis shifted to waiting times and by the end of 2005 the maximum waiting time should be three months for an out-patient appointment and six months for in-patient treatment (Department of Health, 2000:143).

Hospitals are now monitored via a series of performance targets, including waiting times, and their overall 'score' has implications for funding and intervention from the centre. There are significant incentives for hospitals to meet government targets on waiting times. Indeed, performance monitoring via national targets is perhaps the single biggest driver in the current UK system – it identifies the performance of politicians as well as those managing the service, it controls financial flows in the system, and it consumes a considerable proportion (though not systematically measured) of management time throughout the system.

A new system of 'clinical governance' was introduced in 1997, which applies a statutory duty for quality in NHS trusts. To reduce the wide variations in services and outcomes a rolling programme of National Service Frameworks were established in 1998 in England and Wales to set out quality of care for various conditions. The National Institute for Clinical Excellence was established to draw up guidelines on interventions following clinical and cost-evaluation. A telephone and Internet helpline to access NHS services, 'NHS Direct', was made available nationally in 2000. Other expectations in terms of the application of information technology to health services have not been met, as the chapter by Rigby in this volume identifies. Every GP surgery and hospital was to be connected to the NHSnet by 2002, but that has not yet happened.

The present shape of the UK health system reflects exposure to high rates of organisational change, complexity in management tasks, divergence in stakeholder expectations and participation; which are all embedded within a highly politicised system which inevitably grows from taxation-based forms of dominant funding. Deeply held values of universality and free care at the point of delivery deriving from the foundation of the welfare state in 1945, mix not always comfortably with values which have evolved over 60 years and now give additional, but not alternative, emphasis to commitments to quality of health and healthcare, individual and public choice and value for money.

Policy makers and senior executives grapple to create a future based in this context in the realisation that science, technology, commercial investment, professional ethics and the spirits of enquiry and humanitarianism will inevitably result in increasing opportunities and demands for expenditure which can always be well justified. They are also aware that they are in competition for skills, talent, and public and private investment in global market places.

The future shape of the system has to be founded on an acknowledgement of tensions and contradictions within the whole, and systems of accountability for the outcomes of health and healthcare wherein responsibility is matched with authority.

## References

Acheson, D. (1998) *Report of the Independent Inquiry into Inequalities in Health.* London: The Stationery Office

Ahmed, K. (2000) 'Labour Advisors branded "useless"', *The Observer*, Sunday 31st December 2000

Anderson, G., Hurst, J., Hussey, P., Jee-Hughes, M. (2000) 'Health spending and outcomes: trends in OECD countries 1960–1998', *Health Affairs*, May/June

BBC, 13 August 2002, Overseas NHS care gets thumbs up

BBC, 20 February 2004, Europe rules on foreign op costs

BBC News (2003), Vol. 2004.

Bindman, A. and Weiner, J. (2000) 'The modern NHS: an underfunded model of efficiency and integration', *Health Affairs*, May/June

Black, D., Morris. J., Smith, C., Townsend, P. (1980) *Inequalities in Health: a Report of a Research Working Group* (Black Report). London: Department of Health and Social Security

CHI (2004) *Unpacking the Patients' Perspective: Variations in NHS Patients Experience in England.* London, Commission for Health Improvement

Coulter, A. (2002a) 'Patients' views of the good doctor', *British Medical Journal*, 325:668–9

Coulter, A. (2002b) *The Autonomous Patient. Ending Paternalism in Medical Care.* London: Nuffield Trust

Davies, C. (ed.) (2003) *The Future Health Workforce.* Basingstoke: Palgrave Macmillan

Day, P., and Klein, R. (1997) *Steering but not Rowing? Transformation of the Department of Health.* Bristol: Policy Press

Department of Health (1997) *NHS Plan. A First Class Service.* London: The Stationery Office

Department of Health (2000) *Departmental Report.* London: The Stationery Office

Department of Health (2003) *Annual Report of the Department of Health.* London,: The Stationery Office

Detmer, D.E., Singleton, P.D., MacLeod, A., Wait, S., Taylor, M. and Ridgwell, J. (2003) *The Informed Patient: Study Report*. Cambridge: Cambridge University Health mimeo, Judge Institute

Dixon J. et al. (1999) 'Is the English NHS underfunded?' *British Medical Journal*, **314**:58

Dowie, R. and Langman, M. (1999) 'The hospital of the future: staffing of hospitals: future needs, future provision', *British Medical Journal*, **319**, 7218, 1193–5

Dunnigan, M.G. and Pollock, A.M. (2003) 'Downsizing of acute inpatient beds associated with private finance initiative: Scotland's case study', *British Medical Journal*, **326**, 905–10

Evans, B. and Pritchard, C. (2000) 'Cancer survival rates and GDP expenditure on health: a comparison of England and Wales and the USA, Denmark, Netherlands, Finland, France, Germany, Italy, Spain, and Switzerland in the 1990s', *Public Health*, **114**, 336–9

Exworthy, M., Stuart, M., Blane, D. and Marmot, M. (2003) *Tackling Health Inequalities since the Acheson Inquiry*. The Policy Press for Joseph Rowntree Foundation

Foresight (2000) *Healthcare 2020*. Department of Trade and Industry, December 2000

Gibson, L. (2004) 'Move to sell statins over the counter raises concerns', *British Medical Journal*, **328**:1221 (22 May)

Goodman, A. and Shephard, A. (2002) *Inequality and Living Standards in Britain. Some facts*. London: The Institute for Fiscal Studies

Gould, M. (2004) 'UK consultants' fees for private work are amongst highest in world', *British Medical Journal*, **328**:70

Health Select Committee (2002) *The Role of the Private Sector in the NHS*. London: House of Commons, Palace of Westminster

IPPR (2001) *Building Better Partnerships*. London: Commission on Public Private Partnerships, IPPR

Kmietowicz, Z. (2003) 'BMA welcomes review of NHS quangos', *British Medical Journal*, **327**:1308

Koralage, N. (2004) 'GPs reluctant to cover out of hours work, survey shows', *British Medical Journal*, **328**:247

Labour Party (1997) *Britain Deserves Better*. London: General Election Manifesto 1997, Labour Party

Laurance, J. (2003) 'Patients cannot pay rising costs of prescriptions, warns group', *The Independent*, 8 July

Le Grand, J., Mays, N. and Mulligan, J. (eds) (1998) *Learning from the Internal Market: a Review of the Evidence*. London: Kings Fund

Lynch, J.W., et al. (2000) 'Income inequality and mortality: importance to health of individual income, psychosocial environment, or material conditions'. *British Medical Journal*, **320**:1200–04

Mossialos, E. and Thompson, S. (2001) *Voluntary Health Insurance in the European Union*. London: London School of Economics

OECD Health Data (2004) http://www.oecd.org/dataoecd/3/62/31938359.pdf

Owen, J.W. (2002) *The National Health Service and The New Health Economy Securing Our Future Health*. London: Nuffield Trust

Palmer, G., North, J., Carr, J. and Kenway, P. (2003) *Monitoring Poverty and Social Exclusion*. Joseph Rowntree Foundation

Pollock, A.M., Shaoul, J. and Vickers, N. (2002) 'Private finance and "value for money" in NHS hospitals: a policy in search of a rationale?' *BMJ*, **324**:1205–09

Robert, G. (1999) 'Science and technology: trends and issues forward to 2015: implications for healthcare'. *Policy futures for UK health. Technical series*, no. 4. London: Nuffield Trust

Sausman, C. (2003) 'The future health workforce: an overview of trends', in *The Future Health Workforce*, C. Davies (ed.), Palgrave Macmillan, pp. 222–42

Shephard, A. (2003) *Inequality under the Labour government*. London: Institute for Fiscal Studies

HM Treasury (2002) *Budget Report*. London: HM Treasury

Wait, S. (2004) *Benchmarking: a Policy Analysis*. London: The Nuffield Trust (www.nuffieldtrust.org.uk)

Wait, S. and Nolte, E. (2005) 'Benchmarking health systems: trends, conceptual issues and future perspectives', *Benchmarking International Journal*, **12**,4/5 (in press)

Wanless, D. (2001) *Securing our Future Health: Taking a Long-Term View. Interim Report*. London: HM Treasury

Wanless, D. (2002) *Securing our Future Health: Taking a Long-Term View*. London: HM Treasury

Winstanley, D., Sorabji, D. and Dawson, S. (1995) 'When the pieces don't fit: a stakeholder power matrix to analyse public sector restructuring', *Public Money & Management*, April–June:19–26

World Health Organisation (2000) *The WHO Report 2000, Health Systems, Improving Performance*. Geneva: WHO

Young, R. and Leese, B. (1999) 'Recruitment and retention of general practitioners in the UK: what are the problems and solutions?', *British Journal of General Practice*, **49**, 447, 829–33

Zimmern, R. and Cook, C. (2000) *The Nuffield Trust Genetics Scenario Project: genetics and health policy issues for genetic science and their implications for health and health services*. London: The Stationary Office

# 2
# Systems for Health or Healthcare Systems?

*Derek Yach*

## Introduction

Over the years, the phrase 'healthcare systems' has been used to refer to all forms of treatments for diseases, some aspects of rehabilitation, and a few aspects of primary prevention or health promotion. Health departments of countries manage healthcare systems and receive 'health' budgets to do so. This narrow perspective leads to public confusion and a lack of clarity about who is really responsible for broader aspects of health. Do health departments and ministers of health really lead the way in ensuring that government policies are coherent with the health needs of populations? If they did, they would be managing a system for health. This rarely happens; should it? As McGinnis et al. (2002) stated, 'public policymakers need to begin thinking in terms of a health agenda rather than a healthcare agenda or-even more narrowly – a healthcare financing agenda.' This chapter considers how a system for health would differ from a healthcare system.

In recent years many health issues have highlighted the need for such a system-wide approach. The recent SARS epidemic had a significant impact well beyond illness or death in infected people and caused significant harmful impacts within weeks on trade and tourism in affected countries. HIV/Aids in Africa is believed to exert a major negative impact on the continent's development prospects and on its political stability. In an era of heightened concerns about security, many infectious diseases are seen as potential threats to all countries. The recently concluded Framework Convention on Tobacco Control required complex discussions and negotiations to ensure that the multi-sectoral nature of tobacco control was addressed along with demand reduction. All these examples highlight the need for more multi-sectoral dialogue and actions to promote health; and further, indicate the presence in some cases of a gap in global and national governance of health issues with complex determinants and multiple impacts beyond healthcare.

## Which public health issues require a broader systems approach?

The burden of disease has three components: deaths, disease and disability. The determinants of death or disability from a specific cause may differ from the determinants of disease. In general, factors outside of healthcare systems determine the incidence of new cases and thus the state of the problem for any country, while the response of healthcare systems explains levels of complications, case-fatality and disability. Thus, better access to clean water and sanitation reduces the incidence of diarrhoeal disease while access to oral rehydration and in some cases, hospital care, determines whether children with diarrhoea die. For chronic diseases like HIV/Aids, TB, cancer, diabetes and cardiovascular disease, there is a long lag between exposure to risks for disease and the occurrence of clinical disease. Acting on the risk factors (such as unsafe sex or blood supplies, tobacco use or unhealthy diets) or on broader societal determinants of health like female literacy, will reduce incidence, while effective treatment will prevent serious complications and death.

Public health investments do not adequately tackle risk factors early enough. Such risks include food-related factors (such as micronutrient deficiencies; lack of fruit and vegetables; obesity; excess salt consumption); addictive behaviours (alcohol, tobacco and illicit drugs); a range of environmental factors (from global climate change to water, sanitation and air pollution); and unsafe sex. Recent work by WHO (WHO, 2002) has shown that these risks contribute to a considerable proportion of the total burden of disease (Figure 2.1). Reducing these risks requires strong collaboration between many sectors over decades. For them, only a systems approach will be successful.

In contrast, healthcare systems are very successful in preventing certain deaths and complications from many diseases provided treatments are effective and people have access to them. About half of the decline in CVD cardiac vascular disease mortality in the USA over the last two decades is ascribed to better treatment, half to better prevention of risks (Beaglehole and Yach, 2003). For a few cancers, treatment has led to dramatic increases in survival (WHO, 2003). However, this has not been the case with two major tobacco-related cancers: lung and larynx

44

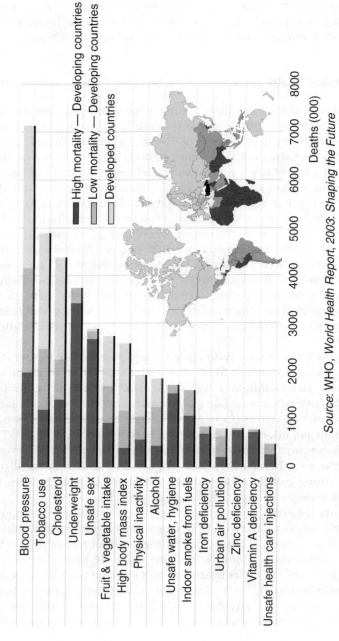

Blood pressure
Tobacco use
Cholesterol
Underweight
Unsafe sex
Fruit & vegetable intake
High body mass index
Physical inactivity
Alcohol
Unsafe water, hygiene
Indoor smoke from fuels
Iron deficiency
Urban air pollution
Zinc deficiency
Vitamin A deficiency
Unsafe health care injections

High mortality — Developing countries
Low mortality — Developing countries
Developed countries

0    1000    2000    3000    4000    5000    6000    7000    8000
Deaths (000)

Source: WHO, World Health Report, 2003: Shaping the Future

Figure 2.1: Deaths attributable to 16 leading risk factors: all countries, 2001

(WHO, 2003). Survival after infection with HIV/Aids has increased to beyond a decade in people on treatment. Importantly, the benefits of such treatment are now visible in terms of increased survival and characteristics of the patients who die. Advocacy groups for patients' rights to treatment have successfully changed drug pricing policies and improved access to diagnosis and treatment for a range of diseases from HIV/Aids, breast cancer and epilepsy.

In contrast, the voices calling for prevention and health promotion are relatively mute. It is not possible to show who benefits from prevention programmes and further many successful prevention programmes take decades to demonstrate that they have reduced death and disease rates. For theses reason, the political pressure for greater investments in prevention and health promotion has till recently been lacking.

Stronger systems are needed to promote health and prevent risks and better healthcare systems are needed to address failures of prevention and conditions for which causes (and also successful interventions) remain unknown (McGinnis, 2002).

## How would a system for health differ from a healthcare system?

The goals of a system concerned about health would be broader, and focus more on determinants and underlying causes of ill-health and ways of promoting health than is the case with most healthcare systems. Healthcare systems usually focus on providing treatment within a system that emphasises quality of care, cost-effectiveness and equity in access to lifelong care. Within government, many sectors play a role in promoting health or causing disease. A system for health would recognise this and ensure that all policies were evaluated in relation to their impact on health and not just from a narrow sectoral perspective. Healthcare systems are funded mainly from health department budgets, some form of social insurance and through private out-of-pocket expenditure. In contrast, a system for health could tap into funding within many sectoral departments – from agriculture and sports, to education and welfare. Healthcare system debates at national level tend to focus on whether programmes should be vertical or horizontal, and how to achieve cost-containment and equity goals. Debates within government on systems for health would address complex and profound issues involving trade-offs between development priorities and between allocations that would benefit current as opposed to future generations. Policy impacts would be required to ensure that decisions are made in a transparent manner.

Environmental impact assessments of major infrastructural projects, new city developments, and social policies have for years been required prior to new projects and policies being approved. However, health considerations are rarely considered in such impact assessments and the result may be profoundly negative for health. For example:

- Urban design decisions rarely consider the impact on physical activity and consequently obesity, type II diabetes and CVD.
- Agricultural policies are not developed from a health perspective but primarily for short-term commercial and political reasons. Thus we have subsidies on products harmful to health, like tobacco; subsidies that protect developed countries' farmers at the cost of developing countries' economies; and few incentives for farmers to grow more desperately needed fruit and vegetables.
- Trade policies often place protection of patents ahead of public health concerns – particularly those of the poorest countries and communities.
- Decisions related to foreign direct investment (FDI) are usually neutral with regard to the impact of new investments on health outcomes and assume that FDI is always good for societies because it brings with it new jobs and economic growth. Contrary evidence suggests that certain types of FDI promote rapid acquisition of unhealthy consumption patterns for products like tobacco, foods with a high fat, sugar and salt content, and alcohol.

Systems for health would be governed at the national level with involvement of the cabinet as a whole and not just regarded, if they are seriously regarded at all, by the ministry of health. In a few countries, ministries of health are often mandated to lead on all issues related to health. This usually occurs when there is a strong and dynamic minister. At the international level, the issue is more complex. Some would argue that the United Nations should take charge of global health policies and governance. However, WHO was initially established to be the source of international guidance on all health matters and not confined to deal only with a narrower subset of healthcare or health service related issues. WHO's Constitution emphasises its overall role in 'health' matters beyond healthcare and over the last 55 years of its existence, this role has only been formally challenged once.

That occurred in 1996 when the International Court of Justice responded to a request by the World Health Assembly to deliver an advisory opinion on the following question: 'in view of the health and environmental effects, would the use of nuclear weapons by a State in war or other armed conflict be a breach of its obligations under international law including the WHO constitution?' The court argued that it lacked jurisdiction to respond to WHO's question because the legality of use of nuclear weapons did not fall within the competence of the organisation. An important conclusion by the court was that WHO, as a specialised agency belonging to a coherent institutional system laid out under the UN Charter is rather subject to a 'principle of speciality'. This interpretation implies that specialised agencies are endowed with sectoral and complementary powers that may neither encroach on each other or the general powers of the UN (Burci, 2004).

This interpretation could have had serious implications for the scope of WHO's work, but in the intervening years governments have not considered applying this principle when considering revisions to the Biological and Chemical Weapons Conventions, while developing the Framework Convention on Tobacco Control or when developing policies to address diet and physical activity. All require actions by sectors and interests way outside the narrow confines of a ministry of health.

## Who has responsibility for resolving complex trade-offs?

Systems for health would consider how best to address the complex trade-offs that exist between sectoral priorities and goals and resolve them by being explicit about the nature of the conflicts and by assigning a high value to health outcomes in the decision-making process. At a national level, resolution of such conflicts would happen in cabinet and may be led by the health department, the treasury or the finance department, or the office of the executive head of state. One of these potential conflicts relates to how much of the national budget should be allocated to healthcare, how much to other programmes that would stimulate health gains and how much to other social and related services?

The recent work of the Commission on Macroeconomics and Health, initiated by WHO and chaired by Jeffrey Sachs, provided a strong rationale for investments in health to be given higher priority within government decision-making and justified the decision by showing that such investment would stimulate economic development and not just reduce rates of deaths and disease. While the commission initially focused on Aids, malaria, TB, tobacco and certain vaccine-related diseases in the poorest countries, more recent work on the macroeconomics of CVD in low-middle income countries, came to the same general conclusions as his original work. Invest more in health – particularly those aspects that will reduce the incidence of CVD.

The Final Report by Derek Wanless to the UK Chancellor of the Exchequer, 'Securing Good Health for the Whole Population', goes much further than almost any other national initiative or review and provides detailed guidance to sectoral ministries about how they could contribute to improving health overall, and especially how they could reduce inequalities in health (Wanless, 2004). What makes Wanless's work so important is that it was commissioned by the UK Treasury and coordinated by them, albeit by drawing heavily on public health expertise. The Final Report must rank as one of the most important contributions to public health anywhere, and certainly has implications for how one can take a step-by-step approach to building true systems for health. Unlike so many other reports cited by him over the last few decades, this one is likely to be backed by government finance and where required, legislation and taxation; and is already strongly supported by a newly activated public health community in the UK.

## What types of conflicts will occur?

Progress in much of infectious disease control is achievable with additional funding for surveillance and effective treatment; for new supply and distribution of drugs and vaccines where existing ones are ineffective or not available; and is also required for general improvements in housing and related infrastructure (water, sanitation and energy). All of these investments are now regarded as non-contentious. Even the tough issues of improving access to drugs in poor countries are being addressed nationally and internationally within the context of the Doha trade round. Conflicts that do remain relate to how sustainable sources of funds for effective action in treating HIV/Aids, malaria, and TB will be developed.

Similar progress has not been made in respect of the major risks for chronic diseases. Figure 2.1 indicates the burden of disease attributable to major risk factors for health worldwide. It is striking to note how many risks, accounting for a huge component of the total burden of disease in the poorest and the most developed countries require changes in the consumption of products in every day trade and commerce.

WHO and most public health agencies often issue calls for individuals to stop smoking; eat less fat, sugar and salt; do more physical activity and eat more fruits, vegetables, nuts and grains. They do so knowing that individual responsibility without supportive government and

*Table 2.1*: Supporters and opponents of selected policy issues

| Major risk factor | Policy issue | Supporters | Opponents |
|---|---|---|---|
| Tobacco | Excise tax | National Finance Departments, World Bank | Tobacco industry |
| | Advertising bans on tobacco products | Some public health specialists/ organisations/pressure groups | Advertisers, media, libertarians |
| | Smoke-free areas | Consumer groups, public health NGOs | Hotels and restaurants |
| | Agricultural subsidies | Enlightened countries | Farmers, rural voters |
| Diet, nutrition | Advertising to children | Some public health specialists/ organisations/pressure groups | Advertisers, multi-national food companies, media |
| | Commodity charges | Fruit and vegetables producers | Sugar farmers, producers, lobbyists |
| | Promotion to children | Sport goods and clubs | Food, toys, media |

multi-sectoral action does not lead to sustained change. Further, unless 'healthy choices are made', in the words of the Ottawa Charter (WHO, 1986), 'the easy choices', unhealthy consumption patterns, will persist, especially among the poor where they often become entrenched as the easiest and most affordable choices.

Table 2.1 summarises a number of policy issues relating to tobacco and diet nutrition that require resolution at a level of government outside of the health department. In the table some traditional opponents to healthy public policies are listed, along with possible supporters of change. Tobacco and diet/physical activity are major contributors to the burden of disease in developed and developing countries.

Because of their disproportionate impact, special emphasis is given to the nature of conflicts and trade-offs that has occurred in these areas. The call to stop smoking has unified a variety of groups from the tobacco industry themselves, the hospitality and entertainment industries, farmers, advertising companies and often the media. All are told a simple message: if people smoke less, many jobs will be lost. It has taken decades of policy work by economists, public health advocates and practitioners to correct myths propagated by the tobacco industry surrogates, some of which have even now got considerable currency:

- Restaurants and pubs will go bankrupt if smoke-free policies are introduced, whereas the opposite is the truth.
- Finance departments will lose revenue from smuggling and reduced tax receipts if excise taxes increase; once again the opposite seems to be true in both cases. Smuggling may have a small impact on revenue but the solution is not to condone crime but rather to strengthen customs and excise controls.
- Farmers in countries like Zimbabwe and Malawi will be unemployed in a few years as tobacco consumption declines. Unfortunately from a public health perspective, consumption does not fall at a rate faster then 5 per cent per year, and usually rates of 2 per cent have been regarded as impressive if maintained for years. At those rates, and in the face of continued population growth, the demand for leaf tobacco will remain high for many decades, and agricultural policies can be put in place if there is political will to do so. The immediate threat to African tobacco farmers comes more from the introduction of mechanisation locally and subsidies in developed countries then from less consumption of tobacco.

A public health statement, 'consume sugar sparingly', that seems like commonsense to most people, evokes strong responses from a wide range of special interests. During the development of a WHO Global Strategy on Diet, Physical Activity and Health, the full range of possible arguments against this simple message about sugar emerged. Soft fizzy drink manufacturers have led the global efforts to deny that sugar causes obesity or dental caries, or that specific levels of free sugars are desirable. Sugarcane farmers in developing countries are concerned that if new WHO/FAO guidelines on sugar consumption were applied globally, they would lose their jobs. The economic stakes are much more substantive in sugar than in tobacco; the size of the lobbying community is far greater and the evidence base on the economics of sugar use is not as well described as it is for tobacco.

For several years efforts were made to be prepared for critique of any efforts to control tobacco use. These included engaging with the Food and Agricultural Organisation, the World Bank, the IMF, UNICEF and other UN partners and jointly agreeing that the key policy goal in relation to tobacco was demand reduction. Supply related issues would need to be addressed but should not block action on making public health gains. In the process, new research by the World Bank showed that tobacco control was sound economic and health policy; and FAO showed that farmers' short-term fears were exaggerated. Within the UN family policy coherence was achieved, and this was later reflected in increased policy coherence within governments. Similar work is yet to emerge with respect to many food policy issues. They are inherently more complex, involve a wider array of players and will need to address the reality that there may be some losers over the long term, but that these are likely to be more than offset by winners.

## Shifting policies: key players need to assume new roles

A shift in thinking away from healthcare systems to systems for health requires individual and collective leadership within many institutions over time. However, institutional inertia, for many reasons, is too often the norm. Major policy makers who could put prevention and health promotion higher on their agenda are often hampered by weak arguments that should emphasise the health gains that would accrue over time. Further, special interests are paid to maintain the status quo while insufficient attention has been given to developing new business models transition policies that allow markets to be more coherent with public health goals. Some policy shifts required by key agencies in order to move towards systems for health are outlined below

### The role of executive: heads of state

Heads of state of the 'G8' – the eight major industrial democracies (the UK, France, Germany, the US, Canada, Italy, Japan and Russia) – recognised health as a global challenge at the G8 Summit in 2000, acknowledging that health is the 'key to prosperity' and 'poor health drives poverty'. This represents an important step towards building a real system that addresses health from a multisectoral perspective. The specifics of their initial focus however, suggest that they intend to limit their support to specific areas such as the establishment of the Global Fund for HIV/Aids, TB and malaria. No subsequent commitment has yet been made for chronic diseases and the complex issues involved in food policy have yet to receive serious attention. The G77, representing heads of state from approximately 130 developing countries, has recently addressed global health issues. Their focus has also been on communicable diseases. The G77 did however support the Framework Convention on Tobacco Control (FCTC) – a turnaround for many G77 members, who previously feared reduced tobacco consumption would negatively affect their farmers. They recognised the validity of the arguments related to the need to focus on demand reduction and were not influenced by lobbyists to use tobacco industry arguments to delay progress. However, their response to the Global Strategy on Diet, Physical Activity and Health has been markedly different (WHO, 2004). Initially they opposed the strategy maintaining that chronic diseases were not a priority for their countries, and further, maintaining that the evidence on sugar was not valid.

The political space created for health in international, multi-lateral fora could be invaluable if it evolved towards being used as an arena to tackle complex long-term choices for health that often require unpopular trade-offs.

## The role of health ministries

Health ministers hold the national responsibility for putting health first in policy and budgetary debates within government. To date they have been ill equipped to fulfil this role. They lack information about the health impact of major development decisions taken by other sectors, and often lack the political clout needed to over-rule development decisions that lead to harmful health outcomes. This could change if they invested a small proportion of their time and investment in building capacity to carry out health impact assessment and to advocate for their conclusions to be incorporated into policy processes. Health departments need to free up staff to focus their energy fulltime on assessing how other sectors can play their parts in being more health promoting. This would require new skills, new assessment tools and new mechanisms to be created within government in order to give greater priority to deliberations about the health consequences of planned policies and programmes. The development of cross-departmental consensus and action will only come if each ministry which must be involved will develop the political will to act for concerns which have traditionally been seen as 'someone else's' problem. This requires that not just the costs but the benefits and the praise for success will be shared. Many governments could learn from the experience of Thailand. They have developed a Health Promotion Foundation funded from a 2 per cent tax on tobacco and alcohol. The work of the foundation has stimulated the types of innovations required to build systems for health.

## The role of the World Health Organisation (WHO)

The main objective of the WHO is to support the 'attainment by all peoples of the highest possible level of health'. Its ability to lever change within other UN agencies that would advance health goals is still largely untapped. However, recent work on HIV/Aids, tobacco, SARS and food safety all suggest that progress can be made when a compelling case for action by WHO's sister agencies is made on health grounds. But similar requirements for success exist at the international level, that is solid evidence, effective and dynamic leadership, political will, opportunities for dialogue, determination to follow through and share the praise and benefits as well as the blame and the costs.

## The role of research institutions

Three or more decades of sustained support for tropical disease research and research training has led to stronger national capacity for research in developing countries and to the development of effective evidence based policies. Similar investments are needed to build national capacity to work across many sectors. This would require those who fund research to work outside of current disciplinary fields and to find ways of stimulating multi-disciplinary policy research that would seek preventive and promotive solutions to major health problems.

## The role of donors

Official development assistance for health has increased in the past five years. The increase is almost entirely due to increased funding for HIV/Aids in Sub-Saharan Africa. Some areas of public health receive very little funding. For example, of the total amount of Overseas Development Aid for health in 2002 of $2.9 billion, about 0.1 per cent was earmarked for chronic disease or related risk factors. The amount spent on health promotion remains small. Some aspects of prevention, notably vaccines, have received increased support in recent years. Private investment in global health far exceeds government assistance, and most targets infectious diseases and humanitarian needs. There is a large unmet need for investments in health promotion and in policies that would lever health improvements through changes in the work of other sectors.

## The role of the World Bank and regional development banks

The World Bank and their regional counterparts have for years emphasised the importance of environmental impact assessment. Major infrastructure programmes involving dams, roads and urban development have been affected by the outcomes of such assessment. Rarely however, have health considerations been taken into account in deciding on whether to support new development projects. Yet as outlined above, the potential exists to reduce adverse health impacts and often to enhance health gains through modest changes to project design. For example, urban development projects in rapidly urbanising developing countries should be regarded as opportunities to enhance physical activity, not retard it; to improve access to fruit and vegetables not make it unaffordable; and to improve safety and security of communities, not threaten it.

## The role of business

A number of leading companies recognise that health promotion and disease prevention need to be given greater priority within the business sector and some are actively trying to develop new business models that are both profitable and good for public health. These include a number of food companies and some pharmaceutical companies. Unilever, Nestle, Pepsico and Kraft have all recently announced intentions to make significant product and marketing changes aimed at being more supportive of public health diet and physical activity goals. These changes include removal of trans-fatty acids from product lines that are widely consumed; reductions in the salt, sugar and saturated fat content of many product lines; greater investment in foods with 'healthier' content profiles; and the development of new products with health and in the case of Unilever, 'vitality', enhancing properties. Together with product changes there have been commitments to review how products are marketed to children with the aim being to remove all false, misleading and deceptive imagery and to ensure that physical activity messages get more emphasis. It is too early to know if these commitments will all be translated into action, and as importantly, whether they will lead to other companies following their lead. If so, there is a huge potential to bring about beneficent public health changes.

Novo Nordisk also announced its commitment to 'rather prevent than just cure'. The CEO and president of NN, Lars Rebien Sorensen announced that NN is preparing to revolutionise the business model on which the research-based drug industry is based and start shifting towards developing a strategy to prevent chronic diseases (Kristensen, 2004). In making the announcement, Sorenson recognised that a wide array of players from the pharmaceutical, food, sports, entertainment and insurance industries would all need to join forces to create new opportunities for prevention and health promotion. At this stage, this is mainly still a vision, but a powerful one that builds on a trend outlined recently by Ilona Kickbusch (Kickbusch, 2003), who writes of 'the increasing privatisation of health promotion' and the emergence of a wellness market. She argues this trend is blurring the lines between food, dietary supplements and pharmaceuticals; is leading to increased investments in employee health programmes; is drawing insurers into including wellness services, from gym membership to massage therapy, into health plans; and is increasingly evident on the services and advice offered on the Internet. The overall impact of this is likely first to increase awareness and use of selected products and services by those already at lowest risk, and only later will benefits accrue to those at the highest level of health risk. But making a start is vital. Policy makers need to be aware of these trends and be ready to intervene where it is possible to accelerate widespread access to new innovations and also be ready strongly to regulate unsubstantiated claims. Taken with advances in genomics, technology changes over the next few decades will re-define our notions of disease and how to detect and manage it.

### The role of global non-governmental organisations

Through effective international advocacy and grass-roots action, highly visible and articulate global NGOs such as Oxfam and Médecins Sans Frontières have successfully advanced the agendas on issues related to drug access for Aids, malaria and other infectious diseases. A similar approach advocating for stronger health promotion and disease pre-vention has yet to emerge. Lessons about how best to advocate for multi-sectoral approaches to prevention could be learned from the emer-gence of the Framework Convention Alliance that brought together 200 NGO's worldwide in support of an effective FCTC.

### From a system for health to a system for sustainable development

Greater efforts need to be made to have health move higher up the political agenda. 'Systems for health' and not just more healthcare, however efficient and effective, are required to tackle the incidence of disease. At the same time those systems for health need to become coherent with broader development approaches and locate their work within the context of sustainable development. This would require more integrated approaches to solutions. For example, food policy that promotes the consumption of a balanced diet rich in fruits and vegeta-bles, transport policies that encourage bicycle use and maximum use of public transport, expanded use of cleaner forms of energy and reduced tobacco use, together would prevent an emerging double burden of dis-eases in developing countries and simultaneously contribute to a more sustainable path of development. Getting there will require the time span set to justify investments. It will also need a shift in the way economists value health and the environment, national politicians and multi-lateral agencies approach health policy, businesses view their area of strategic action and all of us involved in lobbying, consuming, investing and voting, determine our priorities.

## References

Beaglehole, R. and Yach, D. (2003) 'Globalisation and the prevention and control of non-communicable disease: the neglected chronic diseases of adults', *The Lancet*, **362**:903–8

Burci, G.L. and Vignes C.H. (2004) *World Health Organization*. The Netherlands: Kluwer Law International

Kickbusch, I. and Payne, L. (2003) 'Twenty-first century health promotion: the public health revolution meets the wellness revolution', *Health Promotion International*, **18**, 4, 275–8

Kristensen, M. (2004) 'Novo Nordisk's new strategy: from fighting diseases to improving health', *Monday Morning* (Danish newspaper) 13 06–02–2004

McGinnis, J.M., Williams-Russo, P. and Knickman, J.R. (2002) 'The case for more active policy attention to health promotion', *Health Affairs*, **21**, 2, 78–93

Wanless, D. (2004) *Securing Good Health for the Whole Population*. Final Report. London: HM Treasury

Unilever (2003) *Wellbeing and Performance*. The Netherlands: Unilever Health Institute Symposium Series

Waxman, A. (2004) 'The WHO global strategy on diet, physical activity and health', *Development*, **47**, 2, 75–82

World Health Organisation (1986) *1st International Conference on Health Promotion* Ottawa, Canada, November

World Health Organisation (2002) *World Health Report 2002: Reducing Risks; Promoting Healthy Life*, Geneva: WHO

World Health Organisation (2003) *World Cancer Report*. Stewart, B.W. and Kleihues, P. Lyon: International Agency for Research on Cancer

# 3
# The State of the Healthcare System in England

*Calum Paton*

## Introduction

Health policy in England – in the sense of 'high politics' i.e. political decisions as to the shape of the health system – is driven primarily by ideological factors, rather than technical factors aimed at increasing the cost-effectiveness of public expenditure and/or improving quality (Paton, 2001). As a result, the many initiatives geared to the latter ends often have to be implemented in a roundabout way, through institutions which are less than fit for the purpose, creating complexity and obstacles in implementation (Paton, 1999). Reconciling ideologically-motivated yet piecemeal 'chunks' of policy – including Foundation Trusts and various versions of the 'new internal market' – is problematical, not just because of the opportunity cost of the effort but because different chunks of policy imply different incentive systems and even different values. The challenge for the future is to simplify and synthesise policy on the basis of adequate consensus between the state, the medical profession and the public in order to achieve better value for money for objectives which are (at a high level) ideologically and politically driven, and yet are most effectively secured at grass-roots level (Salter, 1998; Klein, 2000).

The rhetoric of post-1997 New Labour under Prime Minister Tony Blair rejects the 'direct provision' state for the regulatory state (Jessop, 2002). Yet the reality is greater centralisation – not because the 'new devolution' based on 'shifting the balance of power' (Department of Health, 2001) is too timid, but because Strategic Health Authorities (SHAs) and (especially) Primary Care Trusts (PCTs) have responsibility, not power. The new arrangements in the NHS without an effective regional tier mean that the key capital and planning decisions (such as the creation of new hospitals, especially under the Private Finance Initiative (PFI), are centralised to the Department of Health (DoH). The challenge for the future here is to achieve an appropriate mix between devolution and centralism which is transparent, stable and designed around health policy functions rather than piecemeal political initiatives.

The first part of this paper provides an analysis of the 'present predicament' of the NHS. The second part builds on this analysis by developing prescriptions for the future. The author draws on other work in his analysis of the state of the healthcare state as well as his direct personal experience as a chairman of a large NHS trust.

## Background

From 1948 to 1991 the NHS was the antithesis of 'command and control' (Paton et al., 1998). Alongside traditional public administration sat medical networks (both benign and otherwise). What Mrs Thatcher hoped to get from her internal market was a means of control to ensure that the commands of central priorities were implemented (Paton, 1992). In the post-1997 world of New Labour control has deepened in pursuit of a wider set of central priorities, putting quality and – to a limited extent – equality on the agenda alongside a technocratic approach popularly described as 'bean-counting' (Paton, 1999). With the new Labour Government of 1997 there was much talk of 'a' or 'the' third way (Giddens, 2000). In Health Policy the 'Third Way' was an alternative to the command and control (first way) and the internal market (second way), mirroring the economy-wide Third Way following 'old-style social democracy' (first way) and Thatcherism (second way). However the characterisation of 1948–91 in the NHS by New Labour can be questioned thereby leaving the Third Way as misleading rhetoric – and its co-existence with the reality of command and control in an uneasy state.

Exworthy and Halford (1999) put both the new managerialism and quasi-markets in context, and point to quasi-markets, quasi-hierarchies and quasi-networks. A hierarchy which does not provide the basis for 'commanding' the doctors is quasi at best. Indeed the quasi-market and the 'networks' approach, which developed within the bosom of the internal market (Flynn, 1992), rather than from the rhetoric of the Third Way, were both attempts to render the medical profession corporately responsible. Alongside creating consistency, coherence and parsimony from the plethora of 'new institutions' in and over the NHS, this remains the biggest challenge – to which clinical governance, consultant appraisals, re-validation and the new consultant contract will, it is hoped, make a big contribution.

This is less a Third Way than the unfinished business of the Griffiths reforms of 1983 from which the internal market was a distraction. Labour's stance around 1992 accepted the Griffiths legacy, rejected the internal market – and sought a framework for performance management which rewarded successful organisations, incorporated clinical assessment and did so in the context of what would now be called 'local health economies' and appropriate regional planning (Labour Party, 1992). Indeed, many of New Labour's keynote 'quality' and even 'performance incentive' initiatives were present in embryo in the policy papers developed earlier (Labour Party, 1995).

The complication now is the policy and institutional inheritance, which has created a 'mobilisation of bias' in policy-making towards a new ideological approach. New Labour inherited the 'Thatcher reforms' to the NHS's structure and culture and also promulgated (especially from 2001 onwards) its own 'mixed economy' agenda for the NHS (Milburn, 2002). It is the assertion of this paper that this plethora of systems and initiatives is obstructing genuine devolution in the NHS.

When the then Secretary of State for Health, Alan Milburn, spoke of a mixture of ideological approaches, on the one hand, he was eager to deny 'Stalinism', and thereby undermine the 'unprecedented ideological onslaught from the Right ... determined to bring down what they now freely describe as a "Stalinist" creation' (Milburn, Speech to New Health Network, 2002). Yet in the same speech, he refers to the 'middle ground between state-run public and shareholder-led private structures ... [embraced by] – both the Right ... and the Left – through the Co-operative Movement.' Is this the same Right that wishes to bring down the NHS, or a different one? If the latter, what is the basis for ascribing the difference? If the former, is it really better to ally, ideologically speaking, with the wreckers, rather than to deny the charge of Stalinism more radically?

What the Right mean by the Stalinism of the NHS is what they characterise as a monolithic, centrally-run, monopoly provider of services. And this is exactly the phrase that Alan Milburn used in the same speech. However, if altruism is the cornerstone of the NHS, then how can it be a 'monopoly' in private terms analogous to a for-profit company which has cornered the market? If key NHS decision makers (doctors, executives) are knights rather than – or as well as – knaves, to use Julian le Grand's pithy terms (Le Grand, 2002), then the analysis is wrong.

The future 'implementation challenge' is to minimise the often contra-dictory effect of decades of structural reforms and encounters with the 'Ghost of Ideological Battles Past' in order to allow the NHS to be run effec-tively. SHAs are now the local 'regulators', yet also responsible for perfor-mance management, strategic planning and indeed institutional develop-ment. Firstly regional DHSCs (Directorates of Health and Social Care), which were then divisions of the DoH, had become the eyes and ears of the ministry, yet in practice sharing performance management with the SHAs. Thus the 'new devolution' (Foundation Trusts et al.) is the velvet glove containing the iron fist of hierarchy – the problem being that the 'hierarchy' is fundamentally about targets upon targets on the one hand, and protecting politicians from responsibility for 'bad news' and 'scan-dals', on the other. As Charles Clarke, then 'chairman' of the Labour Party aptly put it in 2002, 'politicians swim in a media sea'; the defensiveness is understandable, given the need to defend the NHS model.

But the new hierarchy, for all its top-heaviness, is still missing those 'meso'- level institutions to plan and commission for future health in a coherent way. A creative challenge for the future is to re-create meso-level planning institutions around which both managers and clinical professionals can deliver 21st century healthcare.

## Doctors, the state and political economy

The unwritten, informal 'deal' between the state and doctors before 1991 meant that the doctors did not seriously question overall resources or their public-sector pay, and effectively and quietly 'rationed' services (Moran, 1999) in the context of professional and clinical autonomy loosely supported by an ill defined public contract. The new contract for consultants and GPs (2003) and evolving primary care (provider) insti-tutions, are geared to reversing the infor-mal deal. Doctors would get more money in return for less autonomy. The sources of diminished autonomy are of course multiple, not least rising and increasingly art-iculate public expectations. But even so, the autonomy/reward trade-off is neither simple nor uncontestable.

Paradoxically although it could be argued that autonomy for the medical profession was one of the prices of underfunding, that under-funding meant that autonomy could be burdensome since 'doing the rationing our own way' for the doctors was still having to do it. Governments needed doctors to have enough autonomy so that tough decisions were not unequivocally placed at government's door, either by doctors or the public. Doctors might want autonomy in theory, yet get fed up with it in practice; whereas governments will always rely on (partial) medical autonomy! There has always, therefore, been an unwelcome element to 'autonomy' for the medical profession, under conditions of scarcity.

The 'new devolution' is about 'empowering' doctors at the front line and co-opting them. Autonomy will still be relevant so long as it is in line with clinical governance. Doctors can still carry, or at least share, the burden of tough decisions. This is a very British 'managed care', a kind of kinder, gentler version of US 'managed care'. (Poses, 2003; Baldor, 2003; Grembowski et al., 2002; Weiner et al., 2002). But for the future, it is a way forward, for it allows self-regulation by the medical profession as long as standards and outcomes are met. Incidentally, one version of the 'Foundation Trust' model cuts right across this – promoting as it does 'consumer control' by the local community rather than the more sensible 'producer control'.

In the early NHS, the policy was universalism and comprehensiveness; and both limited technology and the prevailing political economy of the industrial welfare state supported this policy. As a result, the state did not have to invest selectively in niche industries and services to ensure international competitiveness (Jessop, 2002). The welfare state helped capitalism reproduce itself through social investment, to be distinguished from social expenses (O'Connor, 1973). In comparison today's 'competition state' makes the state less autonomous, less a guarantor of universalism and yet more complex in its economic role (Paton, 2000).

In health, whatever rationing was necessary was done informally, by doctors acting within the state's distribution of both primary and specialised resources. For example, GPs would 'turn away' the elderly for kidney transplants by custom and practice; or would turn away those for whom hospital referral was difficult due to local lack of provision, or unsuitability for travel. Policy implementation fitted in with the unwritten grand design of policy.

Nowadays, the policy is both to invest in the economy in the context of global capitalism, and to ensure response to increasing consumerism and demands for higher quality. This necessitates more money and more intensive use of all resources whether human or material.

Consider the hypothesis that state-funded health services (such as the NHS) are a cheap means of investment in the workforce and the economy. If firms derive extra profit (surplus value) as a result of healthier workers which is due to social spending, then that extra profit can be defined as the total extra income minus the costs of the social spending (e.g. corporate tax used to contribute to the NHS) which firms make. The residual – the extra profit – is composed of two elements – the contribution which workers make to their own healthcare costs and social expenses (e.g. through tax) which increases their productivity and firms' profits; and the exploitation i.e. 'surplus value' extracted from healthcare workers. This latter element, if it exists, derives from the incomes of healthcare workers being less than the value they create i.e. the classic Marxist definition of surplus value.

Implementation of such a strategy means that doctors and others must be 'on board' (as managers would put it) regarding priorities and whom to prioritise. Otherwise firms will not get what they need from the NHS and/or the public won't. And if this is so, then either firms will make greater use of private occupational healthcare and/or individuals will use the private sector more. Either way, the tax base of the NHS will be undermined, as firms and individuals are less willing to pay for a service that does not deliver what they want.

And if doctors and others are 'on board' with the NHS's mission to invest in the workforce, then economically less central strata in society may find that the NHS's relative exit from general care and rescue makes it less appealing to them.

Thus, to have the active support of the worse-off and less economically productive, the NHS must be fair and universal; to have the support of the middle-classes as consumers, it must be a modern service of three or preferably four-star quality and hotel status; and to have the support of industry, it must provide a healthy workforce at economical cost. Herein lies the challenge for the future.

## 'The new regulatory state?'

The idea of the 'new regulation' is that the state is 'hollowed out'; it regulates rather than provides in a welfare state that mirrors the wider 'post Fordist' economy (Burrows and Loader, 1994). This may involve both local devolution and centralisation.

Ideologically, devolution provides a response to the charge of Stalinism. Practically, it allows Primary Care Trusts to be packaged as devolution even though they were already on the agenda – being New Labour's means of absorbing (and arguably extending) GP fundholding and also the total purchasing arrangements of the end of the Tory years. This absorption was a means of keeping the 1997 promise of NHS 'reintegration without reorganisation.'

Inspection is the quid pro quo of devolution. Regulation is accomplished via performance indicators and inspection, with performance management carried out by Strategic Health Authorities, and MONITOR for Foundation Trusts.

The problem here is that, given the perverse incentives created by the deepened purchaser/provider split between NHS Trusts and Primary Care Trusts respectively, local health economies (covering populations of around half a million or less) have no integrating mechanism other than goodwill or mutual dependence in meeting targets. SHAs tend to monitor performance rather than manage it: that is, they receive what are called Local Delivery Plans from Trusts, but have no ability to align funding flows with service plans. The SHA should be the planner of last resort, but this is rendered difficult by deliberately creating disaggregation under the banner of devolution. In other words the political and ideological agenda, presenting PCTs (in fact the semi-legitimate offspring of the Conservative reforms) as the source of devolution in the NHS, clashes with the analytical policy agenda of achieving objectives and targets effectively and efficiently.

Small-p politics worsens this, by stressing the need for SHAs to 'knock heads together' in the short term at the traded-off expense of promising PCTs more freedom in succeeding financial years. Tensions between system planning, PCT commissioning and patient choice are likely to mean that this promise is unlikely to be realised. If this is the case then it will in itself be a recipe for disillusionment of PCT Boards, and particularly the chairs and non-executive directors who have been appointed under the banner of promoting local freedoms.

Turning now to regulation outside the direct lines of control (Day and Klein, 1987) CHAI (Commission for Health and Audit Inspection, now the Healthcare Commission) is responsible for inspection in ways which bear some affinity with accreditation.

Regulation, especially in an international context, has many meanings. At the theoretical end, 'regulation theory' – or regime theory – in political science refers to how the state's role (in 'steering' the economy) changes to maintain and reinvigorate the capitalist economy in response to crisis (Aglietta, 1979); and therefore how the structure and shape of the state changes. One can draw parallels with the healthcare state, given its 'embeddedness' in the general state (Moran, 1999). At the very least, the language of 'steering but not rowing' has been imported into health policy, as a kind of linguistic policy transfer. The question is, how substantive is this claim?

More familiarly, regulation can refer to economic regulation (of structures, such as the form of markets; institutions, such as healthcare providers; and/or processes, such as the PFI et al.) or to standard-setting via outcomes, primarily quality and equality in clinical and other services. At first, it seemed that New Labour, in abolishing the internal market, would be replacing the former with the latter. Now it seems, as New Labour re-invents the internal market, that it will require both. A practical question therefore arises: should regulation be global, covering all aspects together (as CHAI seems to promise) or will different agencies tackle their own domains, from the structure of the market through the provision of adequate resources to the inspection of quality?

If regulation is global, the distinction between policy, regulation and provision may break down in practice. That is, if inspection covers *inter alia* quality of services, the need for resources and appropriate relationships between providers, it becomes policy – and government will not want that contracted out.

The work remit for the National Institute for Clinical Excellence (NICE), for example, is set by the government. The Bank of England, it could be argued, also has its central objective (the inflation rate) set by the government, which is the criterion to be used in setting interest rates. But NICE is more circumscribed: it is not given a resource envelope and then told to 'get on and do the QALYs' (in order to meet the central objective of maximising health gain within available resources); it makes piecemeal decisions.

If regulation overall is more piecemeal, two important things may happen: firstly, regulation may be shared between 'genuine' regulators (i.e. agencies with autonomy outside the governmental chain of command) and line agencies within the DoH or NHS (e.g. SHAs); and, secondly, different regulators may prioritise differently when 'feeding back' to providers; indeed, may individually 'command' such that the total sum of commands is internally contradictory or 'not do-able' in the here and now. This is of course the current state of affairs, which I experience frequently as the chairman of a large acute Trust which is regularly visited by branches of the NHS, all stipulating different priorities.

Let us consider 'autonomy' on the one hand and health service targets on the other hand. It is clear that the 'new devolution' does not involve the centre relinquishing its role in setting targets, but refers instead to qualified operational freedoms. Whether this is autonomy or a radical exercise of power by the centre is a moot point.

More practically, there is a real debate to be had about whether the centre should specify generic outcomes (e.g. health of populations) or specific targets, and indeed whether politicians should yield to an 'NHS

Board' in setting (definitely) the latter and (possibly) the former. The King's Fund regularly proposes this development, but we have of course been here before. Roy Griffiths in effect recommended an independent Board in 1983, only to be thwarted by the self-interest of the mandarins of the time and the hands-on nature of politicians, augmented by the centralising mission of the Thatcher government (Jenkins, 1995).

At the level of resources for services to meet needs, there is in fact a fundamental tension between needs-based generic resource allocation and target-based allocations. Increasingly under New labour, the latter has come to undermine the former, despite the creation of a new funding formula for allocations to PCTs.

Resource allocation by health authorities allows local decisions about how to produce 'health gain'. Formulae using mortality ratios, direct measures of morbidity and other measures of need are used to allocate resources, and local decisions are possible based on local need. Targets however involve either specific stipulations as to process (e.g. local waiting times) or specific outcomes (e.g. percentage improvements in lives saved in particular clinical areas). They are either applied crudely 'across the board', irrespective of local health profiles, or based on history (e.g. waiting times locally) or are 'rationally' ascribed to each locality based upon that locality's contribution to the national total in line with its health profile.

Only in the last case are targets theoretically compatible with needs-based allocation and even then, if targets are centrally ascribed, the money might as well also be ascribed service-by-service. If this is the case, general formulae for allocation and local decision-making are redundant.

If targets involve criteria for expenditure different from needs-based formulae, there will be a tendency for governments to jerrymander allocations i.e. formally subscribe to the formula (which depoliticises spending) yet in practice restrict it or amend it with earmarked allocations. And that of course is exactly what we have seen in recent years in the English NHS. Even after 2003, upwards of 25 per cent of the budget will be for 'central priorities'.

If we have a target-and-league-table-driven NHS, it makes sense to earmark the funds for the key targets. The main problem with earmarking has been that it has been over-applied for trivial sums and under-applied for significant priorities (such as the National Service Frameworks.) The government seeks to have it both ways – by promising less earmarking while mandating more specific achievements. This, again, is through the looking-glass: this gives central government the power to make priorities without the responsibility for implementing them (the 'new devolution' is the oldest trick in the book).

The challenge for the future is to choose either approach – formula-driven resource allocation or 'targets' – and to stick to it coherently and consistently. In this regard, political sticky-fingers have been progressively mischievous since the late 1980s.

Parallel to this, of course, is the real reason for continuing the purchaser/provider split (now applied only to acute and mental health services, with PCTs both commissioner and provider for the rest): it gives hospitals responsibilities to deliver volumes and quality of service without 'commissioners' necessarily ensuring that the resources are right. It remains to be seen if the new 'Payment by Results' will help. PCTs have a conflict of interest, as hybrid organisations. There is nothing wrong with hybridity if there is not an 'us and them' market culture, but unfortunately the 'collaboration' ethos of 1997 is superseded in practice by a raft of conflicting policy initiatives. In any case, the language of collaboration was always weaker than the reality of the purchaser/provider split. Labour's 1997 promise to 'abolish the market yet keep the purchaser/provider split' was rhetoric: if the market was already history, the split was redundant; if the split was operative, the market was not abolished.

Regarding targets, the main practical challenge is to inject more stability and indeed robustness into the process whereby performance indicators are selectively (and by no means transparently) shaped into the Performance Assessment Framework, producing star-ratings every summer. Star-ratings, despite all their analytical and political failings, can indeed be a powerful spur to better performance, just as league tables for schools cannot be unwritten (Snelling, 2003; Cutler & Waine, 2003). New ratings will, it seems, combine the quantitative and qualitative.

The main problem has in fact been the dissonance between the hundreds of 'high-level' performance indicators; those chosen each year for the star-ratings; and the monthly, or sometimes weekly or even daily, 'reporting' of the headline indicators, i.e. inpatient waiting times, outpatient waiting times, waiting lists, trolley waits and cancelled operations. Boards do not know which to prioritise. 'Relative autonomy' for Trusts may, in practice, be more about the frequency of SITREPs (Situation Reports) rather than something more fundamental.

One major challenge is to ensure that autonomy for Trusts does not militate against cohesion in target-seeking and importantly,the achievement of shared health outcomes within local health economies (i.e. subdivisions of the SHA yet larger by far than most PCTs). It can be observed that ideological anti-Stalinism is a main source of the policy of 'Foundation Trusts' and the even more radical ideas for local independences of various sorts, and yet in this emphasis on differentiations lies obstacles for coherence and consistency. Nevertheless it would be much more sensible to allow depoliticisation of Trust management (the NHS itself will always be political) and greater local freedoms, such as access to capital by local initiative rather than by central choice/diktat as with PFIs. Real devolution means choice as to whether to incur higher revenue costs through new facilities, or not. This is especially important when new 'financial flows' may penalise more expensive Trusts such as those with new capital.

New capital will have to fall within overall Treasury limits for the whole NHS, which is inevitable if all Trusts become Foundations. Ironically, the Treasury will have its way if the Department of Health's Foundation Trust policy becomes universal. An alternative would be to have 'foundation' local health economies, i.e. integrated authorities, as pre-1991 in a superficial structural sense, but incorporating many of the incentives and much of the culture aiding sharper outcome-focused management of more recent years. And this could be achieved without too much more re-disorganisation.

Yet presently we are subject to inconsistency. On the one hand, there is the radical version of the Foundation Hospital, which would dominate the 'new internal market', with a businesslike Board reaching the parts of 'modernisation' that other policies cannot reach. On the other hand, there is the locally-rooted, 'stakeholder'-dominated version, with its 'Auntie Bessie Board' creating a bias towards lowest-common-denominator decision-making. Both versions can be identified in ministerial speeches.

And what about commissioning? Just as 'purchasing' was the dog that never really barked for the Tories, the Foundation Hospital policy (paradoxically) requires central direction of funding flows. PCTs will therefore find themselves 'managed' in order to fulfil wider service plans. This is likely to be beneficial and to bridge the biggest lacuna in today's NHS, traceable to 1991, which is not 'local commissioning' (which is often a red herring in the days of clinical networks) but what might be termed meso-level planning – below the level of central performance monitoring but above PCT level. The SHA needs to get into real strategy and active planning.

The Foundation Hospital should not lead to a divorce from the 'local health economy'. Both NHS Trusts and PCTS are inter-dependent when it comes both to meeting targets and achieving wider goals. In other words, devolution should not be about re-disorganisation 1991-style, but more freedom from the monitoring culture in which chief executives are called to meet SHAs over every waiting-time breach and more freedom from the bidding culture whereby 'kit' and new clinicians are distributed in the wake of ministerial tours rather than flexible planning.

## Different systems and clashing incentives

It is important to choose between different incentive and performance management systems: local collaboration (incorporating the medical professions, unlike the 1974 version); central regulation; central 'command and control'; and the various versions of the market. Before 1983, traditional administration excluded the medics. After 1983 but before 1991, there was general management without the market, but the management model did not really involve doctors corporately, despite its aspirations. After 1991 and before 1997 there was the market with involvement of doctors as medical and clinical directors. After 1997, local collaboration was the 'Third Way' which replaced the market; but this soon gave way to a mixture of direct command and control and central regulation via fining systems for failure to achieve targets. Yet such targets were often not coordinated with local service level agreements, themselves poorly coordinated with the overall local Service and Financial Framework (SAFF), which operated between 1999 and 2003.

Given the emerging shape of clinical services, for reasons of quality and access as well as availability of medical manpower, networks rather than markets make sense. This is compatible with regulation and limited 'command and control', to provide the backdrop to local collaboration. Patient choice should be the linchpin, but commissioner/purchaser-driven markets – or piecemeal, centrally-mandated 'market forces' (the 2003 version) – are less compatible. Meso-level planning allows patient flows to be modelled and funded. It is this which the NHS has lacked post-1991, a lack which New Labour's reforms post-2002 have exacerbated, after incremental improvement post-1997.

The purchaser/provider internal market (1991 version) broke up local cooperation. The new internal market (patient choice of hospital) assumes funding flows which reward choice. But there will still be a 1991-style purchaser/commissioner This is because hospitals which fulfil their Service Level Agreement (SLA) contract will not be fined, but those which underperform will be fined at full cost. This assumes an active purchaser. What about hospitals, or specialties/services within hospitals if the system is really decentralised, which fulfil their SLAs but cannot meet the demand from patient choice? Will they be fined as a result of lengthening waiting lists/times? (Often the distinction between lists and times is academic, despite the rhetoric – unless waiting times targets are micro-regulated, which is itself problematic.) We may not be looking at direct fines, but punishments will come albeit they will be felt indirectly if organisations lose 'star status' and resources in the wake of the loss of a star.

Patient choice and central regulation are maybe incompatible. If so, that will produce demoralisation among clinicians and managers as well as perverse incentives.

And even if central/regional fining/regulation is vastly diminished, who will help the patient and family with their choice – GPs? If so, will they have the information and will to manage the whole system (outpatient and inpatient) in a way that even Health Authorities could not? And even if they do, will PCTs be forced simply to fund such choice (post-2005)? If so they will be just post-boxes like Dutch sickness funds before the 1990s.

In the NHS of Sweden and the social insurance system of France, primary care is not central. Patients self-refer to ambulatory specialist care, in the main. The new system in England may give a push in this direction, alongside EU policy (and indeed global WTO policy.) How can the advantages of the GP gatekeeper policy in the NHS be preserved, without its disadvantages – especially when primary care cannot deliver its aspirations, which require a better mix of general and specialist GPs, plus a better mix of general and specialist medicine in hospitals?

The answer is to have referring GPs – neither fund-holders nor directed by PCT contracts – with their referrals funded in planning agreements. There is also a need for Service Level Agreements – i.e. costed flows by speciality – to be built into Local Delivery Plans (LDPs), and need for all local parties to agree money and services together.

The system whereby special, extra, earmarked monies are awarded in order to meet targets, yet clawed back if they are not met, is short-termist and undermined by perverse incentives. For example, a Trust may be awarded a significant sum to meet the target that 90 per cent of patients presenting to A and E are treated or admitted within four hours. Targets which are a spur to sustainable improvement and therefore sustainable achievement are worthwhile. Yet 'just missing' a target may lead to all the special money being clawed back, which could mean the difference between the statutory obligation to break-even and financial deficit. Achieving the target may be based on the month or even week at the deadline, rather than permanent achievement, and quickly reversed. This is all the more likely if 'all hands to the pump' – and possibly diversion from other activities and patient care – is the means of achievement.

Admittedly the Healthcare Commission assesses performance across the board, and simply transferring problems to other areas (e.g. cancelling elective surgery to ensure there are beds to admit A and E attenders) can affect other targets and the overall rating. But the loss of earmarked funds (it could be up to £1 million) will be more salient than this broader measure, to which the contribution of any one indicator is less significant.

At the level of high politics, performance management was overtly the replacement for the internal market. The trouble was that it quickly became performance monitoring by central government – including a culture of fear and blame, supported by a pyramid of various NHS and DoH agencies stretching to ministers at the pinnacle. Returning to the market is not the answer. Performance monitoring should be devolved to legitimate NHS authorities, and allied to strategic planning of services whose performance can be managed (and not just monitored) by the Strategic Health Authority.

No institutional or technical reform can keep the NHS at arm's length from ministers. Only a cultural change can bring this about. The trouble with all the 'devolution' and 'new internal market' policies is that they are technical/institutional wedges without a change in culture. Ministers are Janus-faced: they understand intellectually the need to 'let go' but cannot – for reasons which may sometimes be personal but which are also rooted in the relationship of the Department of Health to the centres of power of New Labour itself.

To summarise, 'the new regulatory state' is a concept irrelevant to the New NHS, unless it is used to point to 'hollowing out' almost solely by centralisation. Indeed even if we have a 'post Fordist' economy (Jessop, 2002), it may well be that core welfare services are more 'Fordist' than ever. Arguably, the challenge for the state as regards the NHS was to 'incorporate' the doctors into a 'neo Fordist' service, thereby 'modernising' provision from an essentially pre-Fordist system of professional guilds. Doctors were the 'elite' in this sense but not in the Marxist sense of owning the (capitalist) means of production and profit-taking. In the NHS of the future, doctors will be the privileged stratum of the proletariat!

## Re-shaping the healthcare system

In the following section structural weaknesses in the present system, which were discussed above, are addressed with proposals to reshape the healthcare system.

*First proposal.*   Link finance and patient pathways across the whole health economy. This means removing the PCT conflict of interest. GPs should be the first (or, now, one of the first) points of contact with the NHS, and then should refer (or not) according to the precepts of patient pathways and integrated care, in the light of indicators, guidelines and (where relevant) 'protocols'. This means planning by a higher tier, not 'commissioning' by local PCTs. Ironically, the unstable boundaries between primary and secondary care instituted by the Conservatives' internal market reforms and continued in different form by New Labour have created some perverse incentives which also impact upon medical morale.

The 'old NHS' had GPs as low-technology gatekeepers and informal rationers (Moran, 1999), with no financial incentive either to refer or not to refer. Having this type of GP gatekeeper was culturally acceptable in an earlier age, but not in an age of rising expectations.

Yet the Conservative reforms of 1983–97, especially the introduction of GP fund-holding, sought to articulate the rhetoric of patient choice while actually restricting it in practice. GPs could no longer refer freely. GP fund-holding (GPFH) was a curious mix of enhanced primary care services and more formal rationing. GPFH, the policy of 'tipping the balance to primary care' and thereby reducing the independent power of providers of secondary care, became a major plank of the pre-1997 reforms which is now pursued differently with the foundation of Primary Care Trusts in the early 2000s. Now GPs have varying incentives – sometimes to repatriate services from secondary care; and sometimes to refer in order to shift costs.

PCTs have a conflict of interest as commissioner/budget-holder, on the one hand, and co-planner of appropriate services with hospitals and other actors, on the other hand. Additionally, the incentives facing PCTs and GPs are frequently not aligned.

What patients – if not citizens – actually want is access to the best, and frequently most specialised, services. In the best-funded systems, whether private (US), social insurance (France) or Beveridge-like (Sweden), with most consumer choice, the institutionalised GP gatekeeper is conspicuously absent.

The 'new internal market' is fine, if it means patient choice backed up by funding flows of patients to appropriately planned services. That is, planning according to criteria of access, quality, scale (and clinical networks) and cost-effectiveness, should take into account desired referrals from GPs which themselves should take into account patient desires. As always, there is a convergence between 'ideal markets' and 'ideal planning'.

*Second proposal.*   Respond to patient choice by allowing demand to shape supply. The choices made by patients, inevitably shaped and even constrained, should feed into planning, which is an iterative process. That is, planning and choice should be a 'simultaneous equation' to be solved creatively, year-by-year, as services expand, contract, modernise and change.

The alternative is that patient choice means individuals decide in a vacuum where they want to go. This will make either PCTs or GPs irrelevant. It will undermine the 'universal primary care gatekeeper' which makes the UK system cost-effective and equitable.

The GP gatekeeper should be preserved, albeit integrated into modern practice regarding appropriate patient pathways, with funding of secondary and tertiary referrals in line with patient and GP choice. Here, the historic advantages of the NHS (equity and cost-effectiveness) are preserved with more modern patient choice.

If patient choice is to be a reality, then services should be planned through clinical networks and funded by adequately-large commissioners in proportion to patient choice (i.e. workload). PCTs should be provider-organisations, as in Scotland. They can then be small enough to be close to their communities without the pressure to merge in order to be more sensibly-sized commissioners. Furthermore, managed clinical networks can allow a creative compromise between the state's 'targets' and doctors' self-management (and at least partial autonomy). While clinical governance in pursuit of good outcomes is vital, clinical networks can mange the process. Only if they fail is more direct control necessary. This means that 'Foundation' Trusts may be a distraction.

*Third proposal.*   In order to align the UK system with Europe, there needs to be clear ownership and status of NHS organisations. In the future, the European Union will be increasingly important, one way or another. It will either be the source of increased 'liberal' movement – of patients, doctors and health plans – or the basis for increased regulation of the relationship between national healthcare systems and the European Union (Paton et al., 2001). In order to render the evolving NHS and Europe compatible, the complexity of para-statal-based 'dis-organisation' of the NHS should be diminished. Commissioners and providers should be unequivocally state organisations. Patient choice in the UK should be unequivocally compatible with rights to intra-EU mobility; equally, appropriate patient pathways in search of integrated care should not be undermined by 'individualistic' EU Court decisions. This calls for the elucidation of coherent and consistent policy at national and EU level, also covering cross-boundary movements of workers in order to combine choice with collective rights.

*Fourth proposal.* Services, finance and governance ought be aligned in the NHS. Currently, different policy streams have created unhelpful dissonances. Central policy objectives, with related targets (e.g. cancer policy; the NSFs (National Service Frameworks) generally) should be funded on the basis of costed plans, with money allocated to commissioners large enough to embrace clinical networks as a rough principle. This should be the role of the SHAs. Currently, money goes to PCTs, which may 'sign up' to health economy-wide plans collectively, then challenge them or seek to circumvent them individually. Capital and revenue allocations are less joined up than in 1976, when revenue RAWP (Resource Allocation Working Party) and capital RAWP at least led, at Regional level, to attempts to marry the two, imperfect as they were. On governance, the choice is between elected regional government overseeing NHS regions (floated in the 1995 Labour policy document *Renewing the NHS*), on the one hand, and vesting the SHA with legitimacy through appropriate boards, on the other hand.

In this connection, PCTs are a problem structurally, and not just because they are 'new' or because they lack strategic capacity. To make rational choice between, for example, emergency admissions, elective care and financial balance and to meet all the targets requires there to be one organisation seeing the whole picture for a population. Yet PCTs are far too small for this – hence, on the one hand, PCTs' 'shared services' e.g. finance and human resources, and on the other hand, shared functions, e.g. in a locality, one PCT 'leads' on emergencies, another on electives and so on. Solving the scale problem upsets integration; having integrated decision-making is on the wrong scale. As a result, hospitals and NHS Trusts generally may have conflicting demands from a myriad of small commissioners.

One may say, such a situation is simply part of the market which has advantages which outweigh these disadvantages. But is this justified if the arrangement destroys the NHS's comparative advantage of strategic planning of (on the one hand) complex services and (on the other hand) effective interfaces between primary and secondary care? If two PCTs in a locality want to support specialised services at the acute Trust and two others want to refer patients elsewhere, neither may get their wish, as the critical mass of provision may result at neither acute location. This is the old 1990s internal market problem, when market forces destabilised services, especially specialised services. Even 'ordinary' secondary services suffer, for providers need to know well in advance where the patient flows will go: even if consultants did not have employment tenure. The hospital 'market' is not conducive to short-term competition – as we know in theory and learned in England in the 1990s.

*Fifth proposal.*   Performance Indicators and targets should be reduced in number and rendered more compatible between the different agencies. Currently, the Local Development Plan (LDP), successor to the Service and Financial Framework, itself successor to the old annual purchaser–provider contract, is more complicated and adversarial than ever. Moves to make service targets and financial agreements three-year rather than one-year are welcome but only a beginning (and yet to be experienced as a genuine change). The financial negotiation is still annual, and making service-level agreements (contracts) compatible with the LDP is complicated, and requires significant high-level managerial input in the final stages, which diverts attention from other needed areas.

There should be much less 'earmarking' of finance for trivial sums and much more earmarking for significant service priorities if this route rather than general resource allocation accompanied by devolution is followed. Alongside this should go a creative mixture of directly funded (from SHAs) clinical networks, Hospital Trusts and primary care. As with the last internal market, the danger is that newly-created institutions will retard innovative policy and limit its implementation. For example there were newspaper headlines about cancer networks in crisis on 27 August 2002.

*Sixth proposal.*   Avoid conflicting incentive systems and value systems. Incentive systems can produce perverse outcomes and demotivate both professions and managers. A prime forthcoming example would be in how the 'new internal market' is reconciled with star systems and indeed 'fining systems' and how executives 'manage' doctors to achieve results. What of the hospital with good quality, growing reputation, increasing referrals and fixed capacity in the short-term? Will it suffer? Will disadvantage be cumulative? Markets require a level playing field and generalised excess capacity. What of the new rule of standard re-imbursement by procedure; welcome as an alternative to the quality-threatening price competition of the internal market, but a rough tool when dealing with the fine grain of individual hospitals? How will 'cost per case' be reconciled with the need to link capital and revenue planning across health economies?

These issues may seem like 'low politics'. Yet the elision of low politics into high politics has been a hallmark of the NHS since the late 1980s, reflecting the sensitivity of the issue. This was never more politically salient than now. It would be better to devolve within an integrated NHS. Currently, senior NHS executives spend an inordinate amount of time running to stand still. Government should be concerned with reducing the overload of performance management, not adding to it. Such a focus takes away the capacity of the system to deliver.

*Seventh proposal.* Reduce bureaucratic rigidities and overlaps in the system. There are several examples of 'pluralism' in policy-making for health, with involvement (which is rarely coordinated) from the Treasury, the Department of Health, the prime minister's office, various think tanks and various advisers. We also find incompatible criteria used by different inspectorial agencies; failure to match the rhetoric of devolution because of conservatism in financial control and centralism in objective-setting; incompatibility of financial control with longer-term strategic service and business planning and instability of targets.

One graphic example of how central government conservatism hamstrings public management (rather than the reverse) concerns the persistent failure to allow purchasers and Trusts to spend moneys saved from previous years at times of financial need. In the typical health economy of approximately half a million people, up to £15 million may be 'locked away', yet inaccessible through Treasury rules. Regulation of PFI is a labyrinth, to give another example of how centralism is actually enchanced by 'privatisation'.

*Eighth proposal.* SHAs should fund hospitals and networks directly, with PCTs being subcontracted for complementary primary and intermediate services. This proposal would enable an appropriate mix of specialists in hospital, the community (including community hospitals) and primary care to be properly planned. While the GP services could be funded directly by the SHA, all else would flow to one integrated provider. This would make the SHA a planner and commissioner.

Currently, the deepening of the purchaser/provider split creates incentives for purchasers to underspend out of 'prudence', creating crisis for hospitals and even unnecessary disinvestments from services. It also encourages PCTs to seek to meet targets by encouraging hospitals to get into deficit. Hospitals have to reply by breaking-even, then forcing a dialogue about priorities and money. Both Labour and Conservatives are wedded to the split, but where is the evidence that it is the fulcrum of a better system than on integrated one? The rhetoric is of PCTs close to the GP and patient. In fact I contend they are close to neither. PCTs have neither capacity nor scale to commission – they simply repeat central targets, add in some vaguely-costed local aspirations and expect hospitals and other NHS Trusts to make the commissioning decisions, i.e. to make the hard choices about what can be funded.

## Conclusion

This paper began by identifying the ideological driver of health policy. This does not contradict the search for a high-quality, cost-effective NHS, but it may cross-cut and distract. Additionally, there is a divide between 'technocrats' who stress the latter (cost-effectiveness *et al.*), on the one hand, and both 'politicians' and political theorists, on the other hand, who seek legitimacy either for their actions or for the NHS. A technically perfect solution which cannot be implemented because the necessary service (the NHS) and appropriate structures no longer exist is a real danger in the medium and long-term. It cannot be overestimated how much of the NHS's modernisation and improvement agenda for healthcare is aided by the coordinated public service model which the NHS, at its best, represents. Equally, the reciprocal danger is 'political policy' which cannot be translated into practical improvement, or which cuts across other policy streams geared to that end.

It is proposed in this paper that government can lead health policy beyond 'technical' solutions to policy problems. The challenge now is to forge a coherent link between the policy aspiration of 'devolution and autonomy' with clinician self-management. This means: exploring the links between existing acute Trust management and network management; revisiting links between primary, secondary and tertiary care, and their management; providing coherent ownership of policy objectives and targets; clarifying the mix of centralism and local self-management; and reconciling patient choice with networked services.

The ideological component lies in transcending the rather sterile divide – sometimes synchronic, sometimes diachronic; sometimes descriptive, sometimes prescriptive – between hierarchies, markets and networks. Networks can be market-aiding or market-diminishing (Exworthy and Halford, 1999) In the NHS, patient choice within rationally-planned services should be the mantra, not markets.

Hard questions remain. What will be the relationship between Trust Boards, chief executives and – for example – medical directors, on the one hand, and holistic, specialty-based networks on the other? How will 'lead Trusts' lead? How will doctor-managed networks avoid either the marketplace's or the state's embrace; and, if they stay self-managing, how will they manage performance to the satisfaction of the paymaster – government, on behalf of the public – as well as local managers and the public? How will commissioning have to be reshaped to prevent redundancy in a world of provider-led planning, but in a modernised accountable form?

But the potential rewards are great. Again, just one example: a notable phenomenon of the current NHS is not just low medical morale but also low 'top manager' morale. One of the reasons is high turnover; and I suspect that the reason for this is increasingly structural. NHS executives are middlemen between government and the medical profession rather than general managers. They are also in an increasingly volatile and vulnerable position. Targets, accountability and politicians' media-driven approach, on the one hand, and the medical profession's shortened patience with each new cycle of initiatives, are the factors responsible.

A new settlement is needed. It does not require vast reorganisation in the sense of new institutions so much as simplification and elucidation. But it also needs a shared mission, which is difficult to achieve when the mission statement has been so discredited.

The key is renewed trust between the government and the medical profession. Areas of consensus can be developed and communicated. Where consensus is not possible, compromises should be transparent, and likewise communicated. This process is likely to mean compromise between legitimate political targets and clinical aspirations; fewer targets overall; greater clinical accountability within Trusts for performance and outcomes; and explicitly-recognised redrawing of the 'resources/autonomy' conundrum.

# References

Aglietta, M. (1979) *A Theory of Capitalist Regulation*. London: New Left Books

Baldor, R.A. (2003) 'Ethical considerations in disease management: a managed care perspective', *Disease Management & Heath Outcomes*, 11, 2:71–5

Braverman, H. (1998) *Labour and Monopoly Capital*. New York: Monthly Review Press (new edition)

Burrows, R. and Loader, B. (eds) (1994) *Towards a Post-Fordist Welfare State?* London: Routledge

Cutler, T. and Waine, B. (2003) 'Advancing public accountibility? The social services 'star' ratings', *Public Money and Management*, April, 23, 2:125–8

Day, P. and Klein, R. (1987) *Accountabilities. Five Public Services*. London: Tavistock
Department of Health (2000) *The NHS Plan*. London
Department of Health (2001) *Shifting the Balance of Power in the NHS*. London
Department of Health (2002) *The NHS Plan: Next Steps for Investment, Next Steps for Reform*. London
Exworthy, M. and Halford, M. (1999) *Professionals and the New Managerialism in the Public Sector*. Buckingham: Open University Press
Flynn, R. (1992) *Structures of Control in Health Management*. London: Routledge
Giddens, A. (2000) *The Third Way and its Critics*. Cambridge: Polity Press
Gray, J. (1995) *Liberalism*. Buckingham: Open University Press
Grembowski, D.E., Cook, K.S., Patrick, D.L. and Roussel, A.E. (2002) 'Managed care and the US healthcare system – a social exchange perspective', *Social Science and Medicine*, April, **54**, 8:1167–80
Jenkins, S. (1995) *Accountable to None: the Tory Nationalisation of Britain*. London: Hamish Hamilton
Jessop, B. (1994) 'The transition to post-Fordism and the Schumpeterian workfare state', in Burrows, R. and Loader, B. (eds) *Towards a Post-Fordist Welfare State?* London: Routledge
Jessop, B. (2002) *The Future of the Capitalist State*. Cambridge: Polity
Klein, R. (2000) *The New Politics of the National Health Service*. New York: Prentice Hall
Labour Party (1992) *Your Good Health*. London: Walworth Road
Labour Party (1995) *Renewing the NHS*. London: Millbank
Le Grand, J. (2002) 'The Labour government and the National Health Service', in *Oxford Journal of Economic Policy*, Summer
Macdonald, R. (2002) *Using Health Economics in Health Services: Rationing Rationally?* Buckingham: Open University Press
Milburn, A. (2002) Speech to the New Health Network (February), London
Moran, M. (1999) *Governing the Healthcare State*. Manchester: Manchester University Press
O'Connor, J. (1973) *The Fiscal Crisis of the State*. New York: Harper and Row
Paton, C. (1990) *U.S. Health Politics. Public Policy and Political Theory*. Aldershot: Avebury
Paton, C. (1992) *Competition and Planning in the NHS: the Danger of Unplanned Markets*. London: Chapman and Hall
Paton, C. (1999) 'New Labour's Health Policy', in Powell, M. (ed.) *New Labour, New Welfare State?* Bristol: Policy Press
Paton, C. (2000) *World, Class, Britain: Political Economy, Political Theory and British Politics*. London: Macmillan
Paton, C. (2001) 'The state in health: global capitalism, conspiracy, cock-up and competitive change in the NHS', *Public Policy and Administration*, **16**, 4:61–83
Paton, C. et al. (1998) *Competititon and Planning in the NHS 2nd Edition: the Consequences of the Reforms*. London: Stanley Thornes
Paton, C. et al. (2001) *The Impact of Market Forces on the Health System of the European Union*. Dublin: EHMA
Poses, R.M. (2003) 'A cautionary tale: the dysfunction of American healthcare', *European Journal of Internal Medicine*, March, **14**, 2:123–30

Powell, M. (1999) 'New Labour and the third way in the British NHS', *International Journal of Health Services*, 29, 2:353–70

Salter, B. (1998) *The Politics of Change in the Health Service*. London: Macmillan

Snelling, I. (2003) 'Do star ratings really reflect hospital performance?', *Journal of Health, Organisation and Management*, 1 March, 17, 3:210–23

Taylor-Gooby, P. (1985) *Public Opinion, Ideology and State Welfare*. London: Routledge and Kegan Paul

Weiner, J., Gillam, S. and Lewis, R. (2002) 'Organisation and financing of British primary care groups and trusts: observations through the prism of US managed care', *Journal of Health Services Research and Policy*, 1 January, 7, 1:43–50

# 4
# Health Policy Futures and Cost Scenarios for England 2003–2023

*Graham Lister*

This paper explores the main policy directions for health identified in 'Policy Futures for UK Health',[1] drawing on this extensive source to put forward relatively simple assumptions about future health costs (Dargie et al., 2000). It is based on the input of the Nuffield Trust to the 2002 Wanless Review (Wanless, 2002) of long-term healthcare costs,[2] which formed the basis for government expenditure plans for health. In 2003 Derek Wanless was invited to undertake a further review (Wanless, 2004) of the conditions necessary to achieve affordable health services and long-term improvements in health outcomes as envisioned by the so-called 'fully engaged scenario'. The Nuffield Trust again contributed to the consultation and its input is reflected in this paper.

## Methodology

### Scenario planning for health

The method used to generate cost projections for the Nuffield Trust input to the first Wanless Review was to examine the trends identified in the Policy Futures exercise and examine the best available evidence of their potential impact on costs (Lister, 2001). The main drivers of costs are identified as: the rise in consumer expectations, demographic changes, developments in technology, and trends in healthcare work-force pay and methods of work. In each case the impact on health costs depends upon future health policy responses to these social, demo-graphic and economic trends. The main methodological problem was to ensure consistent trend and policy assumptions and to avoid double counting or omission of trend factors. It was also very difficult to allow for backlogs in current expenditure.

Since it is not possible to predict the future course of trends and policy responses with any certainty, scenarios were established that would lead to higher, medium and lower levels of expenditure. These are set out in three scenarios for health futures each of which is internally consistent but none may be forecast with certainty. It has the benefit of setting out a clear framework of assumptions about the trends and policy options. All assumptions about cost increases are stated in real terms and are either step changes or annual rates of increase as noted.

It should also be noted that these scenarios are not based on detailed estimates of changes in health needs or medical practice, they are based on the supply of finance, technology and staff and the demand for higher standards of care. This is because in many cases improvements in health delay death but may not reduce lifetime costs.

The resulting estimates are based on assumptions set out for each scenario, including assumed health policy futures. It would be possible to refine these cost estimates. However, this was not an attempt to predict detailed long-term costs but to provide a quick estimate of the scale of overall NHS cost increases, before the more detailed analyses had been prepared by the Wanless team. Central scenarios in each case are broadly comparable though figures presented here show lower levels of expenditure than Wanless in the first five years but higher rates of growth, thereafter amounting to 12.5 per cent of GDP by 2023 compared to Wanless' central estimate of 11.5 per cent.

## Comparison with the Wanless methodology

The first Wanless Report adopted an approach to forecasting based on an analysis of current spending, disease/condition and type of service and the age and sex of patients. This was then projected using demographic data. The impact of service quality improvement was taken into account by examining how National Service Frameworks (NSFs) would affect costs and projecting these costs across the areas not currently covered by NSFs. Details of the methodology used by the Wanless team to project costs have not been published, but it is clear that, given the paucity of the data, some fairly broad assumptions have had to be made.

The central weakness of the scenarios presented in this paper lies in the assumption that catching up with European levels of expenditure will result in acceptable quality standards. The Wanless report provides a better resolution to this question by linking cost increases to the introduction of NSFs, though it has to be admitted that there is not yet enough evidence that NSF quality targets are being achieved.

The first Wanless Review presents an analysis of the impact of ageing on health costs, though it would have been helpful to take into account the health needs of immigrant communities. It is less convincing in addressing longer-term health cost pressures. For example, it does not appear to take into account the continuing rise in consumer expectations or the likely long-term impact of medical and pharmaceutical developments and globalisation.

The main difference between the assumptions adopted and hence the cost estimates is that while Wanless assumed that the NHS could catch up its shortfall in service quality by the injection of large cash increases over the first five years, the scenarios presented in this paper assume that this will take ten years.

Both papers demonstrate the power of scenario planning to illuminate the policy issues, which underlie such projections. The point is not whether one projection is 'more accurate' than another but how helpful they are in guiding policy choices. In this respect the Wanless Review has been very powerful in generating agreement on the funding needs of the NHS and in identifying key policy issues including the need to link health and social care expenditure plans and the crucial importance of full engagement of society with health issues.

## The cost and policy drivers

The main factors driving health costs are identified in this paper as policy responses to changes and trends in:

- *Consumer expectations*:
  To match the best European standards of health service provision
  To meet growing expectations and demand for greater choice
  To respond to globalisation of lifestyles, food and employment
- *Demographic change*:
  Population change
  Immigration
  Ageing
- *Trends in technology*:
  Pharmaceuticals
  Medical devices and equipment
  Information and communications technology
  Health buildings
- *Health pay and working methods*:
  Recruitment, retention and pay
  Working methods and efficiency
- *The full engagement of all sectors of society with health*

In the following sections the impact of each of these factors on health policy and costs is examined in more detail.

## Consumer expectations

### Matching the best in Europe

The UK public are increasingly aware that higher standards of responsiveness to consumers are achieved by other health systems, note for example, the 2000 WHO World Health Report (WHO, 2000). The long-term cost of health depends upon the quality of care standards applied, but there is no clear picture of what these standards are or how the UK performs. For some years, however, they have been repeatedly told that the basic reason for poor standards is that other countries spend more on health.

Thus one of the policy imperatives, which led to the first Wanless Review (2002) was a commitment, variously expressed by the prime minister and others, for the UK to match the levels of funding and standards of service achieved by other European health systems. This may have led to an assumption that 'catching up' with Europe could be achieved in five years. This goal has been criticised by Rudolf Klein and others because it can be interpreted in different ways (Klein, 2001).

- The increase in UK health funding required to match the 1998 unweighted average of current EU member states was 18.6 per cent (Klein, 2001).
- The increase required to reach the population weighted average was 26 per cent.
- A more meaningful target is suggested by a regression equation linking the level of health expenditure to Gross Domestic Product per Capita[3] (see Figure 4.2). This suggests that at its 1998 level of GDP the UK would need to increase its expenditure by 20.5 per cent to reach the level predicted by the regression equation.

Though some 18.6–26 per cent more resources are enough to match European levels of funding, they will not necessarily achieve the best European standards of healthcare. Scotland already spends 18 per cent more per capita than the average for the UK, with a lower GDP per capita, but few would suggest Scotland matches the best European standards of health service. Resource increases must be matched by appropriate policy measures in order to improve performance and quality as funding is increased.

The following is a list of standards derived from current NHS plans and targets:

*Information and support for self-care and referral* where appropriate from local doctors, nurses and health support workers or by NHS Direct and DiTV.

*24 hour care* available from a responsible primary care team or service, with access to emergency medical services when necessary.

*Primary care consultations* with doctors or nurses within two days for non-urgent cases.

*Out patient appointments* with a consultant, available within two weeks for urgent cases and six weeks for non-urgent.

*Waiting at emergency service points:* A&E, Casualty service Walk-in Centre, less than an hour in 90% of cases and trolley waits of four hours or less.

*Provision of urgent hospital treatment* within three months or less, and non-urgent treatment within six months.

*Choice of hospital for elective services* with the option of treatment in the private sector or abroad if the NHS cannot offer treatment within six months.

*Access to appropriate services* respecting the needs and cultures of patients.

*No undue queues* or delays for diagnostic or treatment equipment or aids.

*Safe discharge* to planned follow up placement or care.

*Treatment under the direct supervision of a consultant* on site.

*Personal nurse management and counselling* respecting the needs of each patient and their carers, providing information, support and follow up.

*Accommodation* in a well furnished room with six beds or less.

*Choice of food* of the standard of a family restaurant.

*Independent information and advice* about health and treatment choices, support by independent advocates coupled with responsiveness to complaints.

*Evidence based treatment and care* meeting national and international standards of best practice, of proven and agreed effectiveness, including cost effectiveness.

*Figure 4.1*: The aspirations of the NHS

Further sections of this paper discuss health policy measures in more detail, but it may be useful to begin by examining the current aims of health policy for England. Figure 4.1 above sets out the current aspirations of the NHS derived from various policy documents and plans. These aims are extremely ambitious and it is clear that there is no single European healthcare system that meets all the standards and targets that have been set.

While it is clear that the NHS does not yet meet these aims, a list of aspirations does establish the shortfall to be met in five or more likely ten years. It would be useful to mount a more detailed study of what patients want and what standards are currently achieved here and elsewhere in Europe. This could provide the basis for a definition of what patients should reasonably expect from the NHS. Such an analysis and policy choice could be embedded in National Institute of Clinical Excellence (NICE)[4] explanations for the public, produced when guidelines are issued to the NHS. It would in effect provide a statement of patient rights.

For the reasons explained later in this paper it is assumed that it will not be possible to make good this aspirational shortfall in less than ten years. To increase funding by 20.5 per cent over ten years would require a cost increase of 1.8 per cent per annum. The lowest estimate of the increase required 18.6 per cent would require increases of 1.7 per cent and the highest estimate 26 per cent would require annual increases of 2.3 per cent per annum.

## Consumer expectations and prosperity

However, meeting current aspirations is not sufficient as it is well known that consumer/patient expectations and hence health expenditures rise with increasing prosperity (Maxwell, 1981). The relationship between health expenditure and GDP per capita at purchasing power parity for EU countries (excluding Luxembourg[5]) plus the Commonwealth OECD countries, shows a significant correlation between health expenditure and GDP as shown in Figure 4.2.

The regression equation shown in Figure 4.2 has a regression co-efficient of 0.85, that is the regression line accounts for about 72 per cent of the variance. The slope of the line is 0.1 suggesting that the growth in health expenditure required to match increased consumer demand due to increased wealth, equates to the annual real rate of growth in GDP per capita. The current Treasury analysis of medium-term economic forecasts suggests a growth of GDP in the range of 1.8 per cent to 2.4 per cent per annum; the long-term forecast growth rate used in the first Wanless review was 2.25 per cent. With a population growth rate of 0.35 per cent (see later) this would produce a growth in GDP per capita of 1.9 per cent and hence a growth in health expenditure at the same rate. The lowest rate forecast for GDP growth of 1.8 per cent coupled with the lowest rate of population growth 0.3 per cent would produce a growth in demand of 1.5 per cent, while the highest GDP growth rate forecast of 2.4 per cent coupled with the highest population growth rate forecast would indicate a growth in demand of 2.0 per cent per annum.

## Consumer orientation and patient choice

Increasing consumer expectations brings a consumer orientation, demanding a more responsive service, offering real choices to patients (Barnes, 1999). This is what consumers are accustomed to from every other service, but surveys show that the NHS lags behind consumer expectations in terms of responsiveness (National Consumer Council, 1998).

The NHS offers patients less choice than many other European systems, where they can chose general practitioners, specialists and

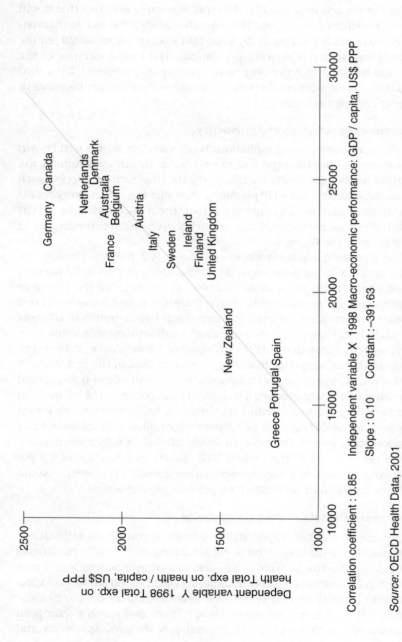

Figure 4.2: Regression of health expenditure against GDP at purchasing power parity (PPP) 1998

Dependent variable Y 1998 Total exp. on health Total exp. on health / capita, US$ PPP

Correlation coefficient : 0.85     Independent variable X  1998 Macro-economic performance: GDP / capita, US$ PPP

Slope : 0.10     Constant : -391.63

Source: OECD Health Data, 2001

hospitals (Lister, 2002). Experience suggests that this is one of the most significant factors in health professionals' attitudes to patients. Without the basic discipline provided by patient choice, based on information about outcomes and other patients' experiences it is doubtful if there will be sufficient incentive to improve quality and responsiveness. This issue has been recognised in English health policy with the establishment of a Patient Access and Choice Team in the Department of Health.

Patient choice in many other European countries entails a choice between public and private hospital providers. While the for-profit, private health sector in England is comparable in scale to most other countries, many other European countries, particularly the Netherlands and Germany, have a very substantial not-for-profit, private sector. Steps to encourage this third tier in the market could improve patient choice and hence the quality of care. Current steps to introduce Foundation Hospital status suggest health policy is moving in this direction.[6]

The choice that patients of the NHS experiencing long waits can expect, is to be offered short waiting times for private treatment by the same consultant operating in both the NHS and private sectors. This situation is unusual in Europe. It would marginally increase costs in the short term to require a complete separation of NHS consultants' public and private sector work but this would reduce any possible incentive to maintain waiting lists and would therefore reduce long-term costs. The new consultant contracts can be seen as a move in this direction.

Low-level co-payments may be considered as a way of encouraging cost-effective choice of services. It would be possible to follow the lead of Sweden, which requires users to pay a charge of €10 for primary care consultations (subject to a limit of €80 per year for all health charges). This would encourage users to choose telephone triage and advisory services for self-care. Low-level co-payment charges for hospital beds and meals might also encourage patients to demand timely treatment and discharge. Low-level charges could also increase patient involvement and choice in planning hospital stays and could reinforce patient responsibilities, for example, to turn up to a booked appointment. There seems to be no good reason why the ingredient costs for meals for people in hospitals should be less than those of people in prisons and no reason why patients would not choose to pay a small charge of say £3 per day to cover the ingredient cost of food (this would double the current spend on food ingredients).

It will be important to specify the nature and level of treatment and choice to which NHS patients are entitled and those services that will not be funded by the NHS. This might encourage private medical insurance to cover additional services excluded from the NHS, such as cosmetic treatments, spa treatments, lifestyle drugs and alternative medicines valued by patients but of no proven efficacy. The issue of which services should be provided as 'core' NHS services and which should be excluded has been approached in several different ways, and at present NICE is required to advise on this.

Many patients are surprised to find that the NHS does not consistently offer support for care of the dying. The Nuffield Trust has called for hospice care to be consistently funded by the NHS, recognising the principle of dignity in death. Half of all deaths occur in NHS hospitals, which have much to learn from best practice in the hospice movement (Nuffield Trust, 2001). Public funding would increase NHS cost by about £200m based on discussion with the chair of the National Council for Hospice and Specialist Palliative Care Services.

Health needs are often shown as an iceberg, with only one-tenth visible above the waterline. Consumer expectations of health and their perceived responsibility for self-care form this waterline. Other chapters in this book (Rogers in Chapter 7 and Greener in Chapter 10) provide further discussion of issues of patient choice and involvement. Future health policy choices will determine how to develop realistic public and patient expectations of health and appreciation of the responsibility of individuals, families and communities for their health and self-care.

## Globalisation

The globalisation of health has been explored at length in a Nuffield Trust Programme.[7] Three major impacts on UK health are highlighted here. First there is the continuing underlying growth in income differentials between those whose production jobs may be exported to lower cost regions and those profiting from world markets in intellectual property. The impact of this will depend upon government policy response; it may be possible to protect the poorest 10 per cent of the population from absolute poverty but relative deprivation is still likely to increase health needs.

Second, it is apparent that consumption patterns are increasingly shaped by global market trends created by multi-national corporations. This, coupled with increasing prosperity, underlies the pandemic of obesity and increasing problems of alcohol abuse and violence. International policy responses will be crucial. If the Framework Convention on Tobacco Control succeeds, it may point the way to the creation of a global governance framework to ameliorate the spread of alcohol and uncontrolled marketing of high salt, high sugar, processed foods and drinks to children (see Yach, Chapter 2, this volume).

Third, it is likely that there will be further global pandemics from new and re-emerging diseases as the speed and volume of travel increases. Such outbreaks are likely to be increasingly costly as the current generation of antibiotics are exhausted through misuse. The outbreak of Severe Acute Respiratory Syndrome (SARS) in 2003 in Asia and its subsequent global spread has been described as the first pandemic of the 21st century. It is estimated that the economic and financial costs arising from the outbreak amounted to some $15 billion worldwide (Kickbusch, 2003). Again national and international policy responses will be crucial. The Nuffield Trust is proposing a programme of action to address global health issues (Lister and Ingram, 2004).

## Demographic change

### Population growth

Over the next 20 years the UK population is likely to grow by between 0.3–0.4 per cent per annum.[8] The most important factors determining the impact of demographic changes on health costs are the total overall increase in population and the increase in the numbers of people in high health need categories, for this purpose two high need groups are most significant: immigrants and elderly people.

The non-elderly, non-migrant population is likely to fall by about 0.1 per cent per year in England, due to emigration and a falling birth rate. This may give rise to a small reduction in demand for healthcare at a rate of about 0.05 per cent per annum (since health utilisation by the under-50s is about half the total).

### Migrants

The number of migrants to England is likely to account for between 0.15 per cent and 0.2 per year of the population. Studies of the health needs of immigrant populations show they have higher needs but often receive fewer health services (The Scottish Executive, 2003). Immigrants' health needs stem from the triple disadvantage they suffer. First, early life experience, particularly maternal and infant malnutrition and exposure to health risks are the most significant factors in long-term personal health needs, second, the stress of migration is a major cause of ill health and third migrants, particularly women are more likely to be isolated and have more difficulty in accessing health services. There is also a 'backlog' of unmet needs in relation to the health needs of ethnic minority and other socially excluded groups. Experts generally agree that the NHS has not done enough to respond to the particular needs of these groups; steps to meet such needs could add to total health costs, but it is difficult to quantify this figure. Policy measures are being set in hand to reduce inequity in access to health through a wide range of policy initiatives including 'Tackling Health Inequalities: a Programme for Action' and the 'Health Gain Collaboration'. Assuming the needs of minority groups will be better met in future, a net increase in demand of about 0.2–0.25 per cent yearly is estimated by the author.

## Ageing

Studies of the cost impact of ageing across the EU, carried out in the Netherlands suggest that UK health costs will increase by between 0.35 per cent per annum and 0.75 per cent, depending on whether age related infirmity is compressed – 'bop till you drop' – or current levels of infirmity continue (Helder et al., 1997).

A broad estimate, which has generally been applied in the UK and has been quoted by successive health ministers, though with little research evidence, is that cost increases of 1.0 per cent per annum are required to allow for the impact of age-related factors on health costs. This figure is assumed as the basis for the 'high' scenario a lower figure of 0.75 per cent has been used for the central, and 0.35 per cent for the low scenario. More research is required in this field, associated with more discussion about fundamental ethical issues which arise concerning choice and appropriate treatment and care in the last years of life.

## Trends in technology

### Pharmaceuticals

The pace of discovery of new pharmaceutical products, which slowed from about 70 new chemical entities per year in 1980 to 17 per year by 2002, is expected to accelerate over the next 20 years, so that by 2022 it is forecast that 200 new chemical entities will be developed each year. This will be driven by three main factors: developments in combinatorial chemistry and equipment make it possible to screen products one million times faster than in 1995 and the Human Genome Project has increased the potential target applications for drugs, from about 500 to 2,500 (Sykes, 2001). The third factor is a policy choice, as NICE is beginning to represent a 'fourth hurdle' in drug development by requiring demonstration of the cost effectiveness of drugs funded by the NHS.

Within the near future the uptake of new drugs for heart conditions and diabetes could give rise to a major increase in NHS costs of some

£2 billion, but some of these costs may be offset later by reduced costs in hospital care. Fastest growth is expected in prescription medicines, which currently account for about 16 per cent of total health costs. The pharmaceutical sector is expected to grow at between 7–9 per cent per annum in real terms over the next ten years. At an average of 8 per cent growth this would lead to an overall increase in total NHS expenditure of 1.3 per cent per year. A recent article shows drug development cost rising by 7.4 per cent p.a. to the year 2000 (DiMasi et al., 2003).

In the longer term, say within 15 years, genetic screening is likely to become significant. It seems possible that tests could be developed for about 30 main conditions and susceptibilities (Zimmern and Cook, 2000). This depends on the development of affordable diagnostic equipment and the training and readiness of GPs to work with screening services and provide the counselling and follow up required. The cost implications could be considerable, depending upon how it affects medical practice. One possibility is that drugs and dosages could be 'tailored' to individual patient needs.

New treatments for diseases such as Parkinson's and Alzheimer's may result in reductions in long-term care costs. New drugs, for example, for diabetes and cardiovascular disease may reduce the cost of inpatient care. It is claimed that drugs reduce total health cost by about 30 per cent of their costs, though there is little evidence on which to base this. Net of savings, drug cost rises would amount to a total cost increase of 0.9 per cent per year. A low scenario based on a drug-cost growth rate of 7 per cent would result in a net increase at a rate of 0.8 per cent while a high scenario based on drug cost increases of 9 per cent would result in a net rate of cost increase of 1.0 per cent per annum.

Over-the-counter (OTC) medicines and other medical products, which make up about 5 per cent of total health costs are expected to increase in real terms due to trends towards self-medication. Growth in sales of diagnostic testing kits for a wide range of conditions and continued expansion of the market in alternative medicines and therapies is expected at about 7 per cent per year. It is expected that expansion of OTC medicines will reduce costs in the NHS, thus no net increase in costs is expected. Policies to support the expansion of the OTC sector includes further measures to integrate community pharmacists in primary care provision (Taylor and Carter, 2002).

## Medical devices and equipment

Medical devices currently account for less than 3 per cent of total health expenditure, but rapid growth is expected over the next 20 years.

Potential developments now in hand include: portable patient diagnostic devices and tests, patient monitoring devices and services including bio-implants, patient knowledge based systems 'Home health advisors,' telemedicine services using video links and sensors, patient education and support for empowerment based behaviour change, and physical and mental wellness programmes. The net cost impact of such developments is assumed to be neutral.

In hospitals a major expansion is expected in the short term in equipment such as Lithotriptors, MRI and CT scanners and Linear Accelerators to make up some of the current shortfall. Beyond this new generations of diagnostic and treatment equipment are expected and in particular more portable and bedside equipment. The development of a range of specialist robotic equipment to support less invasive surgery (portal surgery) is currently underway. Remotely operated devices, controlled through virtual-reality systems, will replace the hand-held scalpel for many complex surgery procedures, for example, to perform heart bypass operations by portal surgery without stopping the heart. The requirement for specialised equipment and skills will lead to further centralisation of complex procedures. More day case surgery procedures will be provided locally. It is assumed that the overall impact of these developments will be broadly cost neutral as they will reduce current costs and time in hospital; they will, however make health services more capital intensive.

Across Europe social health systems will intensify efforts to limit funding of new drugs and technologies to those of proven effectiveness. The direct impact on health costs of excluding certain high-cost services or unproven services may be limited (only affecting 1–2 per cent of costs), but this would enable governments and healthcare payers to influence the development of health and pharmaceuticals technology. Future health policies could include incentives to encourage the development of health technologies that lower costs, following the example of the tax incentive scheme introduced to encourage research into diseases affecting poor countries.

## Information and communications technology

Expenditure on communications and information technology should increase over the next seven years from its current level of about 1.2 per cent of health spend to a level closer to the US level of 4–6 per cent of costs. However, it is important to note these costs include insurance, patient billing and managed care systems. While some US hospitals and systems have extensive patient management systems, many do not.

The 1992 NHS *Information and Information Management Strategy* for England, was intended to encourage the use of integrated healthcare management information systems based on patient administration, order entry, networked systems, contracting and information systems to support commissioning. Expenditure in support of this strategy was partial and incomplete. Expenditure on information technology reached about £700 million per year in 1996, about 1.2 per cent of health costs. By 1998 a further £1 billion additional expenditure was identified as necessary to complete the NHS Information Infrastructure (NHSII) programme based on electronic patient records and medical support systems for patients and clinical professionals. This will amount to an increase of about £250 million per year. Since that date additional expenditures of about £250 million have been identified which will bring annual health information and communications technology expenditure to about 2.2 per cent of total health costs.

In addition, the further development of NHS Direct as a telephone advice service and as an online service coupled with Digital Interactive Television,[9] applications will increase cost by about £150 million per year. It will provide access to health information, initially of a generic nature but becoming increasingly person-specific and incorporating the ability to contact health professionals and self-help groups for health.

Patient-based personal health records including genetic records, lifestyle and health risk information could both give rise to increased demand for health services as patients become more aware of their health needs, and could support a greater degree of health maintenance and self-care. This could make a significant difference to health status over the next 20 years leading to more selectivity and choice by patients as they learn more about the health risks and choices they face in managing their personal and family health.

The NHS Infomation Strategy will introduce 'three tier' web based systems; these offer the possibility to link data from any system to any other via an intermediary system, which would solve interoperability problems. Beyond this, but within ten years, wireless systems using voice recognition and contextual analysis are likely to emerge. This could support a system that responds to what the doctor is saying, keeps medical records, and offers best practice guidance that can be checked by the doctor in real time, rather than requiring subsequent manual input and search.

Current technology offers health professionals and patients access to knowledge and the means to coordinate and integrate care but it is cumbersome and time consuming. Doctors and nurses spend almost as much time dealing with information (about 25 per cent) as they do with patients (about 35–40 per cent). Within ten years, wireless information and communication systems should be available to assist medical professionals and improve the quality of medical decisions with much reduced time input because there will be no need for a second stage of data entry or keyboard search for information. A major policy goal for ICT should be to increase patient contact time, both as a means of improving efficiency and because this will enable doctors and nurses to support patient decisions concerning self-care and other choices. This will improve responsiveness to patients and the quality of medical decisions.

Investment appraisal of information systems to support basic management processes show[10] that it is difficult to justify these investments on the basis of cost savings. However, once the basic systems are in place further investment should offer financial savings. Thus information technology investments are expected to increase overall costs by about 0.25 per cent per annum, over the whole period, this is assumed to result in an increase in overall efficiency as a result of communications and information technology at a rate of 0.75 per cent per annum after year five, by which time the basic infrastructure should be completed.

## Health buildings

Hospitals, diagnostic and treatment centres and GP surgeries are all important elements of health technology. The NHS Estates Agency estimate that the replacement cost of the current building stock of the NHS (excluding GP premises) amounts to some £75 billion. There is a massive backlog in the maintenance and renewal of this stock.

The NHS has 55 per cent less acute hospital beds per capita than the average European system. While the NHS is far more efficient than other systems in its use of staffed hospital beds, achieving a turnover of patients per bed some 45 per cent higher than the average for the EU, the demand for higher standards will require less intensive use of beds. It was found in 1997 that running hospitals at an occupancy rate of over 85 per cent, inevitably leads to unacceptable trolley waits for emergencies but specifications for both Treasury and Public Finance Initiative (PFI) funded hospitals have often been based on expected occupancy rate of 85–90 per cent[11] (NHSE, 1997). Thus, despite trends towards shorter hospital lengths of stay, the NHS needs more beds.

The technology of health buildings is of course intimately related to the redesign of healthcare processes, for example, provision of diagnostic and treatment centres should make it possible to achieve higher levels of efficiency in planned treatments. While day surgery centres and other specialist services may be moved away from major hospital sites, developments in aspects of technology described in previous sections suggest a concentration of high-tech resources in specialist centres. It has been suggested that the model of a hospital of the future may have more resemblance to a village than a factory (Francis and Glanville, 2001). This is also a necessary response to the spread of new forms of antibiotic resistant hospital infections that also dictate a modular design.

Assuming an economic life of 25 years, the rate of investment required to replace the current building stock would be some £3 billion per year. Current capital investment includes direct funding of some £200 million and some 64 PFI schemes costing £8.5 billion in progress. Of these schemes some £2.5 billion are currently under construction. A rapid hospital redevelopment programme takes from five to seven years to complete (a PFI requires at least two years planning and contracting and three years for construction); clearly smaller scale upgrades will be quicker. Thus it does not seem reasonable to assume the backlog in health buildings can be made up in less than ten years.

For the purpose of this scenario exercise it has been assumed that 'catching up with Europe' would encompass the increased cost of such capital investment and its revenue consequences, since most European systems do not have such problems with their capital stock. PFI or Public Private Partnership schemes offer the potential to increase the capital available to the NHS and provide a contracting mechanism to ensure that such investment produces productivity gains (Health Select Committee of the House of Parliament, 2002). If public funds are available and if schemes can be better managed the same could be achieved by this route. In practice it seems likely that a mix of PFI and public investment will continue.

## Trends in health pay and working methods

### Recruitment, retention and pay

A comparison of professional health worker numbers shows that EU health systems (omitting outliers[12]) have on average 87 per cent more doctors and 42 per cent more nurses per thousand population than the UK. These and all other OECD data-based comparisons must be viewed with caution, because definitions of employment numbers may differ (OECD, 2001). For example, the UK count of nurses only includes full-time equivalent numbers of qualified, i.e. state registered level-one and state enrolled level-two nurses and midwives employed by the NHS and does not include nurses employed in the private and independent sectors. A comparison based on the total number of nurses in employment shows that England has about 7.5 nurses per thousand population, which is above the average for Europe, though this figure may need to be adjusted for part-time working and other factors.

One of the most surprising features of the NHS, for doctors from other European countries, is the extent to which hospital services depend upon medical staff in training, and overseas-trained doctors and nurses. There are about 1.5 medical staff in training for each hospital consultant. Other countries would see this as a quality concern; they typically provide more theoretical training for doctors before allowing them practical experience and would ensure consultants were available to supervise their junior colleagues. In this country, on some days of the week it has not been unusual to find junior clinical staff operating alone without their consultants or supervising nurses. Following the report by Sir Kenneth Calman in 1996, progress has been made in increasing the numbers of consultant posts, but there are still shortages at senior levels in some specialties, including: surgery, anaesthetics, medical oncology and intensive care in both medical and nursing professions.[13]

The most crucial shortage is likely to be at primary care level. Here there are already shortages and significant numbers of doctors reaching retirement age. The formation of Primary Care Trusts and new GP contracts are important reforms but may also lead to further loss of staff. There are difficulties in recruiting overseas doctors directly into primary care, since few countries have exact equivalents to UK GPs.

Some 35 per cent of hospital doctors received their initial training outside the UK, about 30 per cent come from poor countries, which suffer from the loss of such expensively trained staff. Recent data suggest the percentage of non-EU trained doctors is still increasing, despite moves to introduce ethical recruitment policies. Over 12,500 nurses were recruited from poor countries into the UK in 2001, however it is important to note that about 7,500 of these were from the Philippines, which has long produced nurses for the international market and has mechanisms for cost recovery.

It takes seven years to train a doctor and four years to train a nurse, and to achieve the level of skills and know-how required for higher-level jobs may require a further six to ten years. Thus despite the increase in the number of training places for doctors by 20 per cent by 2005 as proposed by the Medical Workforce Advisory Committee, and a similar expansion for nursing, this will not immediately meet the most urgent shortages.

The timescale required to produce senior doctors and nurses, even if recruited from abroad, suggests that it is unwise to suggest such problems can be solved in five years. A ten-year period seems more realistic. Treating the problem as if it were a short-term issue can lead to wrong solutions. Doctors and nurses have been recruited from poor countries who can ill afford to lose staff trained at great cost. A longer-term policy would be to look to countries with large numbers of trained doctors and nurses, such as the Czech Republic and Hungary (which joined the EU in May 2004) and develop partnership agreements to extend their medical training and provide English language skills.[14] Such staff would be more likely to work on rotation to the UK without harming the health system from which they are drawn.

At the same time experienced medical and nursing staff from the UK are lost to the NHS because pay and conditions do not meet local requirements. There is a particular problem in London and the South East where inflexibility in pay and conditions has resulted in the loss of very many experienced staff who cannot afford the cost of housing in these areas. These hospitals are staffed with a very high level of new overseas recruits and agency staff, which gives rise to quality and safety concerns. This problem has been recognised in Treasury statements on public sector pay guidelines issued in 2003.

To address staff retention and skill issues, health sector salaries will need to increase by about 2.5 per cent per annum in real terms over the next five years (current rate of pay increase is above this level); this will add about 1.75 per cent per annum to total cost. In the following years pay increases of 2.0 per cent in real terms with high and low estimates of 1.75–2.2 per cent are assumed, raising costs by between 1.2–1.6 per cent.

## Working methods and efficiency

OECD Health Data 2001 show that the UK employs more than the average total number of people in healthcare per thousand population, about 30 compared with a European average of about 23. It appears the UK has a much greater number of people employed who are not defined as physicians, dentists or nurses. Overall it appears that staffing efficiency in terms of activity per employee is lower in the UK than in comparator countries, however, activity per doctor is much higher.

The NHS has a more complex professional structure than most other European systems. It now needs time to re-examine ways of working from the patient's perspective, to break down professional barriers without compromising specialist standards, and simplify patient care pathways. Local Modernisation Review Teams are at work throughout the NHS, and there are many different ways in which modernisation reviews can streamline processes, break down professional barriers and improve efficiency. For example, there may be a reduction in the number of different people caring for a patient during a hospital stay (currently 27 according to some studies), patients may be able to receive all the diagnostic tests required in a single visit rather than requiring repeated visits, and the extent to which tests are duplicated may be reduced. It could also reduce the variation between GPs in their treatment and referral decisions; studies show variations in referring rates of up to 250 per cent.[15]

Health process re-engineering as initiated by the Modernisation Review could lead to long-term cost reductions at above the historic rate. For many years 2 per cent has been set as a target for efficiency improvement. Experience suggests that in many cases the efficiency gains reported have as much to do with data manipulation as real cost reduction. It is doubtful if real efficiency gains have been above 1.5 per cent per annum. This conclusion is supported by a paper by Sean Boyle and John Appleby 'Short Measure', which suggests that the NHS has become less efficient in recent years (Boyle and Appleby, 2001).

Efficiency gains as a result of changes in working methods in practice over the next ten years could reduce staff requirements by 2 per cent per annum for the next ten years and 1.5–2 per cent thereafter. This would reduce overall costs by 1.4 per cent and 1.05–1.4 per cent. Lower levels of efficiency gain have been included in the low cost increase scenario, since greater investment should lead to higher pressure for efficiency improvements. Increases in productivity are also assumed to arise from technology changes; these go hand in hand with changing working methods. There would also be reductions in demand as a result of increased investment in health promotions and support for self-care. Taking these factors together efficiency improvements of between 2.0 per cent and 2.6 per cent per annum could be achieved.

## Full engagement with health

The first Wanless review (2002) noted that only about one-sixth of health improvement can be attributed to health services. This was based on a Nuffield Trust paper by John Bunker, which has recently been revisited (Bunker, 2001). The Wanless report noted a £30 billion difference in cost between a scenario for health services with active engagement with patients and the public and one without such involvement, indeed Derek Wanless himself commented on several occasions that he doubted if healthcare could be made effective and affordable without this engagement. This led to the commissioning of a further review to explore how the 'fully engaged scenario' could be achieved. In responding to this further review the Nuffield Trust sought to define what constitutes 'full engagement'. It concluded, that this requires the engagement of:

- *Public and patients with their health as*:
  Individuals, families and groups responsible for their own good health.
  Participants in health and care decisions as co-producers of health.
  Responsible and knowledgeable users of the NHS.
  Active citizen owners/consumers of NHS and other services.
- *The state in protecting the health of the people through*:
  Measures to support a balanced approach to health risks and gain.
  Measures to support equity in health for the whole population.
  Economic, environmental and social policies for health.
  International policies to address long-term global health issues.
- *All sectors of the economy in supporting health, for example*:
  Employers to protect and improve the health of staff.
  Producers to ensure products and advertising support health.
  Teachers to ensure principles of healthy living are understood.
- *The NHS and all health workers in promoting health, for example*:
  Cost effective investment in specific public health measures (including: health protection, promotion, screening, advice, information, behaviour change, family and community development).
  Support for individual and community based self-care.
  Health promotion as an aspect of all healthcare staff responsibilities.

Engagement requires democratic involvement with local health services. Until recently England was virtually the only major country in Europe with no democratic engagement in health below national level. While UK Parliament determines health policy as do all other European governments, the UK Ministry of Health directly runs virtually all English health services which is not the case in other European systems where regional and local governments play a much stronger role. There are currently many different policy approaches to this issue: the creation of local Patient Forums, patient representation on NHS boards and the election of boards for Foundation Hospitals. It remains to be seen whether these initiatives will solve the problem of the democratic deficit and how they relate to the modernising of governance at local levels in England (Newman, 2001). Such policies may mean some loss of economies of scale in the short term but should release management initiative and improve public engagement in the longer term.

The Nuffield Trust has therefore proposed a series of measures to increase the engagement of all sectors of society with health, including the redefinition of legal responsibilities for public health, through a new Health of the People Act, reforms to improve the leadership and direction of public health policy, steps to increase the responsibility for health borne by employers and producers and measures to strengthen the management of public health research and investment and social marketing for health. In addition the Nuffield Trust is supporting the first phase of the Commission for Patient and Public Involvement in Health's programme through the development of 'Our Health' which is designed to support public and patient organisations in building a constituency for health and local 'champions for health'.

While it is expected that expenditure to support public health will increase from just over 1 per cent of UK health costs to 3–5 per cent, the leadership and management of public health and the actions which are taken are more important than the quantum of expenditure. The first Wanless report suggested cost savings of £1.50 could be achieved for each £1 spent on health promotion and self care, however, a closer look at the evidence suggests that cost savings are very variable. For the purpose of the scenario expenditure on health promotion, disease prevention and self-care including mental health promotion, is assumed to increase by 3 per cent over ten years, offset by reduction in demand by 0.3 per cent per annum in the second ten-year period, which seems to reflect the rate of return that can be achieved on a range of public health interventions (Abelson, 2003).

The most recent Wanless review calls for an examination of the balance between government, employer and individual responsibility for health but did not produce detailed recommendations on this or on the level of expenditure required for public health measures (Wanless, 2004). This was left to a subsequent Department of Health Review *Choosing Health* (Owen and Lister, 2004). The recommendations of this Wanless Report call for strengthening of the leadership, management and information support for public health and its evidence base. It did not make detailed recommendations on the organisational reforms required, leaving this issue to a subsequent review of arms-length bodies.

## Summary of cost and policy scenarios

Figure 4.3 describes the various cost and policy scenarios. The impact of these cost drivers would require real cost increases of 6.58 per cent

1. Meeting European standards: 20% increase over ten years, equivalent to 1.8% per year – low 1.7% – high 2.3%.

2. Consumer expectations: 1.95 % increase per year in line with GDP/capita growth – low 1.5% – high 2.0% per year.

3. Increase of £200 million to provide for hospice care: equivalent to 0.1% increase per year over 5 years.

4. Health needs arising from immigration offset by reducing population: 0.18% – low 0.15% – high 0.2% increase per year.

5. Health needs of the increasing population of elderly people: 0.75% per year – low 0.35% – high 1.0%

6. Medical and pharmaceutical technology average growth impact: 0.9 % per annum (low 0.8% – high 1.0%) based on a 8% (low 7% – high 9%) per annum cost increase in the pharmaceuticals sector and assuming 30% of increased costs are offset by reductions in other health costs

7. Information and communications technology: 0.25% increase per year in costs offset by impact on overall efficiency of 0.5% after five years,i.e. a net saving of 0.25% for years 6–20.

8. Changes in pay of 2.5% per annum over the next five years: assumed to increase costs by 1.75% per annum, thereafter a rate of increase of 2.0% will result in overall cost increases of 1.4% per annum – low 1.2% – high 1.6%

9. Efficiency gains arising from changing working methods: assumed 1.4% over the next ten years and 1.23% in the following period – low 1.05% – high 1.4%.

10. Health promotion, disease prevention and self-care: increase in expenditure of 3% over ten years at 0.3% per annum increase, offset by reduction in demand by 0.3% per annum in the second ten-year period.

*Figure 4.3*: Cost and policy scenarios[16]

per annum for the next five years, 5.63 per cent per annum for years 6–11 and 3.4 per cent per annum for years 11–20. This will mean by the year 2022 England will be spending approximately 12.5 per cent of GDP on healthcare. This is at the level forecast for the unweighted average for the countries of the EU as constituted in 2002 but would be below the forecast for the population weighted average (Barnard, 2003). The forecast arising from the 'low' scenario, coupled with the low forecast for the rate of economic growth would result in health costs rising to 11 per cent of GDP while the high scenario would result in health costs rising to 14 per cent of GDP.

It is also important to 'expect the unexpected': global pandemics, breakthroughs in technology or major changes in demand may be unlikely in any one year but over a twenty-year period they seem more likely than not. In a similar fashion a policy change such as a change in the definition and funding of long-term care could also result in a step increase in costs. The impact of sudden change should be evaluated alongside these scenarios, which tend to assume a continuation of known trends or influences. This should also guard against a complacent expectation that the rate of increase in health costs will slow down in the long term.

## Notes

1. 'Policy Futures for UK Health', edited by Dr Charlotte Dargie with Professor Sandra Dawson and Pam Garside, and accompanying Technical Series particularly No. 1 *The Global Context*, Dr Kelley Lee, No. 3 *Demography*, Charlotte Dargie, No. 4 *Science and Technology*, Glenn Robert , No. 5 *Economy and Finance*, Panos Kanavos, No. 8 *Workforce*, Charlotte Dargie, No. 10 *Public Expectations*, Marian Barnes published by The Nuffield Trust 2000.
2. The Nuffield Trust Submission to the Wanless Review can be found at www.nuffieldtrust.org.uk
3. Drawn from the *OECD Health Data 2001* published by OECD.
4. The author was a member of the NICE Patients Council but all views expressed are personal.
5. Luxembourg is excluded because of its small size and high proportion of cross-border patient flows.
6. Speech by the Rt. Hon. Alan Milburn MP Secretary of State on NHS Foundation Hospitals 22 May 2002 available at http://www.dh.gov.uk/ NewsHome/Speeches/SpeechesList/SpeechesArticle/fs/en?CONTENT_ID=40 00768&chk=jk4/Wa
7. See the UK Partnership for Global Health website at www.ukglobalhealth.org
8. Office of National Statistics Projection as of 15 November 2001.
9. Lord Young of Dartington at launch of Open Health DiTV at the Nuffield Trust 2001.

10. The author helped to write the Goals Paper for the 1992 'Information and Information Management Strategy', for England and subsequently directed investment appraisals for elements of the strategy.
11. The author directed a series of assignments for the planning and contracting of PFI health facilities.
12. Italy is omitted for doctors because they have a large number working in non-clinical capacities. Eire is omitted for nursing as an outlier.
13. See for example 'Unfinished Business', report by Sir Liam Donaldson, Consultation Document on SHO Roles August 2002.
14. Lister, G., 2001, MATRA Partnership Programmes from NSPH Netherlands.
15. See the Worcester Vocational Training Scheme guide to Evidence Based Medicine available at http://www.text.worcestervts.co.uk/clinical/decisions/referrals.htm for literature in this field.
16. The figures show the 'central' scenario with a judgement on the high and low outliers.

# References

Abelson, P. (2003) *Returns of Investment in Public Health: and Epidemiological and Economic Analysis.* Canberra: Population Health Division of the Commonwealth Department of Health and Aged Care

Barnard, K. (ed.) (2003) *The Future of Health: Health of the Future.* London: Fourth European Consultation on Future Trends, Nuffield Trust

Barnes, M. (1999) 'Policy futures for UK health', technical paper No. 10, *Public Expectations: From Paternalism to Partnership: Changing Relationships in Health and Health Services.* London: Nuffield Trust

Boyle, S. and Appleby, J. (2001) 'Short measure', *Health Services Journal,* 13 December, 31–2

Bunker, J. (2001) *Medicine Matters After All. Measuring the benefits of medical care, a healthy lifestyle, and a just social environment.* London: Nuffield Trust

Dargie, C., Dawson, S. and Garside, P. (2000) *Policy Futures for UK Health.* London: Nuffield Trust

DiMasi, J.A., Hansen, R.W. and Grabowski, H. (2003) 'The price of innovation: new estimates of drug development costs', *Journal of Health Economics,* 22:2

Francis, S. and Glanville, R. (2001) *Building a 2020 Vision: Future healthcare environments.* London: Nuffield Trust

Health Select Committee of the House of Parliament (2002) *The Role of the Private Sector in the NHS.* London: Hansard, Westminster

Helder, J.C. and Achterberg, P.W. (1997) 'Future health expenditure in the European Union: Estimates of demographic effects', National Institute for Public Health and the Environment in Bilthoven, the Netherlands, Report number 432504 003

Kickbusch, I. (2003) 'SARS wake-up call for a strong global health policy', Yale Global 25/04/2003 Yale Center for the Study of Globalisation

Klein, R. (2001) 'Estimating the financial requirements of healthcare', *BMJ,* 323:1318–19

Lister, G. (2002) 'Patient choice lessons from other countries', paper to the National Conference on Patient Involvement 2002, London: College of Health

Lister, G. (2001) *The Nuffield Trust Response to the 'Wanless Review: Securing our Future Health, a Long Term Review'*. London: Nuffield Trust note No. 42

Lister, G. and Ingram, I. (2004) *UK Strategy for Global Health*, London: Nuffield Trust

Maxwell, R. (1981) *Health and Wealth International Comparisons of Health Expenditure*. New York: Simon and Schuster

National Consumer Council (1998) *Consumer Concerns 1998*. London

Newman, J. (2001) *Modernising Governance: New Labour, Policy and Society*. London: Sage

NHSE – Economics and Operational Research Division (1997) 'Bed capacity and the trade off between electives and non-electives', Annex to Report to the Chief Executive on Winter Pressures, Leeds

Nuffield Trust (2001) *The Buckinghamshire Declaration*. London

OECD 2001 Health Database. Paris: OECD Health Policy Unit and Institute de Recherche et d'Etude en Economie de la Santé

Owen, J.W. and Lister, G. (2004) *Nuffield Trust Response to Choosing Health*, see www.NuffieldTrust.org.uk

The Scottish Executive (2003) *Improving the health of the Scottish ethnic minority community. Annual report of the steering committee and director of the national resource centre for ethnic minority health 2002–2003.* www.scotland.gov.uk/library5/health/ihsms-00.asp

Sykes, R. (2001) *New Medicines, The Practice of Medicine and Public Policy*. London: Nuffield Trust

Taylor, D. and Carter, S. (2002) *Realising the Promise: Community Pharmacy in the new NHS*. London School of Pharmacy

Wanless, D. (2002) *Securing our Future Health: Taking a Long-term View*. HM Treasury

Wanless, D. (2004) *Securing Good Health For the Whole Population*. HM Treasury

WHO (2000) *World Health Report 2000 Health Systems Improving Performance*. Geneva

Zimmern, R. and Cook, C. (2000) *Genetics and Health: Policy Issues for Genetic Science and their Implications for Health and Health Services*. London: The Stationery Office

# 5
# Why do Good Politics Make Bad Health Policy?

*Scott Greer*

## Introduction: The relationship between health politics and health policy

It is hardly novel to say there is a deep malaise in the health systems of the United Kingdom. Enoch Powell argued in the 1960s that health politics is always gloomy, for it is marked by the propensity of all actors to complain about, rather than celebrate, their resources and treatment (Powell, 1966). Negative stories about doctors have consistently outnumbered positive stories as far back as 1980 (Ali et al., 2001). Against this backdrop, it is easy to dismiss contemporary claims of problems in the health services as yet another instance of politically induced complaint, but evidence is accumulating that in the early 21st century, real conflict and discontent are disrupting the health services of the UK. The malaise shows in the rejection of the new England and Wales contract by hospital consultants, who voted to refuse a contract negotiated by the BMA and DoH that was intended to 'modernise' their work (BBC, 2002). It shows in the problems encountered in subsequent negotiations and renegotiations of the contract for general practitioners worried about their finances and autonomy (Kmietowics, 2003). 'It is hard to believe that the problems with these two contracts are just coincidence' argued the editor of the *British Medical Journal*, 'doctors everywhere don't seem to like the way the world is going. They don't want to be good corporate citizens. They want to be valued professionals' (Smith, 2003:1098). If there is evidence that there is a direct clash between the values of medical professionals and the values of their political masters, then there is reason to think the health services are in trouble. Meanwhile, there is discontent in the management cadres as well. Survey data from the April 2003 survey by the NHS Alliance suggests that half of the managers running English Primary Care Trusts planned to leave within two years (BBC, 2003). If general practitioners, consultants, and managers all show significant levels of discontent at a time when the health budgets of UK governments are increasing dramatically, then we can reasonably ask what is causing the problems.

Regardless of whether the friction between the health and political systems is justified, one of its immediate sources is the combination of reorganisation and managerialism that marks contemporary health policy in the UK. This looks to many professionals like attempts to make them into 'good corporate citizens' at the expense of their professional ethos. The literature on organisational theory, public or private, provides evidence that reorganisation is sometimes dysfunctional, and nearly always expensive and distracting, as staff are trying to find and occupy new roles and start up or shut down different organisations (Isles and Sutherland, 2001, Fulop et al., 2002). The UK health services have been in a maelstrom of structural reorganisation for two decades, with an extraordinarily high degree of change in organisational charts and accountability arrangements (Ham, 1999; Klein, 2000). Meanwhile, everyday activities for clinicians and operational changes have been subjected to a variety of top-down forms of managerialism that try to impose objectives and management styles on them in what has been argued as a peculiar (and not particularly realistic) imitation of private-sector organisations (Pollitt, 1993). In July 2004, we have a dominant language of targets, star ratings, 'earned autonomy', and league tables, with central interventions outliving particular initiatives and governments. One former Labour minister in the UK DoH remarked in a 9 July 2003 talk that in his time in office he would ask his officials to try to count the number of targets imposed on the NHS. At one point they found 459 such managerial targets (Hunt, 2004). Many within the NHS insist that such 'targetitis' erodes morale and effectiveness, distorting managerial priorities and sapping professionals' sense of autonomy and responsibility.

This chapter argues that the problem of friction between politics and the UK health services, and the 'bad' health policy that ensues, is structural. The political system, behaving predictably, produces regular outcomes that gradually erode the organisational stability, coherent goals, and sense of self the NHS requires.[1] It has powerful enabling conditions that encourage politicians that try to micromanage the health services. The particular structure of Westminster democracy and the NHS itself lower the costs of political intervention. While major interventions in health policy require serious political mobilisation in any country, the

UK system is particularly open to seemingly politically low-cost interventions in everything from individual disease treatment to organisational structure.

The first section of this chapter presents the 'multiple streams' model of policymaking applied to UK health policy. It stresses the processes that lead to policy outcomes large and small, and points up both their inherent unpredictability and their substantial disconnection from the health services themselves. The second section examines the institutional makeup of the UK political systems and health services in order to identify what factors put the political system and the health services in such unusually close contact and that so reduce the costs of political intervention. These lead to the conclusion, which considers various changes that might reduce the amount of friction between democratically elected politicians, health services managers, and the professionals who treat the patients. The changes all try to reduce the amount of contact between the hyperactive political world governed by multiple-streams analysis and the professionally dominated world of the NHS. The argument is based primarily on 102 interviews conducted between September 2001 and February 2003. These were anonymous, semi-structured interviews with health service managers and professionals in selected sites in England, Northern Ireland, Scotland and Wales, with officials and interest group representatives, and with politicians and academics in those systems. Participant observation of health service meetings and events across the four systems contributed to the data as well; see Greer (2004) for more details.

## The predictable unpredictability of politics

'You've chosen a bad topic to look at politics here. The problem in health – for all the governments in the UK – is that we are putting billions of pounds into health and we don't see what we're getting' noted a recently retired, Scottish politician in a 12 February 2003 Edinburgh interview with the author. The sentiments are common among politicians. In addition to the disenchantment with public-sector organisations that pervades contemporary thought, politicians in the UK are feeling that the considerable sums of new money put in by Britain's three Labour-led governments should have produced more of an effect than they have. The structure of NHS finance- the fact that its budget is set from general taxation by finance ministers balancing other priorities- means that it is far less prone to the cost inflation that plagues other health systems and that the politics of the NHS are focused on what is secured for the money. The politics of the NHS are mostly about efficiency and (latterly) quality rather than cost constraint; while other countries grope for ways to rein in free-spending doctors, the NHS systems must seek ways to make them do more with their budgets (Freeman, 2000:44-7).

It is natural that politicians would want something for their money, and natural that taxpayers should want them to want something for their money. The question is not whether democratically elected politicians have a right or obligation to take an interest in the way public money is being spent. The question is why their interventions take the form of micromanagement and reorganisation where the justification for such actions is generally invisible to well wishers and participants in the health services. It is not that we lack arguments about and descriptions of the proper role of different stakeholders in public services. There is a strong argument for politicians having 'criteria' power; the ability to set criteria and determine broad policy goals, while other groups have the 'operational' power to design and operate services (Winstanley et al., 1995). It is difficult to identify people in politics or the press who explicitly want politicians to have operational power; there appears to be real strength in and acceptance of the argument that the role of democratically accountable politicians with no expertise is in broad policy and criteria decisions rather than service management. Furthermore, the time frames of health policy should discourage politicians from micromanagement. There is a fundamental mismatch in political and health service timetables. New doctors can take a decade to enter the services, but a decade is three, or more, generally elected parliaments and politicians are unlikely to be able to wait or counsel their voters to wait. Politically astute professionals and managers speak of the need to give politicians 'quick wins'. This is the need to give them short-term, identifiable benefits in order to give the services space to develop longer-term projects. The problem is that it is difficult to generate enough quick wins to persuade the politicians they have enough to justify their possible requirement to levy more taxes.

Despite a focus on quick wins, political frustration with and intervention in organisation and management is endemic. This chapter argues that the disruptive forays by politicians into operational issues can be explained by a well-established political science theory, namely the approach known as the 'multiple-streams' approach. This theory argues that the policy process has a very substantial element of randomness but that the randomness is channelled in particular ways. It explains much of the peculiar and incessant variation in health policy.

While the political system is predictable in the ways it will produce unpredictable outcomes, and the outcomes can be explained, *the system and its inputs are largely disconnected from the health service it is charged to run.*

## The multiple-streams approach

Like many good theories, the multiple-streams explanation of policy decision sounds very simple. Its origins are in the classic work of Cohen et al. (1972) and Kingdon (1995), who specified its use in politics. Zahariadis (1995:27–45) provides an improved formulation with a specific focus on the UK. The approach begins with the ingredients of a policy. The most basic formula for a policy outcome is a combination of a problem (something that seems to demand a response); a politician (who can and might actually do something) and a policy (something to do). If one of the three is absent, it is unlikely anything will happen. When the three come together, a 'window of opportunity' opens in which something happens, and a policy is likely to be the result. This fundamental indeterminacy – based on whatever and whoever happens to be in the right place at the right time and on how long the window stays open – reflects the fact that the political system is in what is termed an 'organised anarchy', or a system in which there is no overall hierarchy among components or borders (Cohen, March and Olsen, 1972). In politics, groups move in and out and increase and decrease in importance and there is no ultimate locus of authority. Those who fight in democratic politics almost invariably live on to fight again.

*Politics* is, in the UK, the ideology and strategy of governing parties (Zahariadis, 1995:34). It incorporates the line-up of interest groups, the number and kind of players in the game, and the politicians' sense of the overall mood in the country, whether impressionistic or based on survey data. All of these come together to give politicians a sense of the political costs, benefits, feasibility and likely outcome of a policy. It also incorporates an important factor, namely individual ministers' need to 'make a mark' at something. It flows in ways that are much studied by politics specialists, endlessly documented by journalists, and much discussed by politicians themselves, as they respond to their perception of wavering public opinion and results of focus groups, internal party pressure, the makeup of the government and its advisors, and the shifting 'conventional wisdom' that fascinates political classes anywhere. In sum, it is the extent to which a party sees a reason to address a problem or proffer a solution. It is not directly governed by the events in the policy sector and it can cause governing politicians to seek out solutions, before fully appreciating problems.

*Problems*, nonetheless, are often 'presented' to politicians. Kingdon (1995) usefully distinguishes between 'problems' and 'conditions' (p. 109). A problem is something seen as requiring attention and amenable to attention. A condition is something disagreeable that we can or must live with. Poverty is a condition – the poor are always with us – but child malnutrition or pensioners without heat are problems that need solutions. Issues travel back and forth between the two categories; variable quality in the NHS was a condition, from the point of view of politicians, until the scandal of incompetent paediatric heart surgery in Bristol made it a political problem (DoH, 2001). Problems typically gain their status through media attention and can often compel politicians to respond. Sometimes politicians or policy entrepreneurs can engineer a condition's transformation into a problem in order to have something on which to act. This happened with quality improvement in Scotland before devolution or the scandal of Bristol. Problems, however, tend to erupt unpredictably – a slow news day combined with an enterprising reporter can create a political problem where none saw one before.

*Policies* also have lives of their own. Rather than being devised as solutions to problems already identified, they exist relatively independently, sustained by a support structure of professionals, academics, and adherents in the health services, professions, and among civil servants (often sharing ideas and worldviews that crosscut institutional positions, Jenkins-Smith and Sabatier, 1994). Policy 'entrepreneurs' sell their ideas, proposing their chosen policies as the responses to any number of problems. The business metaphor of 'entrepreneurs' is not an accident; they sell wares by identifying clients, creating or identifying needs, and modifying their pre-existing product appropriately. With luck, they are in the right place with a plausible policy just when a politician needs a solution to a problem. All their years of preparation, analysis and argumentation have served to make their solution seem feasible and acceptable, rather than outlandish, and give it a better chance of being the outcome of this process, which is actually fundamentally indeterminate.

The policy ideas therefore tend to become what are known as 'Christmas trees', or policies laden with justifications, answers adorned with questions they are supposed to answer. A policy idea becomes decorated with new justifications as time passes and policy entrepreneurs try to sell it as the solution to an increasingly large number of new problems.[2] Thus, primary care commissioning, information technology, data collection and general management have by now accumulated explanations of why they solve almost any problem. They interact; healthcare markets have been sold by the same Stanford Professor, Alain Enthoven, as the way to avoid requiring data collection (because markets are automatic) and as the way to require data collection (because markets build in incentives to do so), (Enthoven, 1979, 1989). The policy is often more important to these entrepreneurs than the problem; problems are temporary and come and go, while the policy is long-lived and carries conviction.

The policy, problem and politicians all flow in their interdependent but separate streams, but occasionally flow together. When they do, a policy decision can emerge. Plausible ideas ardently proposed (and a few implausible ones) couple with a problem, often media-generated or noticed because of a well-timed press release and the entry on to the stage of a politician who must make a mark to thrive and survive – and a policy is made. Policy emerges from this organised chaos of newspapers, think tanks, MPs, MSPs, MLAs, AMs, radio programmemes, civil servants, conferences, professors, scandals, parliamentary timetables and opportunism in a way that never necessarily suits anybody working in the health system.

## Implications of the multiple-streams approach

At a minimum, the 'multiple streams' model suggests that 'evidence-based policy's' appeals for technocratic expertise will have a difficult career. Whilst policy entrepreneurs base their arguments and conclusions on social science and considerations of feasibility and data play a major role in debates, they are still advocating fundamentally political ideas (Majone, 1989). Then, regardless of evidence, the conflicting agendas, the unpredictability, the scepticism of politicians who have heard many 'evidence-based' arguments, the multiple actors and accidents of timing that shape policy, resist technocratic decision making. The government machine goes to work, defending the political decision, and the result is civil service jokes about 'policy-based evidence' (Constitution Unit, 2003). A multiple-streams approach is not compatible with a science-based model of policy development; at most, the appeals to evidence and science that have justified professionals' involvement in policy for decades winnow out some ideas by raising technical standards and obliging all policy entrepreneurs to argue and persuade in a language favorable to expert intervention (Zahariadis, 1995).

At a maximum, this model suggests that the political system is structurally given to interventions that are difficult to justify; if the policy idea has suddenly been enacted because of a favorable conjunction with politics and a problem, that is no guarantee that it is a good or appropriate idea. Each of the streams is subject to important distortions that are unrelated to what we might call the management or professional imperatives of health systems. The political stream is subject to the many factors that govern a government's political success or failure; reshuffles, elections, polls and individual ministers' decisions are all capable of changing the direction of the public mood. Politics is shaped by interactions with events remote from health policies or problems. A war with Iraq can sour labour relations and cause a reshuffle as ministers quit the government. The terror attacks of September 11 2001 in the United States can (and did) provoke abrupt changes in England's public health regime since the Chief Medical Officer was present with his ideas for reorganisation just when the government needed a visible response and the public was awake to the problem of massive terror attacks in the UK (DoH, 2002). Political journalist Andrew Rawnsley argues that the NHS in England shifted direction because Frank Dobson's services were required as Labour's candidate for the Mayor of London, and a wave of reorganisation began when his replacement Alan Milburn was told to 'modernise' the service (Rawnsley, 2001).

## Institutional conditions of instability

The political system, any democratic political system, any permeable system of the type Cohen, March and Olsen (1972) call 'organised anarchy', produces health policies that do not necessarily reflect the goals and imperatives as seen by those who work in the services. That creates a problem. Despite the strong sentiments of many managers, political intervention is of course appropriate and usually justified; the health services must serve the people who are their paymasters. But political intervention, such as reorganisations and tight managerial oversight, can be counterproductive. The question is how to find the balance between political demands, formulated through a policy process that does not produce stable or 'rational' outcomes, and the goals of those charged by profession or managerial responsibility with operating a health system. In turn, this requires examination of the institutional setting of the multiple-streams policy process in the United Kingdom's health systems.

What, then, are the attributes of the NHS and the British political system that make it easy for governments to intervene in even small matters? What is it that allows the political system to choose different policies so easily and quickly while the window of opportunity is still open? To some extent the charms of change are universal, intervention is universal and bad policy is universal (Brunsson and Olsen, 1993). Other countries also have waves of intervention and reforms, often as Light (1997) describes for no easily identifiable good reasons and political systems that make their public services disagreeable and ineffective (Wilson, 1989:113–15). Nevertheless, the structures of the UK state and the institutional structure of the NHS lower the political costs and the organisational costs of interventions, and make frequent policy initiatives more likely.

## Political costs of change

In striking the balance between political accountability and organisational stability, institutions matter. The changeability of any policy varies with the number of veto points in the policy system as well as the strength and number of institutions. Veto points are opportunities for important groups to stop a policy idea; multiplying veto points decreases the odds of any policy change because they are each a hurdle it must clear (Immergut, 1992). These are not just 'hard', legislative veto points, such as those created by referenda, separation of powers or judicial review; there are also softer veto points when a crucial group can threaten to withhold an important resource. Classically, there are three resources that matter. Firstly, advice or comment on technical feasibility, which can diminish the appeal of a policy. Secondly, acquiescence by groups with key roles in implementation and ability to scuttle the change and thereby to make a prediction of implementation failure a reality. Lastly, acceptance of the group's public legitimacy and ability to affect parties' strategies and perceptions (Beer, 1965:320).

Looking now to institutions, let us look first at the 'hard' political institutions. The Westminster system of parliamentary government makes it easy for governments to act and the NHS' existence as a direct part of the state makes it easy for governments to act upon it. The Westminster system and the design of the NHS lower the political costs of managerial intervention. Westminster-system governments, even if increasingly constrained by law or government coalitions, concentrate power and autonomy in the executive and therefore allow it great freedom of action within the specification of accountability of government to parliament and parliament to the people. The doctrine of parliamentary sovereignty brooks few limits; local government and local autonomy in general, the traditional check on the centre, has been progressively eroded over the last century (Harris, 1983; Loughlin,

2000), while judicial oversight, based in European human rights and EU law is new and yet to have its full impact. The unimpeded Westminster parliament, towering over its institutional landscape, also focuses power on the government rather than on the wider assembly. This means that the freedom of action of the government is considerable and checked mostly by periodic general elections. Other governments, more constrained by interpenetrated levels of territorial politics, judicial oversight, or weaker parties, lack such freedom of action and must usually work harder to mobilise political force for a policy change. The devolved governments (with the intermittently suspended exception of Northern Ireland) remain Westminster-style systems that concentrate power and accountability in the government, even if their proportional representation broadens the representation of parties in government). The devolved governments that are functioning – Scotland and Wales – have certainly continued reorganising their health services (Greer, 2003). Devolution did not produce radically more constrained governments; the flexibility and lack of fiscal intervention or formal control by the centre is remarkable in comparative territorial politics (Banting and Corbett, 2002; Bell and Christie, 2002; Simeon, 2003:222–3). In other words, formally, the logic of the Westminster system of party government explains much of the executive's power over the health service.

Furthermore the 'softer' institutional veto points in the policy process are also rare. The degree of micromanagement and incessant change is possible partly because the NHS is a relative rarity in comparative health policy. It is more directly subject to the state than other advanced industrial health systems. It is a single large organisation hierarchically dependent on the government, with very few other players (employers, unions, multiple layers of government, or professions) directly involved in shaping and administering the system. There might be and are powerful interest groups – unquestionably the medical profession and the unions have power. They might have significant resources because of their role giving advice, acquiescence, or acceptance, but they are rarely written into the core structures in the way German healthcare enshrines unions and employers or Canadian healthcare builds in provinces (for introductions, Tuohy, 1992; Freeman, 2000). Internationally, this degree of state autonomy in policymaking is rare because health systems financed out of general taxation and directly run by the state are relatively rare. Spain's main system, whose creators studied different models and selected the NHS model when it set up its health system in the 1980s, is the most similar; Greece and Italy also chose a NHS-like model after considerable comparative study (Linos, 2004). Crucially, systems which are not directly run by the state invariably have more countervailing powers in health service policy decisions – they have more veto points, with actors whose power goes beyond that of interest groups. Governments can occasionally mobilise tremendous will in many different systems and surmount the resistance of healthcare system insiders, but their ability to intervene in small-scale managerial decisions is limited by these other players.

There are few systems in Europe with a comparably strong government able to reach down deep into the health system. Continental welfare states (in the categories of Esping-Andersen, 1990) tend to use corporatist committees and Scandinavian welfare states tend to work through local government and often local government finance. Both of these kinds of systems give a stronger place to important groups (unions, employers and local governments) that can use veto points and disconnect the central state from much of the power over, and much of the blame for, health issues. The dense institutionalisation of these health systems channels conflict over health policy through a number of key actors including the state, and this means that there are more restraints on minor policy change.

The liberal states whose political systems are institutionally comparable to the UK, such as Australia, Canada and the Republic of Ireland, all have powerful parliaments and governments that can redesign policy fields almost at will. They also, however, have one or two additional checks on central organisation. The first is private operators with provider power that are more integrated into their health systems than the UK. The second is the ability to benefit from the interplay of multiple levels of government to frustrate change. This means that despite the strength of Westminster-style parliaments, there are strong veto players and the process of organisational transformation is drawn out. The result is that it is more costly in terms of time, political effort and opportunity costs to try and change the organisation or management of these countries' health systems. The health systems are ultimately the responsibility of the state, but there are important actors that can slow changes and/or defend their own organisational or professional autonomy.

By contrast, the institutional structure of the NHS is akin to that of Westminster. It centralises authority, blame, power and accountability in the government and its individual responsible ministers led by the Secretary of State. Like Westminster democracy, countervailing powers are few and far between. The territorial level of the health services in Britain, like local government is very weak – the management structures between the individual hospital and the Department are entirely pliable and have been reorganised almost without cease since 1983. This is not to understate the power of interest groups, above all medical professions; a cursory review of major works on the politics of the NHS shows their influence on policy quite clearly (for example, Eckstein, 1959, 1960; Fox, 1986; Webster, 1998; Ham, 1999; Moran, 1999; Klein, 2000). They might be important political actors with great strength in their policy fields but they are not written into the structure of the field. There is no requirement for joint decision-making that might slow the rate of policy change as there is for German governments with the requirement they must work through corporatist funds, or federal–provincial negotiations as enshrined in the institutional structure of Canada. Furthermore, the articulation of interests are often confined to those of the specific interest groups represented. Amidst the flurry of organisational changes in Northern Ireland, Scotland and Wales since devolution, the BMA's role has been to safeguard doctors' positions and influence, and the NHS Confederation to safeguard managers' positions and influence (Greer, 2004). The result, crucially, is that there is no formal structure requiring anybody other than the government to make decisions about health services organisation and the structure of influence in politics does not guarantee that the most powerful actors, such as the BMA or even the NHS Confederation, will approach their intervention from a broad-brush, holistic health service design perspective.

The combination of a health system that is formally directly responsible to politicians with a highly centralised and institutionally relatively unencumbered government drastically lowers the political and official costs of change. The formal structure of the state under Westminster systems allows policy to move through quickly, while in other political systems the multiple veto points of multi-level government, separation of powers or formal corporatism slow change, subject it to more scrutiny and make each suggestion less likely to occur.

## Organisational costs of change

The political system lowers the political costs of micromanagement and reorganisation; the design of the NHS lowers the organisational and implementation costs of micromanagement and reorganisation. The direct dependence of the health services on their political masters is well documented and explains the shibboleth that the NHS (or NHS Scotland, or NHS Wales, or the NHS in Northern Ireland) is 'Stalinist' (see Paton, Chapter 3, this volume). It certainly is Stalinist in the sense that most large organisations are: jobs and activities exist at the discretion of the top leadership. The top leadership in the NHS happens to be the Secretary of State or the devolved health minister rather than a corporate chief executive. The main difference, then, is that the last century of capitalism has seen managers become the leaders of most big companies, with other stakeholders (including shareholders) firmly in the background. As long as their organisation's share price is acceptably high, most managers are fairly free. This naturally gives big corporations more focus than public-sector organisations, which are subject to the conflicting demands of many well-represented groups, and gives private chief executives more freedom (Chandler, 1977:490–500; Chandler, 1990:621–8; Williamson, 1985:324–5).

Thus, the charge of 'Stalinism' is only half-right and to that extent banal; it is of interest only if we are to say that any listed corporation is 'Stalinist'. Such unchecked power is rarely if ever found in public corporations and is even less likely in the NHS if the single figure is thought to be the NHS CEO, or even Secretary of the State. The NHS, like any big organisation, is a hierarchical organisation from the point of view of organisation charts or managers. But unlike them, the NHS lacks a fully-fledged corporate structure unless one sees ministers and their activities as the proxy for shareholder owners.

Instead, the NHS directly subjects hierarchical health service organisations with a sizeable management corps to a conflictual, unpredictable, and often very vague political process dominated by multiple-streams decision-making. Westminster systems lower political costs of intervention by minimising veto points and reducing the number of other groups with formal vetoes. Formally, there is nothing left between the government and the smallest activity.

But what about the organisational costs of change? Do organisational costs of reorganisation and micro management not act as a break on continual change? The costs of micromanagement and reorganisation are well documented in academic literature on organisational theory and public policy. Reorganisation takes up time, it diverts organisations from their goals and people from their work; it damages the morale of those reorganised or micromanaged; it requires significant investment in new organisational start-up costs; and for a time it confuses organisations' goals and priorities. Furthermore, these costs cannot be reduced by political institutions alone and must somehow be surmounted to create a system in which intervention is easy. Even if it is possible for the ministers of the UK governments to sideline or quieten or suppress the impact of professional organisations and unions when formulating policy, it is far more difficult for them to change clinical practice. That politicians would want to pay the costs inherent in attempts to organise or reorganise a health system is not intuitively obvious. Surely healthcare should be seen as an even more unrewarding and costly field for political intervention than most? Intervention is difficult and implementation fiendishly difficult. It has a pronounced tendency to develop according to its own logics, subject only to occasional interventions from outside the health policy system that require massive mobilisations of political energy (Tuohy, 1999). There are three reasons for this. First, because like any system it changes as a result of previous policies' interaction with its actors – policies shape politics, and healthcare is unlikely to evolve in the ways politicians expect (Schattschneider, 1935; Pierson, 1993). Second, it is particularly notable for its complexity, powerful interest groups and unpredictable interactions of different factors. Third, in addition to these problems, health management and policy necessarily is unstable. It is about top-down controls over independently minded professionals (Sutherland and Dawson, 1998). This entails two serious problems. On one hand, professionals themselves resist interference by non-professionals; the whole functional justification for professionalism is that highly trained and ethically sensitive specialists are required for decisions that cannot be made according to simple rules. Entrusted with such roles and obliged to make crucial decisions, and then socialised to expect respect, professionals such as those in medicine tend to resist managerial or other impositions from outside. They do this from a strong basis; doctors and nurses are more popular than managers and politicians.

Furthermore, professionals ultimately hold the trump card in health policy and politics. *They ration.* Healthcare comes down to repeated asymmetric dyadic actions in which a professional, usually a doctor, diagnoses a patient and decides on a treatment in conditions that cannot be rationalised or even subjected to meaningful organisational interventions. These interactions are the basis of healthcare provision, and they are a nut uncracked by managerial intervention. The country where management of professional decisions (and information technology use) has been most seriously tried, and tried virtually without budgetary constraint, is the United States. There, the track record has not been good; there appears to be no number of managerial staff adequate to 'control' medical professionals' decisions. So, to spiralling medical costs the American private sector now can add spiralling managerial and information technology costs (Woolhandler and Himmelstein, 1991; Himmelstein et al., 1996; Employee Benefit News, 2003:66).

All of these factors mean that health policy interventions should seem unusually costly and doomed to fail. Yet the UK political systems have demonstrated that constant intervention can go on for decades and continue to remain appealing to political leaders. Much of this, I argue, is due to the presence of professional management in the NHS. They are the solution to the collision of an unstoppable force – politics – with an immovable object – healthcare professionals. Management, first seriously introduced in the NHS in 1983 as part of Margaret Thatcher's first waves of managerialist public service reforms, is the object of the vast majority of political intervention. In quotidian health politics, it is managers as heads of various organisations who are obliged to meet government targets and it is managers as heads of various organisations who suffer when the targets are not met. Board chairs serve at the pleasure of the government, and are quite susceptible to pressure; chief executives and their staff also are largely unable to stand up against political interventions and thus focus on damping down political pressure. One high-level manager in a large hospital trust (theoretically several steps removed from politicians) put it simply, when I asked in a March 2002 Glasgow interview what a chief executive had to do to advance. The interviewee replied that being a good chief executive meant making sure there were no surprise headlines for the minister; balancing the books; and keeping the clinical professionals happy so they did not cause problems in the hospital or in politics. In other words, the good chief executive tries to prevent too much friction between politics and professionals; in the terms of Winstanley et al. he or she tries to smooth the interfaces between criteria and operational power (Winstanley et al., 1995). The job is about fire prevention and fire fighting as much as management.

When reorganisation is imposed, most of the institutions recognised by the public as 'the NHS', that is hospitals, clinical networks and GPs, stay but their organisational settings come and go. In England since 1989 health authorities have been abolished and strategic health authorities created; trusts created and merged repeatedly and foundation hospital status invented; primary care groups created and turned into primary care trusts; NHS regions turned into parts of the NHS Management Executive, given new frontiers, and then abolished; the Management Executive (a managerial central organisation) partially merged with the DoH; Health and Social Care districts created to replace them and slated to be abolished a little over a year later. In most of these cases, with the partial exception of the changes to primary care, the practice and clinical professionals have been left largely alone. The enabling condition for reorganisation and micromanagement is something that buffers politicians and professionals from each other; the management cadre of the health services performs the link function. By contrast, in Spain, which had copied the NHS system before the introduction of management in 1983, the government's efforts to change practice have typically collided directly with professionals and professional organisations. This leds to highly charged political disputes throughout the 1980s and early 1990s (Rodrígues and de Miguel, 1990). The presence of a constantly reorganisable managerial layer might not help the performance of the health services as it sets up and closes down new organisations, but it does provide the malleable target for political intervention that the professions would not be.

## Political intervention and the UK's health services: possible solutions

The problem, then, is that the NHS is a theoretically hierarchical system with a direct, unmediated relationship with the 'organised chaos' of the political system. This means that the relatively unpredictable political system, with its three streams poorly connected to the health service, is constantly creating direct and often remarkably detailed interventions in health policy. The lack of restraint on the government or direct central experience of the costs incurred by change, means the policy can slip easily through a small window before it closes. It is this close connection between ministers as politicians and the management of the health service that is unusual in international comparison, and it is explained by the centralisation of the Westminster systems of the UK and by the otherwise effective NHS design that links its organisation, management and finance directly to the central government. Assuming that the basic model of universal, publicly funded, non-insurance-based healthcare is so entrenched in the UK as to be permanent, the question then is what might raise the political or organisational costs of political interventions, or make them less appealing, and thereby reduce the instability to which multiple-streams policymaking points?

One 'default' political solution is for there to be little or no government. This is the occasional state in Northern Ireland, where the party system gives politicians little incentive to divert themselves from constitutional politics into health policy. When the Northern Ireland Assembly is operating (as it has, intermittently, from 1999 onward), politicians see few votes to be won in health policy and many to be lost. Unlike their peers in healthier political systems, Northern Irish politicians can immerse themselves in constitutional politics, pay little attention to policy, and pay little electoral price. This unhealthy political situation is matched by an unhealthy population and a troubled health system, but at least there is no strong tendency among Northern Irish politicians to interest themselves in the organisation of the health system. The experience does at least make the point that no government means no public policy. For better or for worse when Westminster directly runs Northern Ireland, more policy does get made.

A second political solution would be to try to induce politicians to behave differently. There are a number of political patches that can be used to try to dissipate the connection between multiple-streams of policymaking and actual organisational outcomes. Blame for problems can be shifted to a different territorial level such as happened with NHS regions, boards and districts, before Margaret Thatcher's reforms increased state power in the health system. More broadly, there is the possibility that there can be broadly based learning processes among politicians. It has only been twenty years since the advent of the policies inspired by a 1983 letter from Sir Roy Griffiths created a significant managerial structure allowing politicians to intervene in decisions systematically and a cadre of managers available for easy reorganisation (NHS Management Inquiry, 1983). It has only been a little over a decade since the Thatcher government produced, as in so many other spheres, a dramatic expansion of state power and intervention in health services. The reforms of the 1980s produced both agencies with the power of the state and the remit to manage them on the government's behalf, and that meant the state had to assemble the resources to intervene in the basic structure of the NHS; the result is 'more state, more market' (Giaimo and Manow, 1999; Giaimo, 2001).

More cynically, it is something of a mystery why the need to fill news cycles with health stories leads to meaningful policy activity such as the abolition of whole layers of organisation. Diverting and possibly helpful media events such as campaigns for fitness or against alcoholism should be able simply to decrease the amount of policy activity, thereby allowing policy, politician, and problem to go their separate ways again. More optimistically, there might be institutional learning. Politicians and their civil servants might, over time, work out the costs and benefits of constant intervention and cease to reorganise and set as many targets. A consensus could develop, for example, that frequent reorganisation is not a technically feasible way to improve health system outcomes. Such a learning process would be a remarkable event in a political system that since 1979 has intervened more frequently and in more detail.

A third political solution is to abandon trust in central government's self-restraint and instead increase the checks and balances among different parts of the healthcare system. The outside agencies created since

1997 by the Labour government in England, Scotland and Wales to provide stable, quality regulation could be seen as restraints. However, these organisations, such as the Commission for Health Improvement, the National Institute for Clinical Excellence, and the Health Technology Board for Scotland, have highly politicised work programmes and, as their 2003 mergers show, turn out to be just as susceptible to reorganisation as NHS management. In other words, if the government creates the structures, it is unlikely to create groups that can truly stand up to it.

Pursuing the analogy between the NHS and Westminster, the few political organisations that can stand up to Westminster are the Scottish Parliament and National Assembly for Wales, and they are both backed by broad, powerful social coalitions. In the NHS, only the professions and the unions have been able to exercise anything like a veto on small policy changes. In short, to create such a solution, the government would have to introduce new players with control over the process of policymaking and real power through financing or delivery responsibilities – groups with which it must contend and which can veto incessant small changes in the health system. Broadening the base of representation on a level of health service management such as Strategic Health Authorities in England or Health Boards in Scotland would introduce more players, such as local government, with a solid basis from which to challenge. Alternatively, regional government in England could some day take pressure and accountability from London, and by being closer to its professionals might be more inclined to listen. Scotland and Wales have continued reforming their health services, but their policies are far more predictable than Whitehall's.

Those political solutions all try to limit a theoretically sovereign Westminster Parliament, legally and politically a difficult task. Raising the organisational costs of intervention, rather than the political costs, might work better. An organisational solution would try to build on the professions and tried formulae for autonomy as the basis for stable governance in the NHS. The United Kingdom has some important organisations that have successfully avoided political intervention while remaining politically responsive, and which could serve as models (Futures Group, 2002). The successful model seems to be a combination of a high-profile appointed board with an organisational focus on professional decision-making. The BBC is the greatest example of an organisation that responds to its environment but does not brook political meddling. The model of the BBC, or other institutions around the world that build their independence on the basis of professional self-government (such as the American National Institutes of Health), seems to begin with strong internal domination of decision-making tied to the values of the professions at work. Thus, for example, the BBC has an appointed board subject to close political and media scrutiny but the rest of the organisation governs itself; combined with stable, hypothecated funding (the TV license fee). The political costs of government intervention are high and the organisational costs higher yet. The 2003–2004 Hutton enquiry into the BBC showed that the organisation is hardly insulated from politics, but also showed the depth of institutional and popular support for the model of an independent organisation (Hutton, 2004). If, beneath the board level, the professionals of the organisation then allocate resources they will be reliably autonomous and resistant to intervention.

The Scottish White Paper of 2003 makes significant progress in this respect by transferring increasing authority from managers and organisations such as trusts to 'managed clinical networks', which would be allocative mechanisms dominated by doctors (Scottish Executive Health Department, 2003). If they are implemented, they should be strongly resistant to subsequent managerial or political intervention. This kind of model, combining professional values and political insulation, both increases the professionals' responsibility for how they spend the public's money and makes political intervention harder and more visible. This would require making the professionals and the appointed board clearly responsible for their activities, and presumptively de-legitimise any interest the minister might have in a matter better managed at local level.

All of these options would carry a price. The same centralisation of the UK state that made the NHS *possible* makes it vulnerable to the incessant reorganisations that undermine it. The power of a Westminster parliament allowed Aneurin Bevan to nationalise a great swathe of British life without many concessions to others, and gifted Britain with a cheap, effective and popular health service that comes closer than any other to integrating health and health services, that emphasises primary care in a way few can, inspires devotion in many people, and is the envy of many other countries. That same power of a Westminster parliament, however, allows whoever is Secretary of State for Health to make important, and wrenching, policy decisions so often that their merits dissolve into a blur of damaging, incessant reorganisations. The question for Britain's politicians is how to make the NHS work, how to get something for the taxpayers money which meets public expectations and how to juggle their own intentions, desires and political problems and opportunities. That is also the question of how to improve the fit between the decisiveness of a Westminster government and the need for stability of giant organisations to create and to be seen to create improved health services. British governments, unlike most of their peers, still have great freedom to pursue comprehensive policy ideas, whether good or bad, and stand before the electorate with full responsibility for them. The problem is that the workings of a healthy democratic system that gives the government such power can also slowly destroy the health service that is one of its greatest achievements.

## Notes

1. Following public usage, which has not caught up with rebranding since devolution, I refer to the NHS when I refer to the shared core of values, images, and organisational form in the four 'home country' health systems created in 1948 and only recently allowed much leeway to diverge as a result of devolution (Greer, 2003).
2. I am indebted to Nigel Edwards of the NHS Confederation for this point.

## References

Ali, N.Y., Lo, T.Y.S., Auvache, V.L., and White, P.D. (2001) 'Bad press for doctors: 21 year survey of three national newspapers', *British Medical Journal*, **323** (6 October):782–83.

Audit Commission (2004) *Achieving First-Class Financial Management in the NHS: A Sound Basis for Better Healthcare*. London: Audit Commission

Banting, K.G., and Corbett, S. (2002) 'Health policy and federalism: an introduction, in *Health Policy and Federalism: a Comparative Perspective on Multi-Level Governance*, ed. K.G. Banting and S. Corbett, 1–37. Montreal and Kingston: McGill-Queens University Press

Baumgartner, F.R. and Jones, B.D. (1993) *Agendas and Instability in American Politics*. Chicago: University of Chicago Press

BBC (2002) *Deadlock over consultant contract*, 31 October

BBC (2003) *Health managers set to quit*, 21 April

Beer, S.H. (1965) *Modern British Politics*. London: Faber and Faber

Bell, D., and Christie, A. (2002) 'Finance – the Barnett formula: nobody's child?, in *The State of the Nations 2001: the Second Year of Devolution*, ed. A. Trench, 135–52. Thorverton: Imprint Academic

Brunsson, N., and Olsen, J.P. (1993) *The Reforming Organisation*. London: Routledge

Chandler, A.D. (1977) *The Visible Hand: the Managerial Revolution in American Business*. Cambridge, MA: Harvard University Press

—— (1990) *Scale and Scope: The Dynamics of Industrial Capitalism.* Cambridge, Massachusetts: Harvard University Press

Cohen, M., March, J.G. and Olsen, J.P. (1972) 'A garbage can model of rational choice', *Administrative Science Quarterly*, 1:1–25

Constitution Unit (2003) *Northern Ireland Monitoring Report.* Spring

DoH (2001) *Learning from Bristol: the Report of the Public Inquiry into children's heart surgery at the Bristol Royal Infirmary 1984–1995.* London: Department of Health

DoH (2002) *Getting Ahead of the Curve: a strategy for combating infectious diseases (including other aspects of health protection).* London: HMSO

Eckstein, H. (1959) *The English Health Service: its Origins, Structure, and Achievements.* Oxford: Oxford University Press

—— (1960) *Pressure Group Politics: the Case of the British Medical Association.* London: Allen & Unwin

*Employee Benefit News*, February 2003, p. 66

Enthoven, A.C. (1979) Consumer-centred vs. job-centred health insurance', *Harvard Business Review*, 57:141–52

—— (1989) What Europeans can learn from Americans', *Healthcare Financing Review Annual Supplement*, ex. series:49–77

Esping-Andersen, G. (1990) *The Three Worlds of Welfare Capitalism.* Princeton, NJ: Princeton University Press

Fox, D.M. (1986) *Health Politics, Health Policies: the British and American Experience, 1911–1965.* Princeton, NJ: Princeton University Press

Freeman, R. (2000) *The Politics of Health in Europe.* Manchester: Manchester University Press

Fulop, N., Protopsaltis, G., Hutchings, A., King, A., Allen, P., Normand, C. and Walters, R. (2002) 'Process and impact of mergers of NHS trusts: multicentre case study and management cost analysis', *British Medical Journal*, 325 (3 August):246–9

Futures Group (2002) *The Future of the NHS: a Framework for Debate.* London: Kings Fund

Giaimo, S. (2001) 'Who pays for healthcare reform?' in *The New Politics of the Welfare State*, ed. P. Pierson, 334–67. Oxford: Oxford University Press

Giaimo, S., and Manow, P. (1999) 'Adapting the Welfare State: the case of health reform in Britain, Germany, and the United States', *Comparative Political Studies*, 32 (8 December):967–1000

Greer, S.L. (2003) 'Policy divergence: will it change something in Greenock?' in *The State of the Nations 2003: the Third Year of Devolution in the United Kingdom*, ed. R. Hazell, 195–214. Exeter: Imprint Academic

—— (2004) *Territorial Politics and Health Policy: the UK in Comparative Perspective.* Manchester: Manchester University Press

—— (2005) (forthcoming) 'The fragile divergence machine', in A. Trench, (ed.), *Devolution and Power in the United Kingdom.* Manchester: Manchester University Press

Ham, C. (1999) *Health Policy in Britain*, 4th edn. Basingstoke: Macmillan – now Palgrave Macmillan

Harris, J. (1983) 'The transition to high politics in English social policy 1880–1914', in *High and Low Politics in Modern Britain*, ed. M. Bentley and J. Stevenson, 58–79. Oxford: Oxford University Press

Himmelstein, D.U., Lewontin, J.P. and Woolhandler, S. (1996) 'Who adminis-ters? who cares? Medical administrative and clinical employment in the United States and Canada', *American Journal of Public Health*, 86:172–8

Hunt (Philip) Lord (2004) Talk given at the University of Birmingham, 9 July 2004

Hunter, D.J. (1994) 'From tribalism to corporatism: the managerial challenge to medical dominance', in *Challenging Medicine*, ed. J. Gabe, D. Kelleher and G. Williams, 1–22. London: Routledge

Hutton, Lord (2004) *Report of the Inquiry into the Circumstances Surrounding the Death Of Dr David Kelly CMG*. London: TSO

Iles, V. and Sutherland, K. (2001) *Managing Change in the NHS: organisational change: a review for healthcare managers, professionals and researchers*. London: NCCSDO (National Co-ordinating Centre for NHS Service Delivery and Organisation R&D, Department of Health)

Immergut, E.M. (1992) 'The rules of the game: the logic of health policy-making in France, Switzerland, and Sweden', in *Structuring Politics: Historical institution-alism in comparative analysis*, ed. S. Steinmo, K. Thelen and F. Longstreth, 57–89. Cambridge: Cambridge University Press

Jenkins-Smith, H.C., and Sabatier, P. (1994) 'Evaluating the Advocacy Coalition Framework', *Journal of Public Policy*, 14:175–203

Kingdon, J.W. (1995) *Agendas, Alternatives, and Public Policies*. New York: HarperCollins

Klein, R. (2000) *The New Politics of the NHS*, 4th edn. London: Longman

Kmietowics, Z. (2003) 'GPs vote for "contractus interruptus"', *British Medical Journal*, **326** (24 May):1105

Linos, K. (2004) 'Towards socialised medicine and back? Interests, institutions, sequence and learning', *Conference on Comparative Political Economy*, New Haven: Yale University, 20 May 2004

Light, P.C. (1997) *The Tides of Reform: making government work, 1945–1995*. New Haven: Yale University Press

Loughlin, M. (2000) 'The Restructuring of central-local government relations', in *The Changing Constitution*, 4th edn, ed. J. Jowell and D. Oliver, 137–66. Oxford: Oxford University Press

Majone, G. (1989) *Evidence, Argument, and Persuasion in the Policy Process*. New Haven: Yale University Press

Moran, M. (1999) *Governing the Health Care State: a comparative study of the United Kingdom, the United States, and Germany*. Manchester: Manchester University Press

NHS Management Inquiry (1983) Letter to the Rt. Hon. Norman Fowler MP, Secretary of State for Social Services. Letter sent 6 October.

Pierson, P. (1993) 'When effect becomes cause: policy feedback and political change', *World Politics*, **45**, 4:595–628

Pollitt, C. (1993) *Managerialism and the Public Services*, 2nd edn. Oxford: Blackwell

Powell, J.E. (1966) *A New Look at Medicine and Politics*. London: Pitman Medical

Rawnsley, A. (2001) *Servants of the People: the Inside Story of New Labour*, 2nd edn. London: Penguin

Rodríguez, J.A., and de Miguel, J.M. (1990) *Salud y Poder*. Madrid: Centro de Investigaciones Sociológicas/Siglo Veintiuno

Schattschneider, E.E. (1935) *Politics, Pressures, and the Tariff.* New York: Prentice Hall

Scottish Executive Health Department (2003) *Partnership for Care: Scotland's Health White Paper.* Edinburgh: HMSO

Simeon, R. (2003) 'The long-term care decision: social rights and democratic diversity', in *The State and the Nations: the Third Year of Devolution in the United Kingdom*, ed. R. Hasell, 215–32. Exeter: Imprint Academic

Smith, R. (2003) 'The failures of two contracts', *British Medical Journal*, **326** (24 May):1097–8

Sutherland, K. and Dawson, S. (1998) 'Power and quality improvement in the new NHS: the roles of doctors and managers', *Quality in Healthcare*, 7:516–23

Tuohy, C.H. (1992) *Policy and Politics in Canada: Institutionalised Ambivalence.* Philadelphia: Temple University Press

—— (1999) *Accidental Logics: the Dynamics of Change in the Healthcare Arena in the United States, Britain, and Canada.* Oxford: Oxford University Press

Webster, C. (1998) *The National Health Service: a Political History.* Oxford: Oxford University Press

Williamson, O.E. (1985) *The Economic Institutions of Capitalism: Firms, Markets, Relational Contracting.* New York: Free Press

Wilson, J.Q. (1989) *Bureaucracy: What Government Agencies Do and Why They Do It.* New York: Basic Books

Winstanley, D., Sorabji, D. and Dawson, S. (1995) 'When the pieces don't fit: a stakeholder power matrix to analyse public sector restructuring', *Public Money and Management*, **15** (April–June):19–26

Woolhandler, S. and Himmelstein, D.U. (1991) 'The deteriorating administrative efficiency of the U.S. healthcare system', *New England Journal of Medicine*, 314:1253–8

Zahariadis, N. (1995) *Markets, States, and Public Policy: Privatisation in Britain and France.* Ann Arbor: University of Michigan Press

# Part 2
# Policies and Strategies

# 6
# Strategy in the NHS: Science or Sixth Sense?

*Mark de Rond* and *Penny Dash*

## Introduction

When, in 1959, Charles Lindblom published his influential article 'The Science of Muddling Through', he painted a matter-of-fact picture of strategy development in the context of public administration. His emphasis on the complex, muddled reality of strategy was at odds with what most had hitherto viewed as an inherently rational, objective and controlled process. Not so, wrote Lindblom. His observations on public administration suggested that strategies frequently come about in an incremental, step-by-step fashion. Henry Mintzberg, writing several years after Lindblom, found this to be true also of corporate strategy. Strategies emerge not as sweeping plans but as the product of decisions made at the margin, often to solve problems instead. Plans emerge, as do weeds in a garden; not like flowers grown in the controlled environment of a greenhouse. Indeed, likening the manager to a pottery-maker, Mintzberg (1987) famously depicts her as habitually dithering, impetuous and intuitive. Strategy, it seems, is as much 'sixth sense' as science.

In this chapter we examine what practitioners, gurus and researchers have had to say on the subject of strategy. Three questions are identified as guides for executives. First, what business are we in, and who are our customers? Second, what are our value propositions and capabilities, which make us competitively strong? Third, is there congruence between our answers to the first and second questions? Through brief comparative descriptions of case studies, the chapter illustrates the importance for executives in NHS organisations in the future to develop six capabilities: to define and communicate clear aims, to quantify current performance, to assess future trends which will affect the organisation, to search and use examples of best practice, to innovate within a focused strategy and to communicate with all stakeholders effectively.

## What is strategy? Views of practitioners, gurus and researchers

Since at least the mid-1960s, the field of business strategy has gained significantly in visibility. Despite a proliferating literature (Amazon.com lists well over 3,500 titles when entering the search term 'strategic management'), there remains a fair amount of confusion on the nature and boundaries of the discipline. An excerpt from *The Economist* is telling in this respect:

> No single subject has so dominated the attention of managers, consultants, and management theorists as the subject of corporate strategy ... [What is] puzzling is the fact that the consultants and theorists cannot even agree on the most basic of questions: 'What, precisely, is corporate strategy?' (*The Economist*, October 1993)

But why should this be puzzling? Surely, if the recipe for success were available from any decent bookstore, managers would have a far more difficult time justifying their generous compensation packages (Whittington, 1993). Equally, corporate failure would point to a problem of execution and not development. It seems far more likely that the search for a generic strategy, or a one-best-way, is bound to disappoint since any value provided by it would have been eroded in its discovery (Kay, 1993). Strategy development would occasion the mere transfer and replication of a generic 'best practice'. As John Kay explains:

> One of the hardest things for students of business to accept is that *many problems of strategy have no solution*. The competitive advantages of companies are the product of a market between the capabilities of companies and their commercial, political and regulatory environment. When their environment changes, the required capabilities change. And more often than not, these capabilities will be better provided by different businesses. (*FT*, 2 May 2001; italics added)

Indeed, it only takes a cursory review of the business press to find illustrations of the sort of complexity brought into play by strategic management. Consider some examples.

## Sustaining innovations

Maintaining a momentum of innovation can be difficult, especially for companies whose revenues are generated by the sale or licensing of sophisticated technologies. Consider Netscape. During 1994 and 1995, Netscape changed the world by putting the Internet within reach of normal people. What they appear to have done from 1996 to 1999 was to ride the wave of success, with questionable results. Evidently the company stopped innovating. This at least was the incensed view of one of its former managers. In his resignation letter Jamie Zawinsky bitterly complained that 'the company got big, and big companies just aren't creative ... Great things are accomplished by small groups of people who are driven, who have unity of purpose ... The more people involved, the slower and stupider their union is.'[1]

Or consider the example of the pharmaceutical industry. With revenues of $400 billion per year, it has become one of the biggest and most lucrative in the world. Yet leading pharmaceuticals are at risk of generating too few novel therapeutic agents to sustain their performance in future years. Although research funding has doubled since 1991, the number of new drugs emerging each year has fallen by half. Last year, for example, the FDA only approved 21 'new molecular entities' (new drugs) compared to 53 in 1996. The more they spend on drug development, the fewer drugs they have to show for their effort. Arguably a number of reasons might explain this uninspiring trend, not least the industry's obsession with finding 'blockbuster' drugs (possibly passing up less significant, but still profitable, opportunities). But R & D and sales and marketing costs have also risen sharply (*The Economist*, 13 March 2004). These observations prompt a number of questions relevant to innovative organisations: How can organisations ensure that they do not outgrow their capability to innovate? Are incumbents simply worse at innovating? Is success the bane of innovation?

## Consensus, planning and performance

Despite a popular belief in the need for consensus within organisations on goals, objectives and individual responsibilities, there is little evidence to suggest that these are meaningfully correlated with performance. In fact, one recent study shows the correlation to range from 0.40 to –0.40, implying that consensus can be as harmful as it is beneficial. As for relating formal planning with performance, the correlation is very weak at best (at 0.22). There is even evidence to suggest that the beliefs by members correlate only very weakly with measurable characteristics of their firms.[2] If so, is there any point in formalising strategic planning or in seeking consensus on beliefs and objectives?

## Measuring performance

Measuring organisational performance is difficult, not just because the necessary data may be hard to get at but because it is not clear what criteria best capture performance. John Kay's 1989 study of six UK supermarket chains is insightful in this respect. Whether the accolade goes to Asda, Gateway, Argyll, Tesco, Sainsbury's or Kwik Save depends greatly on the criteria employed: size, return, growth or efficiency. For instance, Sainsbury's did well on size (in absolute numbers) but Asda provided better returns (as measured by gross and net margins). However, when looking at returns on investment (ROI) and equity (ROE), Kwik Save did far better, and when measured by return to shareholders over a 10-year period, Argyll came out first. The problem becomes even trickier when factoring in growth and efficiency measures (Kay, 1993). Given such potential inconsistencies, how are we to measure performance?

## Size, growth and performance

The total market value of mergers and acquisitions announced in 1998 amounted to $2.5 trillion. Exxon merged with Mobil, BP with Amoco, Travelers Group with Citicorp, Daimler-Benz with Chrysler, Pharmacia took over Upjohn, Pharmacia Upjohn acquired Monsanto, Glaxo-Wellcome merged with SmithKline Beecham, Pfizer bought Warner-Lambert and, more recently, Pharmacia. Robert Browning's 'Ah, but a man's reach should exceed his grasp, or what's a heaven for?' may have been embraced rather too enthusiastically, at least during the final years of the last century (Shapiro, 1996). In our zest to fashion bigger empires by merging the assets of several, we seem to have remained blissfully indifferent to research evidence to the contrary. A 1999 study, for instance, found that of the 700 largest deals completed between 1996 and 1999, more than 50 per cent had actually diminished shareholder value. In 2000, Gary Hamel reported a correlation coefficient of only 0.004 (which is not statistically significant) between company size and profitability, whether examined over a 3, 5, or 10 year period (Hamel, 2000). As recently as 12 July 2003, *The Economist* reported that the Boston Consulting Group had, only that week, published research showing that of 277 big M & A deals in America, between 1985 and 2000, 64 per cent destroyed value for the acquirers' shareholders (p. 58). So how important is size really? Can one really risk being left behind in a consolidating world? And how can one overcome the cultural differences that are often blamed for poor integration?

## Management initiatives and performance

Managers are regularly faced with dramatic claims of new knowledge creation. Given the emergence of such 'management fads' some have mockingly wondered whether managers have resorted to outsourcing critical thought. The more memorable fads of the late 20th century include: 'Management By Objectives' (introduced by Peter Drucker in 'The Practice of Management', 1954); 'Quality Circles' (in the 1970s), 'Stick to the Knitting' (by Tom Peters and Robert Waterman in 'In Search of Excellence', 1982), as well as 'Corporate Culture', 'Total Quality Management', 'Benchmarking', and 'Employee Empowerment' (R.M. Kanter in 'The Change Masters', 1983); and 'Business Process Reengineering' (Hammer and Champy in 'Reengineering the Corporation', 1993), and 'Core Competencies' (Hamel and Prahalad, in 'Competing for the Future', 1994). How are managers to discriminate between the various recipes suggested to them by management gurus and consultancies? And how are they to justify their decision to abstain from joining a particular bandwagon to their colleagues, boards and shareholders? More crucially, do such management practices have any material impact on performance? A recent study by Nohria, Joyce and Robertson (2003) examined 200 well-established management fads as employed over a ten-year period by 160 companies, and discovered to their surprise that most of the techniques employed seemed to have no direct causal relationship to superior performance. What mattered instead were only four basic capabilities: (1) the ability to devise and maintain a focused strategy; (2) the ability to develop and maintain flawless operational execution; (3) the ability to develop and maintain a performance-oriented culture; and (4) the ability to build and sustain a fast, flexible, flat organisation. In actual fact, as the authors acknowledge, these are anything but novel. Then why does it remain so difficult for most organisations to put them to effective use?

## Strategy and serendipity

When Napoleon was asked whether he preferred brilliant or courageous generals, he is said to have replied that he would prefer to have lucky ones. The strategic importance of serendipity is well recognised, particularly in technology-intensive industries. Pfizer, Airbus Industrie, 3M, DuPont, Hewlett-Packard, Canon, Danone, Nokia, Honda and Kodak have succeeded, at least in part, by placing bets in unpredictable environments. Pfizer redirected an expensive research project targeted at angina towards male impotence to create Viagra; 3M benefited greatly from 'accidental' products like its Post-It Notes and Scotchguard;

Hewlett-Packard and Canon did likewise with their DeskJet and Bubble jet printing technologies. DuPont did so too with Teflon, as did Kodak with their Weekender camera. But if, as Louis Pasteur mused, 'fortune favours the prepared mind', how does one go about being prepared? What are the requirements in terms of organisational structure, HR management, innovation management, communication flows, knowledge management and planning? How much inefficiency is tolerable, indeed preferable, to allow for chance discoveries? Are some organisations luckier than others? And if so, why?

In sum, at least four decades of dedicated research have hinted repeatedly at the emergent, multi-faceted, and 'messy' nature of making strategic choices. Managers are often forced to respond to scenarios that are unfamiliar. They may have no choice but to act before they have all the relevant information, even if this involves making mistakes, for at least one may be able to correct these mistakes afterwards. They sell to customers whose demands are strong even if not fully rational (Hampden-Turner, 1990). They are called on to provide leadership in organisations with potentially little consensus on goals and objectives, rendering strategy development, as a logical consequence, contestable. They are expected to put in place systems of coordination and control, so as to generate efficiencies, yet also allow for the sort of inefficiencies and 'messiness' that characterise highly innovative environments. Even at the best of times they may be able to do no more than to *satisfice* – or improve on their current position. This process is typically informed not so much by a textbook description of all relevant markets and competitors as by imperfect and inconsistent data, marred by vested interests and bounded rationality. Accordingly, strategic management may be best defined as the ability to see the simple in the complex, not by probing through layers of complexity so as to find an underlying order (for no such thing may exist), but by being able to prioritise inside this complexity – *to see what matters most* – and thus provide explanation, vision, and leadership. This must be based on a deep understanding of organisational capabilities and their continuing relevance to customer needs, and of the subtle discontinuities that threaten an organisation's existence. It is as much an art as a science. Once this is understood, firms can make *informed* choices. These choices will, in turn, enable firms to commit resources but also to kill off those projects that seem less relevant. For strategy is concerned as much with resource deployment as with justifying resource recuperation – and it is tough to kill projects without a strategy (Henderson, 2003).

The mere recognition of complexity, however, does not absolve us from our obligation to provide explanation and advice to aid the design and implementation of business strategies. As managers we are expected to provide relatively straightforward explanations of what is going on and why, and what is expected of those involved. As Pettigrew explains:

> One of the central issues for strategic leadership in the modern corporation becomes the defraying of excessive complexity and ambiguity. The ability to deliver clear, simple, and evocative messages that balance future goals with present needs seems to be a crucial simplifying routine in times of tension and change. (Pettigrew, 2001)

Strategy, at its simplest, is 'means to ends' – the things businesses do, the paths they follow and decisions they take so as to achieve a certain level of success (Thompson, 2001:9). But it is clearly not just about means to ends; it is also about ends in and of themselves. Ends are never set in stone, but are subject to continuous re-evaluation by those involved as they interact with relevant markets, stakeholders, regulators, collaborators and competitors, and are faced with changing economic conditions, terror and security threats, new opportunities and so forth. An observation by the early 20th century philosopher Otto Neurath seems immensely appropriate:

> We are like sailors who must rebuild their ship on the open sea, never able to dismantle it in dry-dock and to reconstruct it out of the best materials.

Or as put by Mintzberg (1989:40):

> The real challenge in crafting strategy lies in detecting the subtle discontinuities that may undermine a business in the future. And for that there is no technique, no program, just a sharp mind in touch with the situation.

Reducing a phenomenon as diverse and complex as strategy risks oversimplification and, when taken to extremes, triviality. Even so, we may abridge its core to three questions without conceding too much relevance:[3]

1. *Where should we direct our energies, and why?* What business are we in, really? Who are our customers – and how do we know this? And what business are we definitely *not* in? After all, it is equally important to know what not to do, or to set limits on what is possible or desirable.

2. *What's our value proposition?* What is it that we are especially good at? What do we bring to the table? And how easy is it for others to imitate or otherwise acquire these capabilities? Do we hold patents that afford us a temporary window of superior profits? Does our reputation help us to earn above normal profits? How do we inventorise and protect these capabilities, particularly when they are embedded in people?
3. *Are our capabilities relevant to our chosen strategy?* Distinctive capabilities can become a source of competitive advantage only when applied to a set of customers (Kay, 1993). Matching responses to the first two questions must yield a consistent picture of the firm and its markets. If the divide is too great, the organisation is at risk of becoming an irrelevance. Clearly, every innovation, product or skill must have a buyer for it to generate a sustainable source of revenues.

We will return to these questions in this chapter, as they comprise the quintessence of business strategy. Following de Wit and Meyer (2004), our chapter proceeds by considering the *process* (or how), *content* (or what) and *context* (or why) of strategy respectively. This allows us to explore strategy from three related angles. The context in our particular case is public healthcare provision in the United Kingdom, and of obvious importance, for it is the context of strategy that legitimises certain courses of action whilst ruling out implausible or unworkable alternatives.

But first we return to Charles Lindblom.

## The strategy process

Lindblom's description of strategy as the outcome of incremental changes rather than of a grand design, flew in the face of the classical ideal of strategy as the successful application of careful reasoning and objectivity to resource allocation in view of an organisation's desired future state. Even if various schools of thought exist on the nature of the strategy process, most fall inside one of two camps. The distinction between the classical, as far-reaching and rational, and the contemporary faction, as gradual and constructivist, is somewhat misleading as the former is mostly prescriptive (in suggesting how strategy should be developed) and the latter descriptive (in depicting how strategy really comes about). Unsurprisingly, the merits of the second, namely its practical use, are also the Achilles' heel of the first. An excellent overview of ten such schools within the strategy field is provided in Mintzberg, Ahlstrand and Lampel (1998). Here, we discuss four of these – strategy as design, planning, entrepreneurship and learning. In our discussion of these four approaches to strategy development we draw extensively on their work. If we have failed to reference specific contributions, this is merely because such frequent referencing would seem to diminish the readability of the chapter. Hence, we hope this 'blanket coverage' is adequate. In discussing these four schools, we highlight the characteristics, limitations and merits of each. The first two of these (design and positioning) seek to prescribe, whereas the remaining two schools (entrepreneurship and learning) are mostly descriptive.

## Strategy as design

Textbook definitions of strategy typically promote a linear and sequential view of strategy development, usually associated with the contributions, in the mid-1960s, of Kenneth Andrews and his Harvard colleagues. At its simplest, they proposed that strategy development be concerned with the idea of creating a 'fit', or a matching of organisational capabilities with opportunities in the relevant markets (Figure 6.1). An analysis of the strengths, weaknesses, opportunities and threats (SWOT) facing the organisation becomes the centerpiece of this process. The search is on for an optimum strategy, one which is consistent with the goals of the organisation, consonant in adapting to the external environment while providing a competitive advantage, representative of corporate values, and feasible using existing resources.

This approach to strategy creation is, however, based on a set of assumptions, some of which may not be immediately obvious. First, it assumes that environmental threats and opportunities, as well as organisational capabilities, are relatively easily identifiable and not subject to disagreement from among those involved in the process. Second, it suggests that the process of strategy formulation is a generally deliberate and conscious process, the responsibility of which lies with the CEO. Also, it assumes that access to good information exists and is affordable and, by implication, is less able to cope with conflicting data, incommensurable claims and paradox. Finally, it assumes that strategies are explicit and will be fully formulated before being implemented. It thus follows that the environment is expected to remain relatively unchanged between formulation and strategy implementation.

Despite its merits and appeal, this approach is not without difficulty. Indeed it may entertain assumptions that are unrealistic. The process of conducting a SWOT analysis, for instance, can be fraught with ambiguity. What an organisation feels as a particular strength may merely be the upshot of the successful application of an underlying capability,

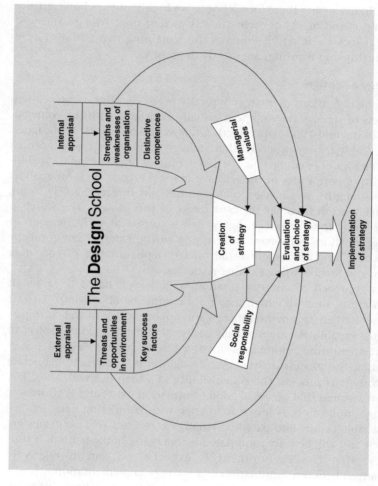

*Figure 6.1*: The 'design school' strategy process (adopted from Mintzberg, Ahlstrand and Lampel, 1998: 26)

or simply good fortune. The same is true for weaknesses, potential threats and opportunities. Second, managers are subject to cognitive limitations, due to imperfect and incomplete information, and an inability accurately to conceptualise the vast array of possible scenarios facing the organisation. This notion, labeled 'bounded rationality' by Nobel laureate Herbert Simon, suggests that no one can process satisfactorily the plethora of variables affecting available choice. The best any business can hope to do is to make a decision that is good enough, or to satisfice. Also, information cannot reasonably be expected to be transmitted up the organisational bureaucracy without significant loss or distortion. Further, strategy is, more often than not, a compromise solution rather than an optimal resolution. Moreover, it is not always possible to formulate strategy in highly unpredictable environments, and most markets are becoming increasingly unpredictable. Making strategy thus promotes inflexibility as the more articulated a strategy becomes, the less flexible it is likely to be. This could prove detrimental in very dynamic or uncertain environments by risking a 'premature closure' of the strategy-making process. In fact, the design view of strategy is characterised by the absence of any organisational learning. A feedback loop between implementation and design is markedly absent. And finally, the artificial separation of formulation and implementation implies a detaching of thinking from acting.

It has, however, made some very distinct and valuable contributions. For example, the design school contributes a vocabulary (still very much in vogue) and the idea of ensuring a fit between organisational capabilities and opportunities provided by the market. And sometimes organisations do need 'grand designs' and a strong leader capable of synthesis and designing strategy. A relevant example is IBM's remarkable turnaround in the early 1990s under its newly appointed CEO Lou Gerstner. Also, arguably, in 'real-life', managers are neither 100 per cent certain nor 100 per cent uncertain about the future. They formulate strategy precisely to avoid the future being a mere extrapolation of the past, as the late H. Igor Ansoff cautioned. Less subtly, the obvious alternative, a strategy of 'trial and error', is but poor medicine for companies on the brink of failure and difficult to sell to shareholders. Trial and error method is likely to be less efficient than a rational model, in which improbable strategies are ruled out and the consequences of others can to some extent be anticipated. At least the classical approach (design school) brings the strategy process out into the open, including any assumptions made by those developing the strategy. 'Plans are useless', surmised Eisenhower, 'but planning is not'. Finally, and most significantly, it addresses all of the three questions that comprise the core of strategy. This is not true of the other schools, as we shall soon see. And perhaps this is its most important contribution, and its enduring characteristic.

## Strategy as planning

The planning school surfaced at about the same time as the design school with the publication of H. Igor Ansoff's *Corporate Strategy* (1965). It accepts many of the same assumptions, but differs in the level of detail pursued. In fact, the comparative simplicity of 'strategy as design' has given way to the drafting of a detailed blueprint. The process begins with the setting of specific objectives, preferably quantifiable objectives, the merit of quantification being that it allows for ease of communication and control. It relies heavily on forecasts and, in practice, commonly extrapolates the future from the present (e.g. by multiplying last quarter's budget by a factor of 1.14 to reflect a 14 per cent growth in market share). Strategy selection is likewise focused on quantifiable (and often financial) measures: the Payback Period, NPV, IRR, MIRR, etc., with the usual consequence that each criterion is only as good as the assumptions underlying it (e.g. cost of capital, rate of inflation, size of cash inflows). The CEO is still responsible for strategy development and implementation but her role is one of approving rather than designing. As with the design school, strategies are fully formulated before being implemented, with no feedback flow between implementation and design.

The notion of strategy as planning has been severely criticised for being too cumbersome, unreliable and inflexible. First, as a chain is only as strong as its weakest link, strategies will only be as good as the forecasts on which they are based. And our archives contain ample examples of forecasting failures. Second, there is no built-in flexibility to deal with the unexpected. In fact, such a detailed, 'blue-printing' approach would appear to require that the world holds still while planning and implementation unfold. Third, it seeks to circumvent human idiosyncrasies by systematising the planning process. But in so doing, it risks dehumanising strategy development. Also, thinking is yet again detached from acting by insisting on complete formulation prior to implementation. And finally, quantified data is arguably limited in scope and richness and often fails to include non-quantifiable, but potentially significant, factors (e.g. expression on customer's face, the mood on the factory floor, gossip, rumours). Besides, much hard data arrives too late to be of use. However, the planning school does highlight the importance of analysis as a support function. It can make communication and control easier to achieve and may work in very stable and predictable environments.

## Strategy as a process of entrepreneurship

The entrepreneurial school accepts the importance placed on leadership by the design school and even puts it at centre stage. Its orientation, however, is different. It emphasises the innate skills of leaders, such as intuition, good judgement, gut feeling, wisdom, and a clear vision of the future of the business. This vision is deliberate yet malleable, rendering the making of strategy purposive but also emergent. Given its reliance on a single vision, the strategy process is strongly contingent on the personal traits of the leader. Hence, the study of strategy should incorporate a detailed examination of such traits.

As before, the entrepreneurial school is predicated on several beliefs. The most obvious of these suggests that strategies exist primarily in the mind of the leader as a vision of the organisation's future. They are thus strongly rooted in experience and intuition. The leader promotes this vision single-mindedly, even obsessively, with close personal monitoring of strategy implementation and making adjustments when necessary. Such a person-centric view of strategy, despite its novelty, invites criticism. Clearly, it presents strategy formation as all wrapped up in one individual – strategy thus remains a 'black box' which we know little about, except that it is related to the vision, intuition, and personality of a single individual. If so, this renders the organisation highly vulnerable. Likewise, corporate failure would inevitably call for a new leader as the natural solution. Also, 'visioning' can fix organisational attention too tightly in one direction at the risk of losing perspective. It also risks fostering a culture of dependency and unquestioned conformity.

## Strategy as learning

If the world is indeed as complex as claimed by the critics, then how should one proceed with strategy formulation? Given that, in most industry contexts, strategic blueprints are impractical, and designs too inflexible, organisational learning through trial and error would appear to be the only logical alternative. Historically associated with the work of James Brian Quinn (1978), this school of thought claims to have a strong empirical foundation. It assumes the complex and unpredictable nature of the environment, coupled with the diffusion of knowledge bases necessary for strategy, precludes deliberate control – strategy-making must take the form of learning over time, in which formulation and implementation become indistinguishable. The role of leadership is thus not to preconceive deliberate strategies, but to foster and manage the process of learning and retention within the organisation.

Whilst rendering a more realistic account of strategy development, the school is not without critics. Under a process of incrementalism, central direction could dissolve into tactical manoeuvering, not strategy. Tactical manoeuvering risks causing the organisation to drift strategically, having lost focus and its place in 'the big picture'. Also, it can make people more interested in innovating new (and more interesting) things than improving an existing initiative. More poignantly, learning by trial and error can be expensive when considering the time and resources invested in non-starters or high-risk experiments.

But it does highlight the importance of organisational learning, particularly in complex and fast-changing environments, and by virtue of its empirical grounding, it can perhaps claim to give a more realistic account of how organisations actually go about strategy-making. And good description may ultimately lead to better prescription.

## The strategy content

### Market power theory

Having touched upon the process of strategy, and the diversity of perspectives, we return to the three questions that, in a very real sense, characterise the corpus of strategy: 'Where do we put our efforts, and why?' 'What's our value proposition?' and 'Do our capabilities suit our strategy?'. The first two point to an enduring, and unresolved, debate in strategy, namely which does a better job at explaining performance variations between organisations? Is it the environment (primarily the industry) in which a firm operates? Or is it something about the firm itself that affords it superior performance over time?[4]

The industry perspective garners support from the early work of Michael Porter. Informed by the contributions of economists Edward Mason and Joe Bain, and the Structure-Conduct-Performance school of Industrial Organisation,[5] Porter (1979) suggested that variations in performance could be explained by industry structure. Every industry, including healthcare provision, can usefully be characterised by the presence of five basic forces: the threat of newcomers entering in the industry, the bargaining power of suppliers, the bargaining power of buyers, the threat of substitution (acting as a price ceiling), and the degree of rivalry between competing providers of the goods or services in question. One's strategy should be to position oneself to take advantage of these forces or to shelter oneself from their ability to erode future profits. The foundation of Porter's industry analysis is thus *efficiency*. In a Darwinian sense, those that are fit (or efficient) will survive, and those that are not will be 'selected out'. In the context of these industry forces, Porter suggested that there are only two generic strategies that can ensure survival in the long run: one either competes on cost or on value. As competing on value can be split into 'differentiation' and 'focus' strategies, one usually speaks of Porter's three generic strategies (cost, differentiation and focus).

The 'cost' strategy implies the pursuit of the lowest possible cost base. This strategy is useful not because it will result in price leadership (price is, after all, determined by the market), but because it will allow firms to fight and win a price war, provided it enjoys the lowest variable costs in the industry (allowing one to price below the variable costs of competitors and still cover one's own variable costs). A 'value' strategy, by contrast, suggests a differentiation approach, by staking out a high-quality position (even if this is just a perception of high-quality or differentiation). These two generic strategies are mutually exclusive, as they require a fundamentally different resource configuration.

For most industries, firms are located somewhere on the cost-value spectrum. As McAffee (2002:37) points out, Southwest Airlines pursues a cost strategy. Its lower-than-average cost-basis allows it to compete on price. But, of course, Southwest doesn't literally minimise costs. It could pack even more customers in its Boeing 737s and stop giving out peanuts, though this might put off some of its current customers. Hence, Southwest Airlines minimises costs for a modest level of value. That it provides value is evidenced by it having won numerous awards for its service quality.

Hence, there are examples of organisations that seem to have successfully combined two of Porter's three generic strategies. Also, in some markets (e.g. luxury goods) cost is largely irrelevant and competition is based primarily on differentiation. Moreover, if indeed industry characteristics are as important as Porter suggests, then one should be able to explain variances in firm profitability as a function thereof. Rumelt (1991) took issue with Porter by demonstrating that his proposition fails to find empirical support. Rather, less than 10 per cent of profitability appears explained by industry characteristics, leaving at least 90 per cent of variances not explained by choice of industry. Indeed, as much as 46 per cent may be related to choice of strategy. McGahan and Porter (1997) responded by limiting Rumelt's conclusions to manufacturing, arguing that they are less relevant to other, non-manufacturing industries. Finally, if some industries are indeed inherently more profitable than others, this surely cannot be true in the long run. If one assumes that industries and markets are transparent and information travels relatively fast, these industries would attract newcomers who would quickly compete away any excess profit potential (Kay, 1993).

## The resource-based view

This leads us into an alternative argument about the nature and source of competitive advantage. If industries and markets cannot sufficiently explain differences in performance, is the answer to be found inside the organisation? Is it perhaps something about the firm – specifically its resources and capabilities – that allows it to reap superior profits over a sustained period of time? This resource-based view (RBV) suggests that an organisation can achieve and sustain a competitive advantage by configuring its tangible and intangible assets in a way that is difficult or indeed impossible to perfectly imitate, or by having resources, skills or capabilities that are durable, and not appropriable, perfectly transferable or replicable (Barney, 1991; Grant, 1991; Peteraf, 1993; Rumelt, 1984, 1991; Wernerfelt, 1984). These need not be single resources but could comprise a configuration of several capabilities. This, for instance, appears to be the case at Southwest Airlines, having successfully combined short-haul flights, low-cost operations, quick turnaround times, efficiency in maintenance and service by flying only one type of aircraft, a friendly culture that fosters belonging and loyalty, and highly motivated staff into a formula that most competitors would find difficult to replicate. Rumelt put it well:

> In essence, the concept is that a firm's competitive position is defined by a bundle of unique resources and relationships and that the task of general management is to adjust and renew these resources and relationships as time, competition, and change erode their value. (Rumelt (1984:557–8)

The implication for strategy development is thus to craft a strategy that makes the most effective use of core resources and capabilities. This may be helpful particularly in rapidly evolving markets, where the organisation's own capabilities may be a more stable platform on which to define its identity (Grant, 1991). The single most important problem with the resource-based view is that it can be difficult to operationalise. For example, how does one avoid mistaking the symptoms for the causes of success? What exactly is a *core* resource or capability? Is it a product (e.g. Nestlé's Kit Kat chocolate bar), a business model (e.g. Amazon company's approach to the marketing and distribution of books via the Internet), a reputation (e.g. Volvo's reputation for safety in car manufacturing), a brand name (e.g. Coca Cola as a global brand of soft drink), a cache of intellectual property (e.g. Capital One's database of credit cardholders), a patent (e.g. the patent on the corrugated coffee holder used by Starbucks), a social network (e.g. The Body Shop's ties with Third World producers of cosmetics and lotions), staff training (e.g. General Electric's management training programmes), a process (e.g. 'the Boeing way' of aircraft product management and design), an ownership and governance structure (e.g. the John Lewis Partnership of department stores), or a corporate culture (e.g. Southwest Airlines)? In a climate where business process reengineering is popular and often entails a 'back to basics' approach, how does one refocus the organisation when these basics themselves are, well, out of focus?

Ironically, whereas market power theory and the resource-based view seem to provide contrary explanations for business success, they are not unrelated. Whilst some industries may temporarily afford a comparatively higher profit potential, the firms that are likely to thrive are those equipped with the finest, and best protected, resources, organised in such a way as to bring a unique value proposition to the market. Likewise, having unique and well-protected resources may prove of little value when irrelevant to a market, when facing indiscriminate or price-insensitive consumers, or when operating as a monopolist. It is thus not surprising that market power theory and the resource-based view help answer the 'where do we put our efforts, and why?' and 'what's our value proposition?' respectively. They are sides of the same coin, both being useful and necessary. And of course they are preconditions for answering the final and most important question of all: 'do our capabilities suit our strategy?'

## The strategy context: the national health service (NHS)

So what can healthcare services in general, and the NHS in particular, learn from these ideas on strategy?

Traditionally, responsibility for strategy development within the NHS has sat in Whitehall as part of the political apparatus where perhaps the most common approach to strategy at the political level has focused on 'strategy as design'.

Politicians have sequentially examined the strengths and weaknesses of different mechanisms of operating the NHS and sought to make changes to the organisation so as to improve its functioning. For example the market driven reforms to the NHS introduced by the Thatcher government in the early 1990s were based on a SWOT analysis of the NHS, drawing on comparisons with alternative structure and funding mechanisms for healthcare systems in different countries. The analysis implied that more market driven healthcare systems resulted in more customer responsive care and more efficient management. Hence a market driven concept (the separation of the purchaser of healthcare from the provider of healthcare) was applied to the NHS. In keeping with the notion of 'strategy as design', the aim was for an 'optimum strategy' for the future of the NHS but in reality this strategy suffered from many of the constraints outlined above.

At other times 'strategy as planning' has been deployed. For example the NHS Plan (Department of Health, 2000) was developed out of a clear quantifiable objective to address the problem of long waiting lists in the NHS. The Plan laid out a strategy to reduce waiting lists through the expansion of capacity. It relied heavily on forecasts – forecasts in terms of numbers of people wanting or needing NHS procedures over the following 10 years, numbers of staff available, numbers of procedures that could be produced per operating theatre or per operating team. It largely extrapolated future activity levels from present demand and activity. And, as with 'strategy as design', the strategy was fully formulated before being implemented with no feedback loop between implementation and design.

Both of these approaches to strategy development focused on the development of a strategy for the NHS largely formulated by politicians and their political advisors with little, if any, involvement of the mainstream organisation, including doctors, nurses and local managers. But these centrally driven approaches to strategy have clearly not been ideal.

First, there has been, and remains, a high level of disconnect between the development and the implementation of the strategy leading to difficulties in implementing change across an enormous and diverse organisation. This characteristic features elsewhere in this volume; see for example, Paton, Chapter 3 and Greer, Chapter 5. The commercial sector has largely rejected centralist approaches to strategy development over the last 10–20 years. During the 1970s and 1980s 'seagull consulting' was relatively commonplace. Groups of external players (usually based in management consulting companies) determined a future strategy in a 'darkened room' remote from the rest of the organisation and 'dropped' it on the desk of the chief executive. But rarely did this result in any long-term beneficial change and has now been replaced by a more inclusive, devolved form of strategy development.

Second, there is ambiguity over the purpose of the NHS, as described more fully in this volume; see Paton, Chapter 3 and Mark, Chapter 9. While most commercial organisations have a clear sense of purpose (to increase shareholder value), the NHS has failed to define its role. For example, some see the objective of the NHS as to improve health status while recognising that healthcare services play but a small part in improving health. A strategy to improve the NHS becomes confused as a strategy to improve health status in which as Yach (Chapter 2, this volume) argues, changes to housing, diet, exercise, employment status, and so on are equally, if not more, important as healthcare services. Others see the NHS as a publicly owned body and so believe that any attempts to improve it should be driven by the public in the local area – often resulting in strategies aimed at 'saving our hospital' rather than improving healthcare per se.

Third, politicians have tended to justify the need for a 'strategic review' of the NHS in terms of the need to unpick a previous government's attempts to improve services rather than to define a clear rationale for change. Decisions are made on the basis of public perception and so likelihood of re-election becomes the driving force for change rather than developing a high quality organisation – a short-term focus rather than a longer-term perspective. For example governments have repeatedly failed to invest in IT in the NHS (Wanless, 2002). While this would have been a substantial contributor to better health outcomes, shorter waiting lists and more efficient operations, it was never seen as a politically astute move – far more worthwhile politically to invest the money in more visible changes such as additional staff.

Fourth, there has been, and remains, a lack of skills to develop a strategy fit for an organisation as large and complex as the NHS. Few politicians and their advisors have first-hand experience of either managing a large organisation, or of developing strategies for them. There is little awareness of techniques deployed in the commercial world – for example 'deep customer discovery' to understand the needs of customers (including patients, carers, the general public) in order to build services to meet those needs; 'customer segmentation' to recognise different needs of different customer groups and design differentiated services focused around the needs of these different groups; business process re-engineering to drive through more efficient internal operations; robust analysis to underpin strategy and change initiatives; benchmarking or studies to examine how to learn from other organisations and so on.

Finally, the centralist, politically driven approach has resulted in a cadre of managers who, as described elsewhere in this volume (Paton,

Chapter 3 and Greer, Chapter 5), are disempowered to develop services to improve care. Organisations within the NHS merely implement what their political masters have decided. There is little room for manoeuver with top down targets (including 346 in the NHS Plan alone) and often directives as to how to deliver and achieve these targets. This disempowerment of managers has, not surprisingly, resulted in an organisation largely bereft of the skill set required to develop meaningful plans, for the future development of services. And without meaningful plans services are not going to develop and improve in an optimal way.

But are these constraints an inevitable result of a publicly funded, publicly accountable service like the NHS?

The policy implementation literature suggests that a rational, top-down approach to strategy development is likely to fail because of the factors identified above, namely a disconnect between the development and the implementation of the strategy leading to difficulties in implementing change across an enormous and diverse organisation such as the NHS; multiple and sometimes conflicting objectives; working to political imperatives; and lack of strategic competency amongst senior managers.

In the classic text on policy implementation, Pressman and Wildavsky's (1973) 'Implementation: how great expectations in Washington are dashed in Oakland' the authors present such challenges in the case study of a federal development programme begun in the 1960s that focused on increasing employment amongst the ethnic minority population. Subsequent contributions in the policy implementation literature have advocated 'bottom-up' or 'learning' or 'integrated' (Barrett and Fudge, 1981; Sabatier, 1998) approaches to strategy development. These all point towards a greater emphasis on local strategic development.

The current government policy is to devolve power to local organisations within the NHS, for example, Primary Care Trusts (PCTs) (Department of Health, 2002a). This should allow these organisations more freedom to develop and implement their own strategies for the future development of services.

But what are the implications for strategic development at the local level? What needs to happen in order to ensure that these organisations are able to perform effective and meaningful strategy development in order to ensure the delivery of high quality healthcare services to their population?

The remainder of this chapter addresses strategy development at a local level by examining:

- The skills and capabilities required to develop strategy within organisations.
- The incentives required to ensure that organisations develop robust strategies for the future.
- The management structures which will need to be put in place to ensure the successful implementation of strategies.

## Skills and capabilities will need to be developed within organisations

Being able to develop a coherent, robust strategy requires a set of skills and capabilities currently lacking in many NHS organisations. A number of these skills and capabilities are examined in more detail below, using case studies to compare how strategy is developed in the commercial sector and in the NHS. In each comparison one of the authors, Penny Dash, was involved.

### An ability to define and communicate a clear vision or aim for an organisation

Managers need to define a set of objectives for their organisation. These objectives will need to be made clear, be widely shared and be 'owned' amongst staff throughout the organisation. For example healthcare organisations could set as their aim a need to:

- Improve clinical outcomes;
- Improve patient or user satisfaction;
- Improve efficiency of services.

But this is not as easy as it sounds. Different factions within a healthcare organisation are likely to hold strong views as to the relative merits of any one objective. For example doctors have traditionally seen improved clinical outcomes as the most important aim while many managers have been increasingly focused on improving efficiency. Patients or lay representatives or may be focused on their own particular illness or provider, sometimes taking a somewhat parochial view that each and every service should be available in their local organisation – a strategy which might improve levels of patient satisfaction but would be in conflict with the other two objectives.

In contrast, commercial organisations tend to have a clearer sense of what their priorities are. They recognise that they need to deliver services that meet identified customers' needs if they are to survive and thrive. This clear vision or aim leads them to analyse customers' needs and ensure structures, processes and incentives are all focused on

## Case study to illustrate importance of clear objectives

|  | Developing a 'patient centred' NHS | Improving customer service in a bank |
|---|---|---|
| Aim | To develop a 'patient centred' healthcare service | To increase customer recruitment and retention |
| Driver for change | Response to view of some stakeholders and interest groups that NHS is not 'patient centred' | Requirement to increase customer recruitment and retention to increase sales, market share and shareholder value |
| Fit to overall strategy of organisation | Unclear – 'patient centred' service has little meaning to many customers and employees. Unclear how it fits with other stated aims – for example 'equity', 'efficiency' 'clinical effectiveness', 'access to care' | Clear fit to overall strategy of becoming leading retail bank in the UK |
| Approach | Policy developed by small group of politicians, policy makers, and various patient interest groups. Little analysis of current customer satisfaction, customer needs, or how other organisations develop customer service and customer focused processes. | Analysis and proposals developed by small group including staff from all levels of organisation and management consultants Analysis based on in depth interviews with customers, current levels of customer recruitment and retention, comparison with other organisations, examples of good practice. |
| Outcome | Recommendation to organisation that future policy development be 'patient centred' | Restructuring of organisation to ensure processes and structures are customer facing. Increased levels of customer satisfaction leading to increased sales |

different customer segments. This clearer vision or aim simplifies strategy development.

The case study above highlights the difficulty the NHS has had in defining what its core objective is with regard to 'customers'. The term 'patient focus' has been extensively used but means many different things to different people, ranging from involving the patient in discussions about his or her care, to developing a culture of customer service through to allowing patients to choose their own provider. This lack of clarity has resulted in confused directions from the centre, and a lack of understanding as to what or how to implement at a local level. In comparison, the retail bank was clear as to its objectives and so found it easier to develop and implement a 'customer focused' organisation.

## An ability to quantify current performance

Being able to measure and assess current performance (the starting point) is a key requirement to identifying areas for future improvement. Yet few healthcare organisations are able to do this.

Robust assessments of clinical outcomes are in their infancy – even crude measures such as death rates or readmission rates are often erroneous, and these are not sufficiently sensitive to detect differences in performance between individuals, teams or organisations. There is little ownership of the need to measure clinical outcomes amongst healthcare professionals, and even less insight and understanding into what these measures are or could be, and how they could be used to drive improvement.

What measures there are have tended to focus on financial criteria, comparing the cost-basis of each individual healthcare organisation. But few can accurately cost each and every procedure and there is little, if any, benchmarking data to facilitate proper comparisons. This leaves managers wanting when it comes to driving through change. For example there are few comparisons of throughput between hospitals in the UK, let alone overseas, making it difficult to identify or justify a need for change. There are no comparisons of GP productivity and so it is difficult to understand whether or not there really is a shortage of GPs.

The case study below compares two different approaches to formulating strategy within an organisation; one the NHS, the other a pharmaceutical company. It highlights the difficulty in formulating strategy in the NHS due to a lack of data. This lack of data inevitably makes it difficult to design services in order to deliver high quality care.

**Case study to illustrate the importance of good quality data in deciding future strategy**

| | Reconfiguration of services in Strategic Health Authority (SHA) | Reconfiguration of manufacturing plants in pharmaceutical company |
|---|---|---|
| Issue | Decide on future location of hospital services | Decide on future number and location of manufacturing plants post merger of two pharmaceutical companies |
| Driver for change | Difficulty providing high quality care due to small size of existing units | Need to reduce duplication and optimise efficiency & quality |
| Fit to overall strategy of organisation | Confused – unclear whether aim is improved quality of clinical care, increased user satisfaction or improved efficiency | Overall strategy focused on maximising synergies arising from merger opportunity |
| Approach/process | • Team of people working across the SHA – mix of clinicians, managers management consultants | • Team of people working with the organisation – mix of front line operational staff, management consultants, senior managers |
| | • Strong desire from public and politicians to know the evidence behind proposals, and the expected impact of change on clinical quality and finance | • Strong desire from board to know the logic behind proposals, and the expected impact of change on quality/finance |
| | • Analysis looked for data about current performance or benchmarks to predict likely impact of changes but little available | • Report drew on benchmark studies to make the case – benchmarks and experience from other organisations (pharmaceutical and other industry sectors) |

## Case study to illustrate the importance of good quality data in deciding future strategy (*continued*)

|  | *Reconfiguration of services in Strategic Health Authority (SHA)* | *Reconfiguration of manufacturing plants in pharmaceutical company* |
|---|---|---|
|  | • Lack of clear starting point data made analysis difficult, resulting in weak communication messages | • Clear starting point data made comparison with forecast relatively straightforward |
| Outcome | Protracted consultation resulting in planning blight for several years | Restructuring completed within one year resulting in cost and quality improvements |

## Making analytical assessments of the impact of future trends on the organisation

For many of the reasons outlined above, there has been little systematic assessment of what future trends are likely to impact healthcare services. The few existing studies tend to be either overly anecdotal or overly complicated and lacking in empirical analysis (Department of Trade and Industry, 2000).

Better development of strategy at the level of individual healthcare organisations will require a better sense of the future drivers of change, at a local level but also at a national level; a greater willingness to look broadly at trends and experiences across the UK and beyond; and a more pragmatic approach to analysing trends and their likely impact on healthcare organisations.

In contrast to the NHS, work done by strategy consulting companies tends to be based on robust analysis that is used to draw conclusions as to how and where organisations could change (McKinsey, 2001; Boston Consulting Group, 2003). For example, a Strategic Health Authority needs to develop a sense of how demand is likely to change over the next 5–10 years. This can be looked at simply by analysing population growth and changes in socio-demographic make up of the population, with perhaps a token acknowledgement of the impact of new medical technology in the broadest sense. But this effort falls short in two important respects. First, it lacks a robust quantified assessment of the likely impact. Second, it risks omitting far more important trends, such as increasing consumerism or the entry of new healthcare providers (for example a supermarket chain) or technology advances allowing far more healthcare to be delivered automatically without the same level of requirement for highly trained healthcare professionals. Building knowledge at a local level will require managers to be able to access and interpret a wide range of data sources to identify likely future trends.

## An ability and a willingness to search for examples of best practice

In order to build high-quality services, able to respond to future trends, healthcare managers need to be able to access examples of best practice. This may require looking outside the NHS and looking outside healthcare organisations. For example, the NHS struggles to recruit and retain a workforce but has failed to learn from non-healthcare players. This could include retailers such as Asda who have continually won 'best employer' awards and have, over many years, refined their approaches to staff management. Or one could look at airlines such as Easyjet who

## Case study to compare development of HR strategy

| | NHS HR strategy | Industrial company HR strategy |
|---|---|---|
| Aim | Decide on future pay, benefits package, training and development for NHS front line staff | Decide on future pay, benefits package, training and development for staff following a merger of two organisations |
| Driver for change | Shortage of key staff | Desire to stabilise business and ensure a high quality workforce for future |
| Approach | Development of future projections of workforce based on existing ways of working and planned levels of training | Analysis of current workforce, assessment of key drivers of recruitment and retention; examples of good practice; analysis of impact; models of future demand and supply |
| Approach/process | • Team of people working at central level – mix of front line operational staff, senior managers, politicians<br>• Lack of analysis – no clear starting point data & little understanding of key drivers for recruitment and retention within services | • Team of people working at central and local level – mix of front line operational staff, senior managers, HR specialists<br>• Analysis focused on starting point, key drivers of recruitment and retention; examples of good practice; analysis of impact; models of future demand and supply |

**Case study to compare development of HR strategy** (*continued*)

*NHS HR strategy*

- Report drew on a few case studies from around the NHS. No research base, few benchmarks and experience from other organisations
- Communication via publications rather than direct to employees

Outcome    Some success but limited

*Industrial company HR strategy*

- Report drew strongly on benchmarks from other organisations, other merger experiences
- Proposals widely communicated and tested with employees

Good retention

have radically changed the reliance of an industry on people and sought to both automate procedures (e.g. e-booking) but also eliminate unnecessary procedures (e.g. seat allocation or on-board catering).

The case study above illustrates the traditional reluctance of managers within the NHS to look for examples of best practice from outside the service. The case study compares two different approaches to developing a robust human resources strategy within an organisation: one the NHS, the other a large industrial manufacturer.

With the vast majority of NHS managers and staff only having worked in the NHS, an external focus may not come easily. Specific mechanisms will need to be put in place to encourage and support the examination of a wider range of different industries and organisations. This could be achieved through the recruitment of managers who bring with them a wider set of experiences; through the development of existing staff perhaps encouraging participation in courses with managers from a broad range of industries or by secondment; or through the greater use of external advisors or consultants acting as a repository of best practice or new ideas.

### An ability to develop innovative proposals for the future

Developing a successful strategy for the future requires innovation, ideas and a culture of entrepreneurship. Developing these skills within the NHS will need a new approach to risk taking. For example, organisations need to be encouraged to react to customer analysis by offering new or differentiated products. They need to test out different types of automation to explore which might offer the greatest benefits. Some of these innovations may fail, some may succeed. But individuals and organisations need to be encouraged to try.

### Developing top-quality communication skills

Perhaps the most important aspect of any strategy process is the ability to communicate objectives, assumptions, processes and conclusions. Proposals need to be substantiated by analysis showing the rationale for change. The implications of proposals for individuals and for organisations need to be outlined.

### Organisations will need incentives to develop robust strategies for the future development of their organisations

The above skills and capabilities are worthless unless there is a clear incentive for organisations to change and develop. It could be argued that in the past, there has had to be a top-down politically driven approach to NHS strategy development because individual organisations have traditionally failed to innovate and change to meet user expectations. Indeed the current government started its programme of reform through a series of top-down initiatives to stimulate greater change at a local level. For example:

- Setting standards for good quality care, such as National Service Frameworks to set out what a package of care should look like for various conditions, or guidance from the National Institute for Clinical Excellence (NICE) into the use of drugs or procedures
- Setting up inspection bodies such as the Commission for Healthcare Improvement (CHI) – now the Healthcare Commission – empowered to monitor the performance of NHS organisations and award them with differential 'star ratings'
- Introducing incentives, such as being granted greater freedoms in return for better quality care (measured as higher star ratings) and greater intervention if deemed a 'failing organisation'.
- Providing support. For instance, the Modernisation Agency was set up as part of the NHS to act as an internal consultancy organisation supporting change and reform within individual organisations.

Now the government is moving beyond this by devolving greater power to change and innovate to local organisations, stimulated through the introduction of competition. Outlined in a Department of Health document, *Delivering the NHS Plan* (Department of Health, 2002b) the government introduced the concept of 'plurality of provision'. This proposal will lead to an increasing amount of NHS work being outsourced to private sector providers. While still in its infancy, the initiative has seen new private sector providers start to compete with existing NHS players to provide care funded by the NHS (Dash, 2004). While price will be fixed, the ability of new private sector providers to produce care at substantially lower cost than NHS providers (largely due to improved process management), will allow them to invest more in additional services in order to offer a better quality product to the NHS.

Added to 'plurality of provision' is the notion of choice; when a patient needs a diagnostic test or an operation, the GP will offer the patient the choice of provider, or even a voucher for the patient to use at a place of their choosing. This may, for the first time, result in real competition between providers which in turn should encourage a greater need at a local organisation level to develop a robust strategy for the future.

## Management structures will need to be aligned to strategy development

Finally, in order to develop and implement a strategy successfully, an organisation needs to be focused on change and able to 'pull' levers to bring about change. This requires a board which is aligned behind a change programme, clear lines of accountability throughout an organisation and robust communication efforts to ensure understanding, buy-in and commitment to change.

Many NHS organisations have traditionally failed to deliver because these attributes have not been in place. In particular, the unique management structures for doctors have tended to make it difficult to bring about change in which they did not want to participate. Doctors within the NHS see themselves as self-employed autonomous professionals, not part of an organisation focused on improvement. This contrasts with other, more successful healthcare organisations, such as California's Kaiser Permanente, where the medical staff see themselves as employees of the organisation and work as part of teams (Feachem, Sekri and White, 2002). This may, though, be about to change with the advent of new contracts for medical staff within their existing employer organisations and/or the development of 'chambers' from which medical staff 'sell' their services to healthcare providers (Dash, 2002).

## In conclusion

Healthcare provision in the UK has, to date, been dominated by the NHS. The epitome of a large politically driven, centrally controlled bureaucracy, the NHS has struggled to develop and implement robust strategies for the future development of customer-focused healthcare services.

At the beginning of the 21st century the UK government is seeking to change the fundamental structure of the NHS, encouraging PCTs and individual consumers to shop around for healthcare from a 'plurality of providers'. With a more market-driven system the government hopes and believes that providers will respond by innovating and redesigning services to ensure improved clinical quality, greater efficiency and, above all, 'customer focused' care. These changes will need to be underpinned by the development, articulation and implementation of robust strategies for the future development of services.

This chapter has set out to explain what strategy is, how it is deployed in the commercial sector and how it could be applied to the NHS. The chapter has shown, from the broader strategy literature, what we can learn and appropriate for use in the health sector. The analysis points towards the benefits of local strategic development of the sort already advocated in this volume by Paton (Chapter 3) and Greer (Chapter 5). By developing local management capacity, supported by local data collection and analysis, with a greater willingness and capability to look outside the NHS and outside the UK, organisations within the NHS have the potential to build robust plans for the development of improved services. This is one route to create a more strategically focused NHS with enhanced performance for the future.

## Notes

1. From 'Resignation and Postmortem' by Jamie Zawinski. His letter used to be accessible at: www.jwz@jwz.org but seems no longer publicly available.
2. These two studies are cited in William H. Starbuck (http://pages.stern.nyu.edu/~wstarbuc/mob/strategizg.html). The original studies were carried out by Grinyer, P.H. and Norburn, D. (1975), and by Payne, R.L and Pugh, D.S. (1976).
3. These are familiar questions in strategy and have surfaced repeatedly in the literature (e.g. Markides, 1999).
4. A detailed discussion of these various explanations for performance variances is provided in M. de Rond (2003).
5. The S-C-P school argued that industry *structure* determined firm *conduct* (or strategy) which, in turn, determined its *performance*.

## References

Ansoff, H.I. (1965) *Corporate Strategy*. New York: McGraw-Hill
Barney J. (1991) 'Firm resources and sustainable competitive advantage', *Journal of Management*, **17**:99–120
Barret, S. and Fudge, C. (1981) *Policy and Action: Essays on the implementation of public policy* (edited). London: Routledge
Boston Consulting Group (2003) *European Physicians and the Internet*. Boston Consulting Group, March
Dash, P. (2002) 'Plan B on the consultant contract', *Guardian*, 1 November
Dash, P. (2004) 'New providers in UK healthcare', *British Medical Journal*, Feb., **328**:340–2
de Rond, M. (2003) *Strategic Alliances As Social Facts: Business, Biotechnology, and Intellectual History*. Cambridge: Cambridge University Press
de Wit, B. and Meyer, R. (2004) *Strategy: Process, Content, Context* (3rd edition). London: Thomson Learning

Department of Health (2000) *The NHS Plan. A Plan for Investment. A Plan for Reform*. London

Department of Health (2002a) *Shifting the Balance of Power: The Next Steps*. Department of Health, January

Department of Health (2002b) *Delivering the NHS Plan*. Department of Health, April

Department of Trade and Industry (2000) *Foresight: Healthcare 2020*. Department of Trade and Industry, December

*The Economist* (1993) 'Eenie,meenie, minie, mo', March 20, p. 76

Feachem, R., Sekri, N. and White, K. (2002) 'Getting more for their dollar: a comparison of the NHS with California's Kaiser Permanente', *British Medical Journal*, **324**:135–43

Grant, R.M. (1991) 'The resource-based theory of competitive advantage: implications for strategy formulation', *California Management Review*, **33**:114–35

Grinyer, P.H. and Norburn, D. (1975) 'Planning for existing markets: perceptions of executives and financial performance', *Journal of the Royal Statistical Society, Series A*, **138**:70–97

Hamel, G. (2000) *Leading the Revolution*. Boston: Harvard Business School Press

Hampden-Turner, C. (1990) *Charting the Corporate Mind: From Dilemma to Strategy*. Oxford: Blackwell

Henderson, R. (2003) 'Developing and managing a successful technology and product strategy', Executive education seminar for the Cambridge-MIT Institute, June, The Moller Centre, Cambridge

Kay, J.A. (1993) *Foundations of Corporate Success*. Oxford: Oxford University Press

Lindblom, C.E. (1959) 'The science of "muddling through"', *Public Administration Review*, **19**, 2: 79–88

Markides, C.C. (1999) 'A dynamic view of strategy', *Sloan Management Review*, Spring: 55–63

McAfee, R.P. (2002) *Competitive Solutions: the Strategist's Toolkit*. New Jersey: Princeton University Press

McGahan, A.M. and Porter, M.E. (1997) 'How much does industry matter, really?' *Strategic Management Journal*, **18** (Special Issue):15–31

McKinsey & Co. (2001) 'A model for disease management', *McKinsey Quarterly*, **4**

Mintzberg, H. (1987) 'Crafting Strategy', *Harvard Business Review* 65, **4**:66–75

Mintzberg, H. (1989) *Mintzberg on Management*. New York: Free Presss

Mintzberg, H., Ahlstrand, B. and Lampel, J. (1998) *Strategy Safari*. London: Prentice-Hall

Nohria, N., Joyce, W. and Roberson, B. (2003) 'What really works', *Harvard Business Review*, July: 43–52

Payne, R.L. and Pugh, D.S. (1976) 'Organisational structure and climate', in M.D. Dunette (ed.) *Handbook of Industrial and Organizational Psychology*. Chicago: Rand McNally, 1125–73

Peteraf, M. (1993) 'The cornerstones of competitive advantage: a resource-based view', *Strategic Management Journal*, **14**:179–91

Pettigrew, A. (2001) 'Crosstalk: Hambrick and Pettigrew on Leadership.', *Academy of Management Executive*, **15**, 3:36–45

Porter, M.E. (1979) 'How competitive forces shape strategy', *Harvard Business Review*, **57**, 2:137–145

Pressman, J.L. and Wildavsky, A. (1973) 'Implementation – how great expectations in Washington are dashed in Oakland; or, why it's amazing that Federal

Programmes work at all, this being a saga of the Economic Development Administration as told by two sympathetic observers who seek to build morals on a foundation of ruined hopes (The Oakland Project Series)'. University of California Press

Quinn, J.B. (1978) 'Strategic change: logical incrementalism', *Sloan Management Review* (Fall):7–21

Rumelt, R.P. (1984) 'Towards a strategic theory of the firm', in B. Lamb (ed.), *Competitive Strategic Management*, 556–70. Englewood Cliffs, NJ: Prentice Hall

Rumelt, R. (1991) 'How much does industry matter?' *Strategic Management Journal*, 12, 3:167–85

Sabatier, P. (1998) *Theories of the Policy Process* (edited). Westview Press

Shapiro, E.C. (1996) *Fad Surfing in the Boardroom*. Oxford: Capstone Publishing

Thompson, J.L. (2001) *Strategic Management*, 4th edn. London: Thompson Learning

Wanless, D. (2002), *The Wanless Review: securing our future health; taking a long-term view*. HM Treasury, April

Wernerfelt, B. (1984) 'A resource-based view of the firm', *Strategic Management Journal*, 5:171–80

Whittington, R. (1993) *What is Strategy: and does it matter?* London: International Thomson Business Press

# 7
# Ethics and Policy in Healthcare: Status and Prognosis

*Wendy A. Rogers*

## Introduction

Policy is the tool that is used to translate ideas or ideology into action. The ideas may be political, social, philosophical or economic; they may come from political parties, from communities or from corporations. In healthcare, policy is subject to many pressures: practical considerations to do with capacity and cost, political considerations to do with acceptability to the electorate, a philosophical commitment to a certain vision of healthcare, and pragmatic trade-offs. These pressures are surely enough to guarantee a certain incoherence, yet this paper raises a further area for discussion, to do with ethical values informing aspects of health policy.

At one level, we all value good health and share the belief that it is better to be healthy rather than unhealthy. This creates a moral imperative both to treat and prevent ill health. This moral imperative has also been accepted as a social imperative, reflected in the very existence of the National Health Service (NHS) in the UK. However this basic agreement over the value of good health does not protect health policy from political and other pressures, or easily translate into a package of 'top priorities' which we can afford, or even which we must afford. As a result, the values that underpin specific health policies may be multiple and conflicting, and apparently important values may be overshadowed by pragmatic concerns This paper aims to tease out some of these tensions; to examine the current status of the relationship between policy and ethics, and to discuss ways to improve the prognosis for a healthier relationship.

## Current themes in health policy

What are some of the dominant themes in current health policy? Here I use examples specifically from the UK, however these themes are common across many western nations. Within the over-arching theme of providing a comprehensive and affordable health service, there are a number of sub-themes. Three of these will be considered in this paper:

- the need for evidence-based medicine (EBM) and technology appraisal;
- the promise of patient-centred care and greater informed choice for users of healthcare services; and
- the desire for greater preventive initiatives.

Each of these themes relates to specific ethical values, and to assumptions about the ways that these values should be protected and promoted. Figure 7.1 summarises the policy themes and ethical values which are briefly described, and then followed by further analysis of the way that these values are currently put into practice, and the tensions between them.

### Evidence-based medicine and beneficence

Rapid advances in healthcare interventions can lead to problems of both under- and over-utilisation. On the one hand, new, and often expensive, interventions may be introduced into practice before these have been demonstrated to be better than existing interventions. On the other hand, new and effective interventions may be ignored while clinicians continue to practice according to tradition, habit or local opinion (Coulter, 1996; Sackett et al., 1997; Dawson et al., 1999; Sutherland and Dawson, 2002).

| Healthcare theme | Associated ethical values |
|---|---|
| EBM and technology appraisal | Beneficence (also non-maleficence and equity) |
| Patient-centred care and informed choice | Respect for patient autonomy |
| Greater preventive healthcare | Harm minimisation and utility |

*Figure 7.1*: Policy themes and ethical values

In addition, there are ever-increasing numbers of new drugs and technologies coming onto the market and competing for the healthcare pound. This situation has led to a predictable and reasonable policy requirement to have, as much as is possible, accurate information about new interventions, including information about efficacy and efficiency, followed by consistent decisions about their nation-wide introduction. In March 1998 the then Health Secretary Frank Dobson stated that:

> Scientific and technological advances offer huge opportunities for the NHS if properly harnessed and exploited, but the NHS has come to see them as a threat ... We need a 'third way' between uncritical adoption of the latest gizmo on the one hand, and head in the sand rejection of technology on the other. This means that we need a systematic process for identifying, assessing and then disseminating promising developments. Our new National Institute for Clinical Excellence will sort out the wheat from the chaff so we will know which new treatments should enter mainstream practice immediately. (NICE, 1999a)

The body charged with this task in England and Wales is the National Institute for Clinical Excellence (NICE), which uses the techniques of evidence-based medicine to determine the clinical and cost-effectiveness of new interventions. Once these have been reviewed, NICE offers guidance as to the recommended availability of the intervention within the NHS. If an intervention is approved by NICE, local providers are required to make this available to patients through the NHS.

The processes of EBM involve review of the benefits and harms of specific interventions, in order to make a judgement about their overall effectiveness. The underlying ethical value in this process is beneficence – the desire to act for the good of the patient by offering interventions which are of proven benefit.

Beneficence is a long-standing value in healthcare ethics (Pellegrino and Thomasma, 1981). The aim of acting for the good of patients justifies many practices that would otherwise be unacceptable, such as invasive diagnostic tests or the administration of potentially deadly medicines. Traditionally understood, beneficence revolves around the proper use of complex professional knowledge for the benefit of the patient. Physicians, due to their training and experience, know best which medical interventions will benefit patients; the moral requirement of beneficence maintains that trust and ensures that this knowledge is used for the good of patients rather than for any other reasons, such as commercial gain or self-interest. The practices of EBM are located well within this understanding of beneficence. Expertise, based upon privileged professional knowledge, confers authority upon the assessments of clinicians, and similarly it is expertise that confers authority upon the judgements of EBM.

There are two other ethical values directly linked to EBM and the work of NICE. The first is non-maleficence, or the duty to do no harm. Non-maleficence is an integral part of EBM as the process of reviewing evidence includes looking at harmful effects as well as beneficial effects. Interventions that are directly harmful to health, or that do not confer any benefit, are not recommended, justified by appeal to the principle of non-maleficence. The second value linked to EBM is that of equity. Through national guidance, NICE attempts to ensure national availability of approved interventions, aiming at equity of access. This is a direct attempt to minimise regional variations that previously led to unequal access to some healthcare interventions (known as 'post-code rationing') as this was widely seen as inequitable (NICE, 1999b).

## Patient-centred care and respect for patient autonomy

Patient-centred care emerged into political prominence with the NHS Plan published in July 2000. This referred to a patient-led NHS and promised more power and information for patients (Department of Health, 2000). One of the core NHS principles from this plan stated that:

> The NHS will shape its services around the needs and preferences of individual patients, their families and carers ... The NHS will treat patients as individuals, with respect for their dignity. Patients and citizens will have a greater say in the NHS and the provision of services will be centred on patients' needs. (Department of Health, 2000)

After decades as passive recipients of care, NHS patients were to have a more active role in a health service aimed at facilitating informed choices about treatment and respecting patient preferences. The ideal promised in the plan is that of a health service in which patients receive comprehensive information about proffered treatments and their alternatives and, after discussion and reflection, are able to make individual decisions which reflect their own values.

The commitment to foster informed choice and to shape services around the needs and preferences of individual patients relates to the ethical duty of respect for patient autonomy. Respect for patient autonomy has become the dominant, although contested, value in western healthcare ethics, reflecting an increasing emphasis upon individual rights together with a rise in consumerism in healthcare (Wolpe, 1998). This has been most obvious in North America, but the ideas that patients should be treated as individuals, informed about their health-care and given the right to choose what happens to them, have become accepted within UK health policy. Respect for autonomy has become such a central theme in healthcare ethics in part due to concerns about the paternalism that often accompanies medical care based solely on beneficence. In a paternalistic approach patients have been treated as passive recipients of care, with little opportunity or encouragement to be informed about their treatment, let alone to question it or express preferences for alternative courses of action. In response to concerns of this kind, the NHS has made shaping its services around the needs and preferences of individual patients a core principle.

## Greater prevention, utility and minimising harm

The NHS plan has a commitment to public health and the prevention of disease (Department of Health, 2000). Prominent amongst the targeted areas are cancer and heart disease, because they are the biggest killers in the UK, and because they are amenable to preventive interventions. Cardiovascular disease, for example, has identifiable risk factors which can be modified to reduce the risk of disease. Some cancers have a lengthy course in which early identification of the disease state may lead to improved survival. This has led to the development of national preventive programmes, such as the breast cancer and cervical cancer screening programmes, the current pilots for bowel cancer screening, and guidelines for the primary and secondary prevention of cardiovascular disease.

The current National Screening Committee (NSC) definition of screening is:

> A public health service in which members of a defined population, who do not necessarily perceive that they are at risk of, or already affected by, a disease or its complications, are asked a question or offered a test to identify those individuals who are more likely to be helped than harmed by further tests or treatment to reduce the risk of disease or its complications. (UK National Screening Committee, 2004, p. 6)

When some of these screening programmes were introduced, the emphasis was upon maximising population coverage and various - mechanisms (such as incentives for GPs to reach targets for cervical cancer screening and immunisation rates) were introduced to this end.

The emphasis is now changing, with a focus upon potential participants making informed choices about whether or not to take up screening, as per the NSC definition. Despite this change, screening coverage targets still exist, and screening programmes are evaluated in terms of the proportion of the population screened, rather than using a measure that might identify the number who made an informed choice about screening.

The theme of greater prevention appeals to a principle of harm minimisation. Reducing or preventing harm is another long standing and deeply held ethical value in healthcare. Screening programmes and other preventive initiatives are aimed at reducing or preventing harms in the population, by lowering population levels of morbidity and mortality caused by the index diseases. Harm reductions achieved by preventive programmes can be significant at a regional or national level, but for each individual who is screened, the reduction in risk of harm may be quite small. This is known as the prevention paradox (Rose, 1999). The ethical move from a focus upon individuals, as is usually the case in clinical care, to one on populations is achieved through utilitarian reasoning which balances the sum of benefits and harms at the population level. This kind of reasoning may be quite alien to many healthcare professionals who are more comfortable with weighing up harms and benefits for individual patients. One important feature of screening is that its success depends to some extent upon population coverage; to make the predicted health gains, a high proportion of the population must participate in screening, even though many of these people are unlikely to benefit directly, and the burdens, such as side-effects from the screening intervention, may fall upon those who do not benefit.

## Tensions between these values

There are obvious tensions between the different ethical values that underpin current themes in health policy. If acting beneficently requires that healthcare professionals carefully implement the specific recommendations of evidence-based medicine, this leaves little scope for patients to exercise autonomy by making their own informed choices. Indeed, this is the very task that EBM will already have performed in its judgement of the best available intervention. However, this conclusion is incompatible with placing patients' needs and preferences at the centre of the NHS, unless we are certain that patients will always come to the same conclusions as those performing EBM reviews. This however cannot be assumed. There are several reasons why the clinical recommendations made by EBM may not always be those that would be chosen by fully informed patients (Rogers, 2002). EBM can only compare treatments for which research evidence exists, and some options preferred by patients may not have been subject to research assessment. In assessing evidence, various assumptions are made about the parameters that should be used to judge the effectiveness of interventions, for example length of symptom-free survival, or rate of adverse events. These endpoints are those which have been selected by researchers as both clinically significant and measurable within the time-limited confines of the trial. However, if offered the choice, patients may identify alternative or additional endpoints, such as number and frequency of long-term side effects, ease of compliance, or impact upon lifestyle. Using EBM, patients may be given some (usually limited) information about why a particular intervention is recommended, but they will not be given a range of choices based upon a comprehensive assessment of patients' preferences. There seems to be an irreducible conflict between the beneficence of EBM and a robust commitment to respect for patient autonomy expressed through patient choice.

What about the relationship between maximising harm reduction at a population level and the focus on respect for patient autonomy? Again there is a tension; ensuring that all patients reach a fully informed and autonomous choice about screening or vaccination is likely to be counter-productive in terms of achieving maximum population coverage for the test, especially where this is unpleasant, inconvenient and unlikely to have significant benefits for the individual. An example of this would be the faecal occult blood test used in screening for bowel cancer. The ethical gains made in respecting autonomy may be offset by the harms of incomplete screening and failure to achieve significant reductions in population levels of disease.

This difficulty of adjudicating between apparently conflicting ethical values has long been recognised in clinical ethics. Indeed, this is one of the main criticisms of principled-based approaches (such as (Beauchamp and Childress, 1994) which seem to offer little guidance as to how to proceed when following one principle leads to a conclusion which is incompatible with another principle (Gert, Culver and Clouser, 1997). Before abandoning this line of enquiry however, it is worth taking a closer look at the way that these ethical values seem to be understood in the context of health policy.

## Analysis of the values apparent in current policy

The nature of beneficence assumed by evidence-based medicine is very much the traditional understanding of beneficence, with experts judging the 'best' interventions for patients. As mentioned above, there are reasons to think that the professional view may not entirely reflect patients' views, but leaving aside this problem for a moment, we are still left with the requirement for a strong identity between the patient's best interests with regard to health, and their best interests *simpliciter*, so that the right thing to do, medically speaking, is identical to the right thing to do, all things considered. This conflation of interests is less problematic when patients are faced with potentially reversible life-threatening or very serious illnesses. In these situations, all or most of the patient's interests are contained within their health interests, as without health there will be no other interests. But in less urgent situations, which are far more common, there is a gap between health interests and overall interests. Health is important to most people, but it is not always the most important consideration in any situation. This gap is ignored when policy based upon EBM assumes that medical expertise should be the determining expertise in deciding how patients should make use of healthcare options.

Beneficence can be understood in a broader sense than the narrow health-based sense underpinning evidence-based medicine (Rogers, 1999). This view includes the importance of patients' other interests, such as family relationships, employment, financial considerations, the interest that people have in being cared for, and of course, autonomy or self-determination. A broader view of beneficence directs us towards a greater role for patients to have a say in their care, allowing patients to define their own interests and then to assess the possible contribution from healthcare. This limits the role of healthcare professionals to actions aimed at achieving patient-defined health goals, suitably informed by the best available, relevant evidence. In fact this is similar to the original vision of the EBM pioneers, to inform decisions rather than determine them (Sackett, 1996). If the ethical imperative underlying EBM really is beneficence, there should be little to prevent a shift in process towards a patient-centred form of EBM that would help practitioners to act beneficently in the broader sense, as for example proposed in some models of evidence-informed patient choice (Entwistle et al., 1998; Hope, 1996). This change in emphasis would mean that evidence became a tool rather than an imperative, and EBM would lose its regulatory overtones. However, EBM and assessments of new interventions have become inextricably linked with issues of cost and control. NICE, for example, is explicitly charged with assessing predicted costs of its guidance. Questions of cost are of course, important, but should be overtly addressed as such in terms of what we as a national community can afford with regard to healthcare, rather than hooked on to beneficence-based judgements about the healthcare value of different interventions.

Respect for patient autonomy is the value underpinning the commitment to focus care around patients' needs and preferences. Why is respect for autonomy considered so important, and what do we actually mean by it (O'Neill, 2002; Rothman, 1991)? Western societies place a very high value on self-determination and freedom from interference. This ideal of freedom is jealously guarded, despite the fact that many people live their lives subject to barrages of often covert and/or coercive influences and with their choices severely limited by external circumstances that they are powerless to influence, such as social class, employment, educational level or even physical appearance.

Choices about many aspects of healthcare are influenced by societal factors over which people have little control (Sherwin, 1992). The growing market for cosmetic surgery is one example; this is very much a service driven by patients' preferences, but the forces that lead women to believe that signs of ageing, or small breast size, are unacceptable health defects requiring surgical correction are surely freedom limiting. It would be difficult to claim that these choices are free in the sense of being wholly owned by the patient, as they usually reflect adherence to a cultural ideal of youth or optimal breast size. Perhaps this objection is unrealistic, after all we live in the social world and are shaped by it and it would be paternalistic to deny people their choices on the grounds that their desires, because shaped by society, are inauthentic. Who else could claim the expertise to know better than the individual concerned what is good for them, and on what grounds, as that 'expert' in turn would be influenced by their own social milieu? What this example highlights is the problematic nature of autonomy: we are not free in the sense that all of our preferences arise *de novo* from within.

If this is the case, and our preferences belong as much to society as to ourselves, respecting individual autonomy may not reduce simply to meeting preferences, and we may question the idea that offering patients choices about their treatment meets the ethical requirement of respecting autonomy. Even in a best-case scenario, in which for example, a patient is offered a choice about surgical or medical treatment for a problem, it is not clear in what sense this enhances their freedom. Yes, they have end-stage choice between two particular options, but they have not had any opportunities to influence the selection of those options, and the circumstances of the choice are very much shaped by professional rather than lay interests. To a person who has waited six months or more for a specialist appointment, had this cancelled twice and had to wait two hours in an uncomfortable waiting-room, only to be greeted by a junior doctor rather than the specialist that she expected, offering choices may do little to make that person feel like a self-determining and free individual.

If we think a bit more about the forces that led to an emphasis upon respect for patient autonomy, we might arrive at a different view of how best to achieve this in a health service, and providing choices may not be the answer. In the scenario of the patient waiting months for an appointment and being disappointed with the seniority of the doctor she saw, we can ask what kinds of things might have made her feel more in control, more as if she was an actor rather than an object. One obvious answer is information – information about waiting times and how these are being addressed, information about the kinds of emergencies that lead to cancellations, information about how doctors are trained and supported, so that she knows even if she sees a junior doctor, this doctor has some expertise in the field or can call upon the specialist in the next room.

The provision of information is important as a way of formally recognising the patient as a person. Knowing that the waiting list is six months and that cancellations are due to the unexpected call up of one specialist into the armed forces does not materially change the circumstances, but providing this information indicates respect for the person waiting, and recognises that she has a legitimate interest in knowing what is going on and why. This kind of response captures a different part of the obligation to respect patient autonomy, with the emphasis upon respect rather than autonomy. Respectful treatment reflects recognition of that person's individuality and treats them as an end rather than a means – a person waiting for an appointment rather than a statistic to be manipulated on a list.

It may be argued that several aspects of the respectful treatment described above are to do with process and administration, rather than with actual healthcare. In answer to this, first, it is not clear to what extent process and administration can be divorced from a consideration of care; for patients' healthcare comes in a package. They have an appointment in this hospital, with this length of waiting list, and these procedures. The actual medical interaction is framed by these other considerations, which help to shape expectations and to colour the experience of the patient while receiving care. Of course, prompt appointments and luxurious waiting-rooms do not remove the responsibility from practitioners for providing respectful and high quality care; these are non-negotiable requirements. However, improving the circumstances of care may well increase the likelihood that the patient arrives before the doctor in a fit state to understand and to benefit from the care offered. This might go far towards increasing actual patient autonomy in terms of understanding what treatment is being proposed and why, and making an informed decision, rather than the provision of what may be bewildering options to patients who are too frazzled by the process to take in the necessary information to make a choice.

There is a further point to make about the provision of information, which I have so far taken to be of value in promoting respect for patients. There has been a general push for patients to receive increased information in healthcare, in part through formalised informed consent processes. This is understandable in the context of problems such as the undisclosed high mortality rates in the Bristol paediatric cardiac surgery unit (Kennedy, 2001), and the retention of organs at many institutions (Redfern, 2001). In these situations, the focus of public anger was on lack of information – parents were not told of the unacceptably high death rate at Bristol, or that a 'tissue sample' might be a whole heart or brain. The lack of information prevented parents and relatives from making any kind of informed decision, such as whether to go ahead with surgery or agree to tissue donation. Lack of information directly limited the choices, and hence agency, of those involved. Perhaps more importantly, the perceived secrecy and cover-ups eroded trust in the competence and practices of medical staff. Policy makers seem to have latched on to this anger at the lack of information, so that now provision of information is seen as a universal panacea.

There are problems with this approach. First, the uncritical provision of information does not necessarily solve whatever problem is at stake. Telling parents in Bristol about the high mortality rates would not have solved the problem, which required far more drastic action. Information alone would not have provided the parents with increased agency in any meaningful sense unless they were offered surgery with an alternative clinician or at another unit. Providing information respects the understandable desire that patients may have to know what is going on, but without further action to remedy the underlying situation, the gains for patients may be meagre in terms of creating meaningful choices.

Second, it is not always clear what purpose information serves, and the perceived (or desired) relationship between receipt of information and autonomous choices. Some patient information seems unclear in its aims, such as patient versions of guidelines, or information about some screening programmes. Are these kind of documents aimed at informing patients about all the relevant issues (and who should identify which issues are relevant is another question) so that they can make a well-reasoned choice, or are they about ensuring that the patient makes the 'right' choice, i.e. the one advocated by those producing the materials (Raffle, 2001)? Information is not value-free, but the underlying values are not always made explicit, and neither are the aims.

Third, as O'Neill pointed out in the 2003 BBC Reith lectures, there is no direct relationship between information and trust (O'Neill, 2002b). We have access to unbelievable amounts of information, including league tables for hospital performances and so on, but information in and of itself does not build trust unless we can verify the accuracy of that information. A poor performance on a league table may reflect a health service providing good care to a very sick population, while a good performance may demonstrate facility at manipulating waiting list figures.

Finally, there has been little analysis of the implications of the commitment to patient choice and autonomy. Questions about the capacity of the NHS actually to provide more information in clinical settings and to respond to patients' preferences, or the desirability of providing a greater range of options, have not been clearly articulated, never mind answered.

Minimising harms, at a population level, is the final value to consider here. This may be the most difficult value to promote in the current culture of individualism and self-interest, as harms are minimised at a population level rather than at an individual level. This breaks the nexus between reducing harm and self-interest, as participation in a preventive activity may not confer any benefit upon specific individuals, but instead produces benefits at the population level. Rather than self-interest, the appeal is to the common good or public interest. This can be hard to conceptualise. How can one hundred people having a test to detect an early cancer in one of them be in the public interest? Surely the benefit is to the individual whose cancer is detected, and the other ninety-nine who had negative tests have not benefited, except perhaps in terms of reassurance. The good would still have been achieved even if many of them had not had the test, as long as the one positive person was tested. And that of course is the issue in screening; as we cannot predict who will be positive, the whole population at risk needs to be tested to identify the one. The statistics are hard to grasp as even diseases which are major causes of morbidity can be quite rare at the individual level. There is a need for those making policy in this area to have a strong grasp of statistics and probability. The way that statistics are expressed can be misleading: screening to halve the rate of cancer sounds desirable, but if the cancer in question is fairly rare, this may involve screening two hundred healthy individuals to find the affected one. Put this way, the proposition is not so attractive.

Screening programmes are based upon preventing or minimising disease. The screening programmes that we have reflect a number of factors including the availability of specific tests, historical precedents, public pressure, and public health priorities. Older screening programmes, such as cervical screening, are not based on rigorous proof of effectiveness, while for some programmes such as breast cancer screening, the evidence of programme effectiveness is still being debated, and for others, such as bowel cancer screening, the evidence is currently being assembled. This means that the moral foundation of some screening in terms of preventing or minimising harm is weaker than we might wish for. There is a chance that the programme might not actually lead to an overall decrease in deaths or disease, or that the harms from false positive or false negative results may outweigh the benefits. This is a tricky point – the benefits are measured at a population level, but the harms of erroneous results affect individuals. How should these be compared or balanced? We do not know how many people, given all of the relevant information, might prefer to play the odds and refuse preventive care, thereby avoiding any of the possible complications, and rely upon prompt and effective treatment if and when disease occurs.

## Future prognosis: values for ethically coherent policy

So far I have identified and explored some of the values that underpin current policy, tracked the tension between them, and outlined criticisms of the current interpretations of these values in the policy context. How can we move forward from here? What are the values that might underpin a national health service and how can these values act in a synergistic rather than antagonistic manner? These questions are important if we are to meet the challenge identified by Evans: 'Future health policies ought to be driven by a clear and openly defended choice of core moral values' (Evans, 1999).

First of all, we need to rethink respect for autonomy. There seems to be something futile and even underhand about emphasising individual autonomy in healthcare when many of the illnesses with which people are afflicted reflect, as Yach describes in Chapter 6, their lack of agency in society. Acheson (1998) has documented the excess morbidity and mortality associated with deprivation. Promising to respect patient preferences in a health service that does not have the resources to provide patients with adequate information, and which cannot afford to offer a wide range of services, is at best misleading. The rhetoric about informed choices seems to mask the implicit suggestion that patients are welcome to make their own choices as long as those are the choices that have already been identified as desirable by professionals, for example to take EBM based advice, or to accept screening tests or vaccinations.

A focus upon respect rather than choice might capture some of the ethical importance of respect for autonomy while facilitating transparency about the capacities and limits of the NHS. The NHS can provide services in an efficient and respectful way, avoiding the rhetoric of choice if providing choice is neither possible nor sustainable. Within those limits, patients' rights to choose whether to accept or reject treatments should be encouraged and respected. This limit on open-ended preferences may be acceptable if there has been meaningful patient input at all levels of developing and delivering services, so that the perhaps limited options that are available reflect patient values rather than exclusively professional ones. The recent formation of the NICE Citizen's council may be seen as a move in this direction, although it is not yet clear what force the council will have. These issues are further discussed in Chapter 10 by Greener.

Second, we need to rethink beneficence. The aims of the health service are defined by the statutory duties of Secretary of State:

> to continue the promotion in England and Wales of a comprehensive health service designed to secure improvement
> (a) in the physical and mental health of the people of those countries, and
> (b) in the prevention, diagnosis and treatment of illness. (cited in Newdick, 1995, p. 119)

If beneficence is acting for the (health) good of others, we should have a robust debate about the nature of that good, and the responsibilities of the government in acting for the health good of the population. This calls for a political vision of a healthy society and discussion about the best ways of achieving this vision. As Yach (Chapter 6) details, the evidence about the links between health and social determinants is now well accepted, so that it is no longer plausible to limit considerations of health to the provision of diagnostic and therapeutic services. If we are serious about reducing morbidity and mortality, for example from cardiovascular disease, then the costs and benefits of alternative methods of achieving this should be clearly debated in ways that facilitate comparisons. Perhaps the widespread prescription of statins will achieve significant reductions in heart disease, perhaps a transport policy which supports cycling and walking will do the same, or a policy which puts healthy foods into schools or provides income support for disadvantaged families to make healthy choices at the supermarket. Each of these options assumes a certain vision of the best way to achieve health in a society, reflecting underlying values; these kind of choices are social and political and should be recognised and debated as such. It is intellectually dishonest to present health problems as epidemics visited upon us (coronary heart disease, cancer) that require largely medical solutions when the circumstances that have led to the 'epidemics' remain unacknowledged and/or unaddressed, yet are rooted in our social fabric.

There are important choices to be made in trying to address the health issues that result from the ways that society is structured. The current solution is to emphasise the treatment of ill health through the provision of a more or less adequate health service. Other options, such as greater income redistribution, or structural attempts to reduce inequalities in access to education or employment, are not presented in relation to health policy. Yet these options should be presented explicitly on the political agenda as choices that we are making about the health and welfare of members of our society.

What of the conflict between individualism and the common good? Are patients' rights infringed by appeals to the common good, especially when participation in screening programmes may entail some health risks? Are governments justified in asking citizens to participate in immunisation programmes to maintain safe levels of population immunity? These are difficult questions, made more difficult by the increasingly high standard of living that many of us enjoy and the decreasing returns from increased health surveillance. When infectious diseases were common and fatal, vaccination was a clear benefit, both to protect the individual and to reduce epidemics in the population. Now that many people have never seen a case of, for example measles and its possible aftermath, the individual danger of infection seems so remote that any potential or even postulated risks from immunisation are enough to persuade some parents that it is safer to avoid immunisation.

Perhaps we need a closer examination of the 'common good'. The term implies that the 'good' is held in common, across the population. But population-based health interventions do not distribute their benefits evenly across the population, and can in fact increase inequalities in health (de Walle et al., 1999; Reading et al., 1994). This places severe limits on the common good argument, as we might consider that any health gains for some (relatively advantaged) sectors of the population are offset by increases in health inequalities for more disadvantaged sectors. Unless population-based interventions either reduce inequalities, or the health benefits from them are distributed equally, we cannot try to justify them through appeals to the common good. Rather, we should be alerted to the need to focus specifically upon inequalities, and on ways to improve the health of the least well off in our society.

## Conclusion

This paper has argued that three themes in current health policy can be mapped to specific ethical values. As they stand, there are tensions between these values. If we believe that expertise should be the basis for choosing healthcare interventions, this leaves no room for patient choice; and if we believe that patient choice should be the most important factor, the role for evidence is limited. Similarly, if we want greater preventive healthcare, we cannot privilege informed choice. The current policies do not explicitly recognise these tensions, nor indicate a way through them.

However, we can reformulate the underlying values to achieve some greater coherence. Beneficence can be understood as a broad consideration of patients' interests, in which medical expertise plays a vital, but not a determining, role. This leaves a supportive role for evidence-based medicine in informing patients' choices. Respect for autonomy may be better achieved through meaningful participation in decisions about the healthcare system or about the creation of a realisable agenda for tackling the social, behavioural and institutional determinants of health at population level, rather than through rhetoric about patient preferences at an individual clinical level. Preventing ill health through population interventions cannot be justified by appeals to self-interest or to the common good unless the benefits of prevention reduce rather than exacerbate inequalities in health.

What might ethically coherent policy look like? First, policy themes should be explicitly (and honestly) linked to underlying ethical values.

This is necessary for informed political debate. Healthcare is such an emotive subject that it is easy to obscure the values underlying specific policy objectives in motherhood statements about 'improving health-care'. Explicit discussion of values would lead to greater clarity, and allow citizens to make more informed choices about which policies to support at elections. I am not suggesting that it would be an easy task to translate overt values-based health policy into actions that necessarily preserved those values, but this could be an ideal to strive for.

Ethically explicit policy would not promise the unachievable ('placing patient preferences at the heart of the NHS'), rather it would make more modest yet sustainable claims, thus demonstrating trustworthiness. This will require more information than we have at present, suggesting several lines for further inquiry. For example, we need to debate the merits and practicalities of emphasising respect rather than autonomy in clinical care and ask how the morally significant imperative to respect persons can become embedded into all levels of the health service. At the same time, we need to determine what kinds of mechanisms (citizens' juries, opinion polls, referenda) are best suited to achieving meaningful citizen/patient input into decisions about the healthcare system. We need to ask whether appeals for restraint and/or altruism can be justified with regard to a resource limited health service, and whether paternalism is acceptable at a public health level. We need more information about the relationship between patients' rights and population health, and to debate when a society is sufficiently caring of its citizens to justify appeals to the common good.

These measures may go some way towards avoiding ethical contradictions in health policy, improving the prognosis and leading to greater unity of purpose. We may even hope that greater unity may lead to better health outcomes, and a series of achievable health policy goals.

## References

Acheson, D.E. (1998) *Independent Inquiry into Inequalities in Health: Report*. London: The Stationery Office

Beauchamp, T. and Childress, J. (1994) *Principles of Biomedical Ethics*, 4th edn. New York: Oxford University Press

Coulter, A. (1996) 'Theory into practice: applying the evidence across the health service', *Bailliere's Clinical Obstetrics and Gynaecology*, **10**, 4:715–29

Dawson, S., Sutherland, K., Dopson, S. and Miller, R. (1999) 'Changing clinical practice: views about the management of adult asthma', *Quality in Healthcare*, **8**:253–61 de Walle, H., van der Pal, K. and de Jong-van den Berg et al. (1999) 'Effect of a mass media campaign to reduce socio-economic differences in women's awareness and behaviour concerning use of folic acid: cross sectional study', *British Medical Journal*, **319**:291–292

Department of Health (2000) *The NHS Plan*. Crown Copyright

Entwistle, V.A., Sheldon, T.A., Sowden, A. and Watt, I.S. (1998) 'Evidence-informed patient choice', *International Journal of Technology Assessment in Healthcare*, **14**, 2:212–25

Evans, M. (1999) 'Reconciling conflicting values in health policy', Technical paper 9, in Dargie, C. (ed.) *Policy Futures for UK Health Project*. Nuffield Trust Technical Series

Gert, B., Culver, C. and Clouser, K. (1997) *Bioethics: a Return to Fundamentals*. New York: Oxford University Press

Hope, T. (1996) *Evidence-based Patient Choice*, King's Fund, London

Kennedy, I. (2001) *Learning from Bristol: The Report of the Public Enquiry into Children's Heart Surgery at the Bristol Royal Infirmary 1984–95*. Norwich: The Stationery Office, CN5207 (1)

Newdick, C. (1995) *Who Should we Treat? Law, Patients and Resources in the NHS*. Oxford: Clarendon Press

NICE (1999a) *Secretary of State's Speech*. http://www.nice.org.uk/Embcat.asp?page=oldsite/back/frank_dobson.htmandd=907 (accessed 17–2–03)

NICE (1999b) *A Guide to our Work*. http://www.nice.org.uk/cat.asp?c=137 (accessed 17–8–02)

O'Neill, O. (2002a) *Autonomy and Trust in Bioethics*. Cambridge: Cambridge University Press

O'Neill, O. (2002b) *Trust and Transparency* (BBC Reith Lectures 2002, lecture 4) http://www.bbc.co.uk/radio4/reith2002/ (accessed 21–5–03)

Pellegrino, E.D. and Thomasma, D. (1981) *A Philosophical Basis of Medical Practice: towards a philosophy and ethic of the healing professions*. New York: Oxford University Press

Raffle, A. (2001) 'Information about screening – is it to achieve high uptake or to ensure informed choice?', *Health Expectations*, **4**:92–8

Reading, R., Colver, A., Openshaw, S., and Jarvis, S. (1994) 'Do interventions that improve immunisation uptake also reduce social inequalities in uptake?', *British Medical Journal*, **308**:1142–4

Redfern, M. (2001) *The Royal Liverpool Children's Inquiry Report*. London: Department of Health

Rogers, W. (1999) 'Beneficence in general practice: an empirical investigation', *Journal of Medical Ethics*, **25**:388–93

Rogers, W.A. (2002) 'Evidence-based medicine in practice: limiting or facilitating patient choice?', *Health Expectations*, **5**:95–103

Rose, G. (1999) 'Sick individuals and sick populations,' in D. Beauchamp and B. Steinbock (eds) *New Ethics for the Public's Health*. New York: Oxford University Press: 28–38

Rothman, D. (1991) *Strangers at the Bedside: a history of how law and ethics transformed medical decision-making*. New York: Basic Books

Sackett, D.L. (1996) 'Evidence based medicine: what it is and what it isn't', *British Medical Journal*, **312**: 71–72

Sackett, D., Richardson, W.S., Rosenberg, W., and Haynes, R.B. (1997) *Evidence-based Medicine: how to practice and teach EBM.* New York: Churchill Livingstone

Sherwin, S. (1992) *No Longer Patient: Feminist ethics and healthcare.* Philadelphia: Temple University Press

Sutherland, K., and Dawson, S. (2002) 'Making sense in practice, doctors at work', *International Studies of Management and Organisation,* 32, 2, Summer

UK National Screening Committee (2004) 'What is screening?' Accessed on 20 October 2004 from: http:/www.nsc.nhs.uk/whatscreening/whatscreen ind.htm

Wolpe, P.R. (1998) '"The triumph of autonomy in American bioethics": a sociological view,' in *Bioethics and Society: constructing the ethical enterprise,* R. De Vries and J. Subedi (eds), Englewod Cliffs, NJ: Prentice-Hall, 38–59

# 8
# Making Healthcare Sustainable: a Case Study of the NHS

*Karen Jochelson*

## Introduction

Sustainable development – the idea that growth should meet today's economic, social and environmental needs, without compromising the needs of the future – has been on the international political and business agenda for sometime. Leading multi-nationals have found that eco-efficiency reduces waste, lessens a company's environmental impact, and improves the balance sheet. They argue that environmental and social stewardship reduces potential legal liability, and is a driver for innovation that creates new markets and revenue growth (Arnold and Day, 1998). Governments may pass environmental regulations and talk about sustainable development, but rarely do they apply a discerning gaze to the public sector to evaluate its social and environmental impact, and the potential benefits of applying sustainable development principles to public sector organisation and activities.

This article looks at the publicly funded National Health Service (NHS) in England and suggests that if it began to use its resources in ways that are less wasteful and ultimately less costly, it may reduce damage it causes to the environment and to public health, and in the long term free up resources to reinvest in better healthcare. It begins by assessing the resources of the NHS and the potential impact its activities may have on the environment and on health, and concludes with some examples that suggest the health, environmental and financial benefits of incorporating environmental awareness into the management of the health service.

## Environmental and health impact of the NHS

The healthcare sector is enormous in size and resource intensive. The NHS's planned expenditure for 2004–05 is £77.6 billion. By 2008 this could increase to £185 billion (Wanless, 2002). It employs over one million people nationally and is probably the largest single employer in the UK. It uses almost 23 million square metres of floor space in England – space equivalent to 140 Canary Wharfs, or three times the amount of office space in the City of London (ERIC Returns, 2002; personal communication, City of London Planning Office, 10 July 2001). Its land holdings run to 9,000 hectares, the equivalent of 64 Hyde Parks (ERIC Returns, 2002; personal communication, Royal Parks London, Press Office, 10 July 2001). At this scale it is likely that NHS activities – its consumption of goods and services, creation and disposal of waste, reliance on a car-based transport system, and use of energy – have a significant economic, environmental and social impact locally and across the UK. This section outlines the size of its impact and the likely environmental and health impact of its operational activities.

## Procurement

The NHS spends about £11 billion every year on purchasing a huge range of goods and services ranging from food to electricity and fuel, from syringes to ultrasound equipment, and from transport services to agency nursing staff. Just in London the NHS spends about £2.2 billion each year (NHS Purchasing and Supply Agency, 2001a). It is difficult to come by figure for particular items, but Acute Trusts in London may carry as much as 726 kilograms of mercury (Jochelson, 2002:33) and of potentially recyclable products, use about 13,500 toner cartridges, 560,000 batteries, 32 million paper cups and 23 tonnes of paper a year (Jochelson, 2002b:74).

The scale of NHS purchasing power means that the choices it makes about the type of goods it buys can have an impact on the environment, and hence the health and well-being of staff and patients within a hospital, and the community beyond. For example, indoor air pollution is caused by the use of pesticides, cleaning materials and disinfectants, which can contain toxic chemicals and by the particulates and emissions given off by equipment and synthetic materials used to construct and furnish buildings. Where ventilation is inadequate, poor air quality can lead to 'sick building syndrome', which can have neurotoxic, respiratory, and chemosensory effects and irritate the skin, eyes and throat (Redlich, Sparer and Cullen, 1997). Long-term exposure to particular chemicals can lead also to more serious chronic respiratory ailments (Healthcare Without Harm and American College of Nurse-midwives, 2001:15–17).

Commonly used hospital equipment can also have an environmental and health impact (Healthcare Without Harm and Environmental

Working Group, 1998; Rossi and Schettler, 2000; Solomon and Schettler, 2000). PVC is found in equipment ranging from IV and plasma collection bags to catheters, gloves and thermal blankets. When incorrectly incinerated, dioxin is created. It is carcinogenic, has severe developmental impacts on foetal growth, and can lead to male and female reproductive dysfunction. Plasticisers, or phthalates, are added to PVC to make it softer and are used in IV bags, storage bags and tubing. Phthalates can leach out of the plastic when in contact with liquids like blood and certain fat emulsion products. Phthalates are a potential human carcinogen and a suspected endocrine disruptor in humans and animals. Mercury is found in dental amalgams, thermometers, sphygmomanometers, chemicals for histology fixatives and stains, in some antiseptics and preservatives, batteries and fluorescent lights. It is a persistent neurotoxin, attacks the body's central nervous system, and can damage a developing foetus.

## Waste

The NHS produces 600,000 tonnes of clinical and domestic waste a year. This is made up of the equivalent of 408,900 tonnes a year of clinical, infectious and pharmaceutical waste, which includes, for example, blood bags, human tissue, infectious material, cytotoxic waste and used syringes (Environment Agency. Personal communication, 11 December 2001). It also produces 200,000 tonnes of domestic waste a year, which includes paper, bottles, cans, or kitchen scraps (Department of Health, 1999/2000). In 1999/2000 disposal of clinical waste cost the NHS £31 million and domestic waste cost £11 million (Department of Health, 1999/2000).

Most hospital domestic waste goes to landfill. Clinical waste is incinerated. Landfilling or incinerating waste exact an environmental cost. Both methods destroy finite primary resources that could be recycled. Landfill sites produce methane and $CO_2$, which are greenhouse gases that contribute to climate change. Toxic chemicals deposited in landfill sites include volatile organic compounds, pesticides, solvents and heavy metals. Modern incinerators that are properly operated are less polluting than their predecessors. However, incineration can release particulate matter, acidic gases and particles, heavy metals and organic compounds.

Landfill sites have been shown to be associated with an increased maternal risk of having a baby with congenital abnormalities or low birth weight, though this conclusion is contested (Fielder, Poon-King and Palmer et al., 2000; Elliott, Briggs and Morris et al., 2001; Roberts,

Redfearn and Dockerty, 2000; McNamee, 2001). Studies of workers at incinerator plants and populations and farm animals living near incinerators show evidence of exposure to dioxins, organic compounds, heavy metals, and mutagenic compounds (Committee on Health Effects of Waste Incineration, 2000: ch. 5). Although clinical waste incineration contributes a relatively small proportion of all dioxin releases in the UK annually, it is mainly responsible for dioxin emissions from waste incineration plants (Dyke, Foan, Wenborn and Coleman, 1997; Alcock, Gemmill and Jones, 1998). A critical review of the literature on the health impact of incineration suggests that the findings of many studies are not generalisable and that it is difficult to tie health effects to particular pollutants, particularly where the effects are delayed and intergenerational. Nevertheless, these pollutants have been associated with respiratory disease and impaired lung function, neurobehavioural changes, haematological effects, cardiovascular effects, gastrointestinal and liver abnormalities and reproductive and foetal developmental effects (Committee on Health Effects of Waste Incineration, 2000).

## Travel

Health service staff and visitors to health service facilities are largely dependent on transport by car. By 2000 more than 17 million people in the UK, 70 per cent of those working, usually travelled to work by car (Department of Environment, Transport and the Regions, 2001). If health sector workers follow this trend, this means about 700,000 journeys to work by car daily. National surveys show that over three-quarters of journeys to local hospitals by health service users are by car, as are about half of visits to GPs and pharmacies (Office for National Statistics, 2001: table 12.4).

Transport is the fastest growing source of greenhouse gases implicated in global warming. By 1994, road transport contributed 23 per cent of all carbon dioxide ($CO_2$) emissions and 38 per cent of volatile organic compounds which when interacting with sunlight produce ground level ozone (Department of Transport, 1996: Table 2.10; Department of Environment, Transport and the Regions, 2000: table 2.8). Numerous studies also suggest that air pollution is an aggravating, rather than a causal factor, in ill health and in earlier deaths, especially among elderly people, or those with advanced lung or heart disease (Dora, 1999; Katsouyanni et al., 1997; Health Education Authority, 2000:8–10; Wolff and Gilham, 1991; Schwartz, 1997). The Committee on the Medical Effects of Air Pollution (COMEAP) estimates that in the UK, small particulate matter ($PM_{10}$) annually contributes to 10,500 hospital admissions for respiratory problems and the probable earlier death of 8,100 people in urban areas. It also estimates an additional 500 to 9,900 hospital admissions and between 700 and 12,500 earlier deaths due to the impact of ground level ozone (COMEAP, 1998: tables 1.1., 1.2). In 1997 in the UK, 3,559 people were killed, 42,967 seriously injured and 280,978 slightly injured in road accidents (Cm 4386 1999:87).

Traffic noise is associated with the disruption of memory, attention and problem solving abilities. Busy roads also hinder independence in children and undermine neighbourhood social support networks and so have an impact on the health of communities and mental health of individuals.

This health burden has an economic cost for the NHS. One estimate suggests that each admission to hospital for respiratory problems that could be avoided, could save the NHS £1,400–2,500 (Department of Health, 1999: table 1). This would put the cost of pollution-related admissions nationally at between £17m and £60m. Traffic accidents in 1997 were estimated to cost NHS over £420m per year (London Health Observatory).

## Energy

Hospitals are intensive users of energy, and it is both the design and operation of buildings that are the causes. Hospital design has changed with a shift to deeper plan buildings that use more electricity for lighting, heating and ventilation. The NHS uses 46 million gigajoules of energy, equivalent to 0.64 per cent of the national energy usage (DOH, 1999/2000) and produces about 7.5 million tonnes of $CO_2$ per year (Building Research Establishment, 2001:2). A typical acute hospital consumes energy equivalent to 16 tonnes of $CO_2$ per bed space per year or in total about 8700m$^3$ of $CO_2$ – enough to fill over 60 six-bed wards (Building Research Establishment, 1999:5). With about 23,650 acute beds, London would produce about 378,400 tonnes of $CO_2$ per year – enough to fill 1,419,000 six-bed wards. Hospitals' energy consumption has also risen with their more intensive use of sophisticated medical and IT equipment. Just PC use in acute hospitals in London could consume 11,409,600 kWh a year – enough to run 3,260 average households (Building Research Establishment, 1999:8–10, Jochelson, 2002c:106).

A growing international literature explores the impact of climate change on health and disease patterns (McMichael and Haines, 1997; Haines, McMichael and Epstein, 2000; Epstein, 2000; Epstein, 1997). An Expert Group on Climate Change and Health drawn together by the Department of Health, concluded that the UK is likely to experience warmer but wetter winters and warmer and drier summers. This will have benefits and costs for health in the UK (Department of Health, 2001a:21–8).

On the positive side: the panel estimates that by 2050 excess winter deaths will have declined by perhaps 20,000 per year, from the current annual estimate of 60,000–80,000 cold-related deaths. On the negative side: heat related deaths occurring in the summer could increase to around 2,800 a year; cases of food poisoning linked to warm weather which currently stand at about 100,000 cases per year, will continue to increase by about 10,000 cases per year by 2050. By 2050 indigenous malaria caused by *Plasmodium vivax* could become re-established. Ozone depletion which leads to increased UV radiation is likely to cause an increase in skin cancer and eye damage unless individuals try to limit their exposure. At today's emissions levels, the UK could expect 30,000 extra cases of skin cancer per year by 2050 and 2,000 excess cases of cataracts each year by 2050. UVB radiation also contributes to photo-chemical smog and ground level ozone, which is likely to cause several thousand associated deaths and several thousand episodes of illness per year from respiratory conditions.

It is beyond the remit of this study to calculate an exact economic, environmental or health cost from the activities of the NHS, but by implication its activities bear a cost for individuals and for society in the loss of human and physical resources. A study of a Canadian hospital found that its 'ecological footprint', i.e. the total area of productive land and water required to produce the resources consumed by the hospital, and assimilate its waste, was 719 times larger than its actual land area (Germain, 2001/02). Assuming the NHS uses resources to the same intensity, this would mean its foot print was 16,537 square kilometres, equivalent to a country midway between the size of Northern Ireland and Wales. This excess consumption and waste will contribute to environmental and ecological degradation with an eventual impact on health. This is at odds with government policy which for the past decade has sounded the cause of sustainable development and efficient use of public resources.

## Government policy on sustainable development

In 1990, with the publication of *This Common Inheritance: Britain's Environmental Strategy*, the UK signalled its intent to incorporate prin-ciples of sustainable development into government policy (Cm1200, 1990). This was developed further by the 1999 White Paper, *A Better*

*Quality of Life. A Strategy for Sustainable Development for the UK.* The report recognised that current economic activity was wasteful and polluting, threatened long-term economic opportunity and human health, and where it ignored the needs of the poorest people, was not sustainable. It suggested that sustainable development could ensure 'a better quality of life for everyone, now and for generations to come' if government policy focused on social progress for all, effective protection of the environment, prudent use of natural resources and high and stable levels of economic growth and employment (Cm 4345: para 4.6).

In 2001 the government set up a Cabinet Committee on the Environment, and appointed Green Ministers responsible for integrating environmental issues into their policies and operations. As part of the Greening Government campaign, there are now targets for the government estate ranging from the increasing the use of renewable energy and reducing water consumption, to recovering value from office waste, to using timber from sustainable forests and recycled paper.

Over the past decade there have also been a series of policy initiatives across government in support of its sustainable development strategy. On the social front, as part of strategies for tackling poverty and social exclusion, the government has stressed the importance of building local economies through regeneration and neighbourhood renewal. It has tried to tackle low incomes through tax schemes and raising the minimum wage, and it has focused on improving educational attainment, and reskilling people who are unemployed. A Department of Health consultation paper, *Tackling Health Inequalities* suggests, that the NHS 'as a major employer and major business' can address inequalities and regeneration through 'its investment in staff and capital, the purchase of services, and the development and regeneration of local economies'. It specifically recommends that 'NHS procurement of goods and services helps, wherever possible, to stimulate local economies and enhance the employability of vulnerable groups, especially in disadvantaged areas' (Department of Health, 2001b: para 4.15).

On the environmental front, the government's strategy for waste management, *Waste Strategy 2000 for England and Wales*, aims to minimise the volume of waste, promote recycling rather than disposal, pass the cost of waste disposal onto the polluter, and encourage the creation of new markets in recycled materials (Waste Strategy, 2000). *A New Deal for Transport* (1998), recommended reducing car usage by providing alternative forms of transport – public transport, cycling, walking – and reducing the need to travel by linking transport and land planning. The report was one of the first to make explicit links between transport and its health effects and suggested that the transport strategy could help meet health targets on reducing accidents, and death rates from heart disease and stroke. It also recommended that hospitals be seen to be taking the lead in changing travel habits' by introducing green travel plans (Department of Environment, Transport and the Regions, 1998). In 1997 the UK signed up to the Kyoto Protocol, which required industrial countries to reduce $CO_2$ emissions by 12.5 per cent below 1990 levels by 2008–2012 in the hope of stabilising the atmospheric concentrations of greenhouse gases. The UK has set its own more ambitious target to reduce $CO_2$ emissions by 20 per cent by 2010. To achieve this, the government has tried to stimulate the take-up of low-carbon technologies by business, encourage the growth of renewable energy to 10 per cent of the energy market, cut transport emissions and promote energy efficiency in the domestic, business and public sector through the Climate Change Levy, a charge on the amount and type of energy used by an institution. The NHS has agreed to reduce the level of primary energy consumption by 15 per cent or 1.5m tonnes of carbon from March 2000 to March 2010 with different specifications set for existing facilities and new capital developments (Department of Health, 2001c).

The government is also undertaking a major restructuring of the NHS. Various White Papers have stressed that the role of the NHS is not just to cure the sick, but also to promote good health, and that social, economic and environmental factors contribute to poor health (Cm 4386:ix, 3; Cm 4818–I:5). In other chapters in this volume, Yach, Chapter 2, makes a plea for this reorientation on a global scale and Lister, Chapter 4, looks at the cost implications of what Wanless (2002) called the 'fully engaged scenario'. Ambitious plans to improve the quality of service also cite the need for efficient use of resources (Cm 3807, 1997). These plans have not been explicitly linked to the sustainable development strategy, though could be interpreted within it. Certainly NHS Estates has published a report examining how environmental sustainability can affect the operational management of health service facilities and have financial benefits. Performance management through Controls Assurance Standards now includes monitoring environmental impact, transport policies and waste disposal policies and a new environmental assessment tool aims to raise environmental awareness among trusts (NHS Estates, 2001; NHS Estates and DTI, 2002).

## Progress towards sustainable development within the NHS

It is a long step from policy statements to practical improvement. The author requested interviews with 45 primary care, community health, mental health and acute care trusts in London, and interviewed a total of 21 Trusts (five Primary Care Trusts, two community health, two mental health trusts and twelve Acute Trusts) in London between November 2001 and January 2002.

Based on these interviews, it seems that progress within Trusts is uneven, and that despite information about improving environmental performance, in practice it is low on Trusts' agenda.

At one end of the spectrum is Lewisham Hospital Trust which regards itself as a responsible corporate citizen. In its environmental and social audit of its activities, it suggests that in delivering healthcare 'a hospital should not adversely affect the health, wellbeing and interests of its staff, the local community, ... patients, their families and carers' and that 'a hospital should be alert to how its activities affect the natural environment'. It believes that 'an improved hospital environment and improved environmental management should result in better and more efficient healthcare delivery'. Other Trusts recognised the impact they had on their local communities whether it was as a local employer, a buyer of goods and services, or as an attractor of traffic which clogged local roads. Some Primary Care Trusts saw themselves playing significant roles in the regeneration of their local areas, and ensured that health impacts were integrated into environmental, educational, economic and public service aims of new community plans.

But for most Trusts, their clinical concerns and targets came first. One acute trust chief executive explained: 'We are aware of the broader context we operate in, but the danger is that if we try to do more than our core activity, our service will fail. We need to focus on our core service and do it well. Our aim is to get patients into hospital faster, and process them more quickly. Quality of care is our first concern. We are under pressure to meet targets with limited human resources.' PCTs especially are not investing resources in the environmental and social agenda. They are focused on developing the new primary care structures and meeting targets ranging from treating cancer and coronary heart disease to reducing waiting times.

Regardless of whether trusts have an environmental policy or not, and whether they are in acute or primary care, they all face similar problems. First, trust boards and senior management are unconvinced of the benefits of an environmental or social agenda. One chief executive explained that he wouldn't disagree with priority of environmental issues but his trust was measured solely by its medical activity, financial health and human resource policies. 'As a conscious citizen it (environmental and social issues) is in our remit, but we need to focus our efforts on performance indicators we are measured by', he explained. Estates managers described the difficulties of placing environmental issues on board agendas, despite the need to meet controls assurance standards. As one manager commented: 'the Board's interest is in balancing budgets, dealing with patients, and service strategy. Clinical issues are foremost. They look at the hospital from a medical point of view.' Finance directors were unenthusiastic as they did not see financial benefits from issues they believed were not part of the hospital's core mission. One PCT commented that its board had simply accepted the risk of not doing anything about the environmental assessment for controls assurance, as it felt it did not have the resources and meeting its clinical targets took priority.

Secondly, trusts felt hampered by their limited human resources. Many Acute Trusts had quickly produced an environmental policy to satisfy one of the controls assurance criteria, but then had done little more. Partly, this was because Trusts did not have an environmental officer to oversee the process of educating different parts of a Trust about the environmental policy and working out the practical implications for following it. Environmental issues simply got tagged onto someone's job responsibilities, and since estates employees already felt overstretched, this meant little would be done in practice. Partly, Trusts felt they lacked information about what environmental and social responsibility meant in practice. PCTs especially often inherited small, under-resourced estates departments responsible for overseeing many small sites scattered over a wide area. Some had no idea of what kind of physical assets they owned, nor the running costs. Without a base-line it was difficult to create an environmental strategy and measure its impact. Other Trusts felt they did not have the resources to bring in an external contractor to conduct an environmental audit.

Thirdly, Trusts had limited financial resources and tended to focus on the short term. One Trust said it was willing to consider how to make energy savings across its 40 facilities scattered across several boroughs. But in practice it had no resources, and spent its estates budget on 'propping things up'. The estates manager stated: 'We are trying to provide a service with inadequate means. The reality of our energy system is figuring out which radiator is going to explode. We cannot just cut out waste, we need more money to simply manage what we have, never mind invest for the future.' Many Trusts spoke of the division between capital and revenue budgets, which meant the focus was usually on the purchase cost of an item, and the long-term maintenance cost was ignored. As one estates manager put it: 'In the health system, for construction projects especially, we tend to go for what is cheapest to build, rather than what is cost effective to maintain in the long run. We focus on capital costs, not revenue savings, so it is hard to justify investments.' Where projects incur a small premium in purchase price but offer great savings in running costs over the long term, this clearly makes no sense.

The case studies that follow show some of the difficulties encountered in trying to make parts of the health sector sustainable, but also suggest that if it learns to use its resources differently, it has the potential to save money, reduce the damage to public health, and in the long term free up resources to reinvest in better healthcare.

## Procurement

European Commission directives state that public sector procurement decisions must be guided by fair and open competition; propriety and regularity and value for money (determined by quality and whole-life costing criteria) (HM Treasury). Despite these regulations, Treasury guidance suggests that it is possible for a public body to support its environmental policies through its procurement strategy (HM Treasury and Department of Transport, Local Government and the Regions). For example, whole life costs assess the value for money of a product on the basis of its price and its running and disposal costs. This should favour products that are more energy-efficient (and result in lower energy bills), or are easier to reuse or recycle (and reduce disposal costs) and so may be defined as better value than equivalent products with lower purchase prices. The Treasury guidance also suggests that contract specifications can use environmental criteria. For example, a contract can specify that a product should not release ozone-depleting gases, or should contain recycled materials or be recyclable. The public body cannot restrict selection of tenders only to providers who offer this, but among the tenders submitted it can select the best value supplier of the specified product.

The NHS Purchasing and Supply Agency (PASA) negotiates national contracts or framework agreements for wide range of products and services. It is tackling environmental issues in two ways. Firstly, as part of the 'Greening of the NHS' programme, it has assessed its own operations, developed an environmental policy, and was certified to ISO 14001 (an internationally accredited environmental management tool) in June 2000. It has since published its first corporate environmental report detailing its progress on environmental issues. Secondly, as part of its environmental management strategy it is assessing the environmental impact of its purchasing practices. It is hoping to develop a register of environmentally preferable products or services, which it defines as 'those that are less harmful to human health and the environment when compared with competing products that serve the same purpose' (NHS Purchasing and Supply Agency, 2001a:11).

But it has some way to go. A survey of PASA buyers (the agents who evaluate tenders) in 2001 found that 56 per cent of respondents were unaware of environmental issues, and 40 per cent did not know whether products contained controversial substances (Davey, 2001). The survey showed that some buyers considered running costs as well as price, but only infrequently were disposal, recycling, refurbishment, administrative and other indirect costs taken into account (NHS Purchasing and Supply Agency, 2001b:13). PASA's survey of suppliers showed that 86 per cent of top management placed some importance on their organisation's environmental performance, but only 11 per cent were ISO 14001/EMAS certified, and just 9 per cent had published an environmental report. Sixty four per cent did not make any environmental claims about their products, and among those that did, just 3 per cent complied with recognised standards. Eighteen per cent made no effort to reduce the quantity of packaging applied to products supplied to the NHS (NHS PASA, 2002:3–10).

There is clearly considerable work to be done in making environmental issues part of tender specifications, making whole life costing part of the procurement process and persuading significant suppliers that there is money to be made in developing environmentally sensitive manufacturing processes and products. A few existing contracts demonstrate what is possible. PASA has contracts for the recycling and reuse of prosthetic limbs, and for the reconditioning and reuse of wheelchairs and hearing aids. These contracts, it suggests, allow savings in natural resource use, support government guidelines on waste management which preference reuse and recycling over disposal, and may offer considerable price savings (NHS Purchasing and Supply Agency, 2001b:11). It also offers contracts for the disposal and recycling of special and hazardous waste such as used engine oil and tyres (NHS Purchasing and Supply Agency, 2001c:26–7).

A PASA survey of NHS Trusts was still in progress at time of writing. Initial perusal of replies suggested that Trusts were willing to include environmental criteria in their procurement policies, but needed resources and training to enable them to do this. Author interviews with London Trusts also suggested that few had introduced environmental criteria for purchasing, and many had no policy planned. Three Trusts – St George's, Newham and Lewisham Hospital Trusts – had begun to introduce environmental criteria into purchasing. One South London Trust, for example, had audited tender applications for a pest control contract, to assess whether potential contractors could comply with the Trust's environmental policy in addition to the usual requirements. Many procurement officers believed that environmentally sensitive procurement was likely to be more expensive, but this Trust found environmentally aware procurement decisions could be cost neutral or offer savings. Recycled photocopier paper, for example, was more expensive than ordinary paper, but the next best environmental option – paper made from accredited sustainable forests – was cost neutral. Recycled toner cartridges for printers and photocopiers also gave sizeable savings. This Trust also used its procurement strategy to create a safer and healthier working environment when it decided to remove mercury thermometers and sphygmomanometers from its wards. The hospital has no record of how much mercury it carried, but it may have been as much as 18 kilograms (Jochelson, 2002a:40).

## Waste

Government waste strategy, at least since the mid-1990s, has emphasised the 'waste hierarchy' prioritising waste reduction, re-use, recycling, composting, and energy recovery, over disposal. Yet no Trusts interviewed for this study had systematic policies in place following these criteria. The focus of Trusts' waste management strategies over the past decade has been on developing appropriate waste disposal systems to satisfy legal requirements (the Environmental Protection Act specifies a 'duty of care' on hospitals making them responsible for the safe and lawful disposal of clinical waste or risk a criminal offence), and on reducing the costs of disposal. Efforts at waste reduction have focused on waste stream segregation rather than minimisation.

All Trusts interviewed had problems enforcing waste segregation on wards. Domestic waste is often deposited in clinical waste bags, and so is disposed of at a higher cost (Jochelson, 2002b: 73). Improper disposal of sharps can be dangerous: various studies showed a 4–10 per cent incidence of sharps injuries in domestic staff and porters, who were most likely to be injured when transporting waste bags. These groups usually have the lowest uptake of hepatitis B vaccine, and so are vulnerable to potential infection (Gyawali, Rice and Tilzey, 1998; Smedley, Coggon, Heap and Ross, 1995; Chapman, Verow and Poole 1996; Audit Commission, 1997:25). Recycling projects were often piecemeal, usually championed by individuals with a passion for environmental issues and depended on staff goodwill to take a bag of recyclable material to a central collecting station. Only some Trusts had a Waste Management Officer to monitor waste segregation and volume, educate and train staff and develop a systematic way of collecting material for recycling. These problems are not dissimilar to those described by a 1997 Audit Commission report on the management of hospital waste (Audit Commission, 1997).

Where hospitals develop an effective waste management strategy, they are able to segregate domestic and clinical waste, reduce the volume of clinical waste for incineration, recycle domestic waste and reduce their disposal costs. For example, the Manchester Royal Infirmary (Central Manchester Healthcare NHS Trust) introduced waste segregation, and recycling of paper and cardboard. It found that it could recycle 242 tonnes of materials annually, saving £14,000 in general waste landfill costs, and reduced its waste landfill costs by £7,000 in 1998/99. The Macclesfield District General Hospital (East Cheshire NHS Trust) reduced the waste it sent to landfill from 540 tonnes in 1996/97 to 381 tonnes in 1998/99 with its costs of landfill waste dropping from £33,000 to £18,810 over the same period (NHS Estates, 2000). Waste management and procurement officers seldom collaborate, yet procurement choices can influence the volume and cost of waste created, the environmental impact of purchasing decisions and in the future will help compliance with various EU directives on the disposal of hazardous substances and electronic equipment. Recycling and buying recycled products are one way for a hospital to reduce its environmental impact and its waste disposal costs. Work towards closed material loop cycles either by trusts or equipment manufacturers was not evident.

## Travel

Increasing car ownership and the centralisation of specialist health facilities have attracted greater numbers of staff and patients to hospital sites and cause increased pressure on car parking services. Car parks are expensive to run and divert scarce resources from patient care; expanding car parks only attracts more traffic. Traffic and overspill parking also annoy local residents. Interviews with Acute Trusts in London showed that many sites either had or were developing transport policies. The plans try to encourage walking, cycling, travelling by public transport and car sharing and discourage driving alone. In most cases Trusts' efforts at developing a green travel plan were due to local authorities making it a condition of planning permission for new developments. In 1998 some 25 local authorities reported using planning conditions. By 2000, 152 authorities were doing so (Department of Environment, Transport and the Regions, 2001b: paras 6.10, 6.22).

Some inner city hospitals have virtually no parking at all. For example, Great Ormond Street, with a staff of 2,200 has a 110-space car park, used largely by clinicians working on different sites. Yet many staff still depend on a car for their sole use. A survey conducted by a Hospital Trust in North West London showed that 43 per cent of their staff travelled in their cars alone to work, and of these 60 per cent did not use their car for work duties. A similar survey by a Hospital Trust in South London showed that 46 per cent travelled by car. These fairly low car-use figures probably reflect how London travel patterns differ from national trends with fewer commuters by car.

An example of a well developed and monitored green travel plan, but outside London, is that at Addenbrooke's Hospital, which lies three miles from the centre of Cambridge. The hospital has a staff of 5,000 but only 3,365 car spaces, of which 2,475 are reserved for staff. The lack of car parking spaces and planned hospital expansion forced the Trust to look at travel alternatives. By 1997 they had developed the *Access to Addenbrooke's* scheme. The scheme reduced the availability of car parking spaces to staff who lived locally or had alternative means of transport. Staff who car-shared were given preferential access to the car park, and could rely on an emergency get-you-home service. To encourage biking, the Trust offer interest-free loans for cycles and mopeds, provided training for inexpert cyclists, improved parking, roads and showering facilities and offered a cycle repair service. To encourage use of public transport, Addenbrooke's liaised with the local and county councils and with bus companies on developing bus routes, better timetabling, and better waiting facilities, and sold weekly tickets at a discount. To encourage patients and visitors to use public transport, travel information was sent out with appointment schedules. The impact of the *Access to Addenbrooke's* scheme is evident in changed travel behaviour. Between 1993 and 1999, car usage among staff dropped from 74 per cent to 60 per cent, cycling increased from 17 per cent to 21 per cent and bus usage also climbed from 4 per cent to 12 per cent. Government tax incentives also allow staff using a cycle for work purposes to claim a mileage allowance.

## Energy

The health sector has had a long history of concern about energy efficiency and has met previous energy reduction targets. Yet a telephone survey conducted by MORI in 2001 for the Government's Energy Efficiency Best Practice Programme found that while more than 80 per cent of NHS Trust chief executives and finance directors knew that they could save money by being more energy-efficient, few were treating the issue as a priority (Rowland, 2001). This attitude was also evident from interviews conducted with Acute and Primary Health Care Trusts in London. Some acute hospital Trusts had an energy policy and energy manager to push an energy reduction strategy through the Trust. But other Trusts believed their capital and maintenance budgets were too small to allow energy efficiency investments.

In 2001 there were 148 Private Finance Initiative building schemes approved for the NHS in England with an approximate capital value of £4.5 billion (Audit Commission, 2001:10). This building programme offered an opportunity to use energy efficient and sustainable design to reduce the resource burden and running costs of the health infra-structure. A study of low-energy hospitals by NHS Estates, concluded that energy-efficient design resulted in energy consumption that is 50 per cent lower than in a standard designed hospital of similar function. Lower energy consumption meant lower energy and maintenance costs and a saving of 1,500 tonnes of $CO_2$ per year for a typical 300-bed acute hospital (NHS Estates, 1994:3) For example, Wansbeck General Hospital in Northumberland saved £273,000 over three years in energy bills, and emitted 6,000 tonnes less of $CO_2$ compared to an equivalent hospital (Department of Environment, Transport and the Regions, 1999). St Mary's Hospital on the Isle of Wight emitted 3,141 tonnes of $CO_2$ compared to the standard 4,853 tonnes for a similar traditionally designed hospital (NHS Estates, 1997).

The government has been keen to encourage energy-intensive institutions to install combined heat and power (CHP) systems. For example, the Royal Free Hampstead Hospital in North West London, is a single-site, energy-intensive building consisting of a tower block and 50 lifts. The gas-driven CHP unit installed in 1995 generates electricity more cleanly and cheaply than the grid, waste heat is used to heat water, create sterilising steam, and heat the building. In summer the steam is vented to chillers to cool the building. The scheme has had a positive environmental impact: it is more energy-efficient than buying energy from the grid; gas is cleaner; the new chillers do not use CFCs; and $CO_2$ emissions have been reduced from about 40,000 tonnes before installation to 26,000 tonnes now. The scheme also has had a positive financial impact on the Trust. The system cost £4–5 million, but since the Trust saves about £872,000 a year, it has easily recouped its costs. The Trust is also exempt from the Climate Change Levy and has benefited from the reduction in employer national insurance contributions.

Several Trusts have also signed up to 'green electricity' contracts. The Cabinet Committee on the Environment set a target of 10 per cent of electricity claimed from renewable sources by March 2008. In January

2002 PASA negotiated a new contract that will supply 20 per cent of electricity to NHS from renewable sources without a price premium.

## Conclusion

The government has committed itself to modernising and investing in the NHS. Adding sustainable development principles and goals to daily decision-making might feel like another unreachable target imposed on NHS staff. And at a time when there is confusion among staff and users about the purpose and values underpinning the NHS, sustainable development might appear tangential to a healthcare system. Yet sustainable development complements NHS values in two ways. Firstly, it builds on the idea that the NHS can promote good health. The 1944 White Paper which outlined the founding principles of the NHS, for example, suggested that the NHS ought to exist for 'the promotion of good health rather than only the treatment of bad' (New, 1999:22). A more recent version of NHS 'core principles' by the NHS Confederation in 2000 states that 'the NHS will help keep people healthy and work to reduce health inequalities' and explains that good health 'depends upon social, environmental and economic factors' (NHS Confederation, 2000). Secondly, a commitment to sustainable development principles builds on the public service ethos of the NHS: the idea that its activities are driven by concern for the welfare of others and the common good, rather than by profit (New, 1999:30–2).

If the NHS is to take the sustainable development strategy to heart, it needs to look at it as an opportunity to find innovative ways of running its infrastructure that reduces costs to the environment, health and its budget. For this to happen, there needs firstly, to be a clear commitment from the Department of Health and the NHS that sustainable development is integral to the mission of the NHS to prevent ill-health. Sustainable development should not be marginalised as 'an estates issue', but should inform how the NHS uses its resources, conducts its activities and acts in the community.

Secondly, senior NHS management and policy makers need to recognise the financial and health costs of continuing with 'business as usual', and the potential benefits of thinking and acting differently. Thirdly, Trust boards and senior managers need to recognise that sustainable development can become part of their corporate mission and be integrated into every part of trust management. They need to commit themselves to this publicly, and then begin to look at how to implement sustainable development principles holistically across their organisations, rather than as piecemeal gestures. Finally, sustainable development is about working in partnership. For the NHS, this means developing cross-disciplinary partnerships for health across the organisation.

The NHS is changing, and if it has the will and vision, it can show that using public resources in a sustainable way means not just providing a high quality public service, but using those resources – financial, human and material – in a way that builds community, protects the environment and safeguards health for the future – aims that are congruent with its founding principles.

# References

Alcock, R., Gemmill, R. and Jones, K. (1998) 'An updated UK PCDD/F atmospheric emission inventory based on a recent emissions measurement programme', *Organohalogen Compounds*, 36:105–08

Arnold, M.B. and Day, R.M. (1998) *The Next Bottom Line. Making Sustainable Development Tangible*. Washington: World Resources Institute

Audit Commission (1997) *Getting Sorted: the safe and economic management of hospital waste*. London: The Commission

Audit Commission (2001) *Building for the Future: the management of procurement under private finance initiative*. London: The Commission

Building Research Establishment, (BRECSU) (1999) *Energy Consumption in Hospitals*. DETR energy consumption guide 72, Watford: BRE

Building Research Establishment (BRECSU) (2001) *Energy Efficiency in Hospitals: a pathfinder for management and staff*. General information leaflet 57, Watford: BRE

Chapman, J., Verow, P. and Poole, C.J.M. (1996) 'Comment', *Occupational Medicine*, 46, 5:382

Cm1200. Department of the Environment (1990) *This Common Inheritance: Britain's environmental strategy*. London: The Stationery Office

Cm 3807. Department of Health (1997) *The New NHS. Modern. Dependable*. London: Stationery Office

Cm 4386. Department of Health (1999) *Saving Lives: Our Healthier Nation*. London: The Stationery Office

Cm 4345. Department of Environment, Transport and the Regions (1999) *A Better Quality of Life. A Strategy For Sustainable Development for the UK*. London: The Stationery Office

Cm 4818–I. Department of Health (2000) *The NHS Plan. A Plan for Investment. A Plan for Reform*. London: The Stationery Office

COMEAP Report (1998) *The Quantification of the Effects of Air Pollution on Health in the United Kingdom: Executive Summary*. HMSO, http://www.doh.gov.uk/hef/airpol/airpol7.htm

Committee on Health Effects of Waste Incineration (2000) *Waste Incineration and Public Health*. Washington DC: National Academy Press

Davey, A. (2001) *NHS PASA environmental strategy. Presentation at 'Sustainability in Public Services' conference*, London, 27 November

Department of Health, Estate Return Information Collection (ERIC) (1999/2000)

Department of Health ad-hoc group on the economic appraisal of the health effects of air pollutants (1999) 'Economic appraisal of the health effects of air pollution report', http://www.doh.gov.uk/hef/airpol/eareport.htm

Department of Health (2001a) *Health Effects of Climate Change in the UK: an expert review for comment*. London: The Stationery Office

Department of Health (2001b) *Tackling Health Inequalities: consultation on a plan for delivery*. London: DoH

Department of Health Circular (2001c) *New energy efficiency targets: climate change programme*, April

Department of Health, Estate Return Information Collection (ERIC), 31 March 2002

Department of Environment, Transport and the Regions (DETR) (1998) *A New Deal for Transport: better for everyone*. London: The Stationery Office

Department of Environment, Transport and the Regions (1999) *The Government's Sustainable Development Strategy: what does it mean for the UK health sector?*. Sustainable development factsheets, 22 September, http://www.environment.dtlr.gov.uk/sustainable/factsheets/health/index.htm

Department of Environment, Transport and the Regions (2000) *Transport Statistics* Great Britain. London: The Stationery Office

Department of Environment, Transport and the Regions (2001) Transport statistics: travel to work. Personal travel factsheet 3, March, http://www.transtat.dtlr.gov.uk/facts/ntsfacts/travwork/travwork.htm

Department of Environment, Transport and the Regions (2001b) *Take up and Effectiveness of Travel Plans and Travel Awareness Campaigns*. London: The Stationery Office. http://www.local-transport.dtlr.gov.uk/travelplans/effective/index.htm

Department of Transport (1996) *Transport Statistics*. Great Britain. London: The Stationery Office

Dora, C. (1999) 'A different route to health: implications of transport policies', *British Medical Journal*, 318:1686–9

Dyke, P.H., Foan, C., Wenborn, M., and Coleman, P.J. (1997) 'A review of dioxin releases to land and water in the UK', *The Science of the Total Environment*, 207(2,3):119–31

Elliott, P., Briggs, D. and Morris, S. et al. (2001) 'Risk of adverse birth outcomes in populations living near landfill sites' *BMJ*, 323:363–8

Epstein, P.R. (1997) 'Climate, ecology and human health', *Consequences*, 3, 2:3–19

Epstein, P.R. (2000) 'Is global warming harmful to health?' *Scientific American*, http://www.sciam.com/article.cfm?articleID=0008C7B2-E060–1C73–9B81809EC588EF21

Fielder, H.M.P., Poon-King, C.M. and Palmer, S.R., et al. (2000) 'Assessment of impact on health of residents living near the Nant-y-gwyddon landfill site: retrospective analysis', *BMJ*, 320:19–23

Germain, S. (2001/02) 'The Ecological Footprint of Lions Gate Hospital', *Hospital Quarterly*, 5 (2)

Gyawali, P., Rice, P.S., and Tilzey, A.J. (1998) 'Exposure to blood borne viruses and the hepatitis B vaccination status among healthcare workers in inner London', *Occupational and Environmental Medicine*, 55, 8:570–572

Haines, A., McMichael, A.J. and Epstein, P.R. (2000) 'Environment and health: 2. global climate change and health', *Canadian Medical Association Journal*, **163**, 6:729–34

Healthcare Without Harm and Environmental Working Group (1998) *'Greening' Hospitals: an analysis of pollution prevention in America's top hospitals.* Environmental Working Group/Tides Centre

Healthcare Without Harm and American College of Nurse-midwives (2001) *Green Birthdays*. Washington: Healthcare without Harm

Health Education Authority (2000) *Environment and Health: air pollution*. London: Health Education Authority

HM Treasury, *Procurement Policy Guidelines*. http://www.ogc.gov.uk/ogc/procurement.nsf/pages/HMTreasuryProcurementGuidance

HM Treasury and Department of Transport, Local Government and the Regions, *Environmental Issues in Purchasing: a note*. http://www.ogc.gov.uk

Jochelson, K. (2002a) 'Purchasing policy', in *Claiming the Health Dividend. Unlocking the Benefits of NHS Spending*, ed. A. Coote, 29–44, London: King's Fund

Jochelson, K. (2002b) 'Waste', in *Claiming the Health Dividend. Unlocking the Benefits of NHS Spending*, ed. A. Coote, 71–82, London: King's Fund

Jochelson, K. (2002c) 'Energy', in *Claiming the Health Dividend. Unlocking the Benefits of NHS Spending*, ed. A. Coote, 97–110, London: King's Fund

Katsouyanni, K. et al. (1997) 'Short term effects of ambient sulphur dioxide and partiuclate matter on mortality in 12 European cities: results from time series date from the APHEA project', *British Medical Journal*, **314**:1658

London Health Observatory, http://www.lho.org.uk/hil/transport.htm

McMichael, A.J. and Haines, A. (1997) 'Global climate change: the potential effects on health', *BMJ*, **315**:805–09

McNamee, R. (2001) 'Does exposure to landfill waste harm the fetus?', *BMJ*, **323**:351–2

New, B. (1999) *A Good-Enough Service. Values, Trade-offs and the NHS*. London: IPPR and King's Fund

NHS Confederation (2000) *NHS Core Principles*. London: The NHS Confederation, August

NHS Estates (1994) *Achieving Energy Efficiency in New Hospitals*. London: The Stationery Office

NHS Estates (1997) *Low Energy Hospitals: St Mary's Hospital, Isle of Wight: final report*. London: The Stationery Office

NHS Estates (2000) *Healthcare Waste Minimisation: a compendium of good practice*. London: The Stationery Office

NHS Estates (2001) *Sustainable Development in the NHS*. London: The Stationery Office

NHS Estates and DTI (2002) *NHS Environmental Assessment Tool*. Leeds

NHS Purchasing and Supply Agency (2001) *Selling to the NHS: a guide for suppliers*. London: PASA

NHS Purchasing and Supply Agency (2001b) *Environmental Report 2000/01*. London: PASA

NHS Purchasing and Supply Agency (2001c) *Strategic Report into the Activity of the NHS Purchasing and Supply Agency in the Waste Management Market*. London: PASA, July

NHS Purchasing and Supply Agency (2002) Executive summary – NHS PASA supplier environmental performance appraisal questionnaire. http://www.pasa.doh.gov.uk/environment/wkgrps/escwg/escwg_supplier_execsummary.doc

Office for National Statistics (2001) *Social Trends no. 31*. London: The Stationery Office

Redlich, C.A., Sparer, J. and Cullen, M.R. (1997) 'Sick building syndrome', *The Lancet*, **349**:1013–16

Roberts, D., Redfearn, A. and Dockerty, J. (2000) 'Health effects of landfill sites: whether results are assertions or evidence is unclear', *BMJ*, **320**:1541

Rossi, M. and Schettler, T. (2000) 'PVC and healthcare', in *Healthcare Without Harm. Setting Healthcare's Environmental Agenda.* Papers and proceedings from the 16 October 2000 Conference

Rowland, R. (2001) 'A source of energy info', *Hospital Development*, **29**:34

Schwartz, J. (1997) 'Health effects of air pollution from traffic: ozone and particulate matter', in *Health at the Crossroads: Transport Policy and Urban Health*, eds. T. Fletcher and A.J. McMichael, London: John Wiley and Sons: 61–82

Smedley, J., Coggon, D., Heap, D. and Ross, A. (1995) 'Management of sharps injuries and contamination incidents in healthcare workers: an audit in the Wessex and Oxford regions', *Occupational Medicine*, **45**, 5:273–5

Solomon, G. M. and Schettler, T. (2000) 'Environment and health: 6. Endocrine disruption and potential human health implications', *Canadian Medical Association Journal*, **163**, 11:1471–6

Wanless, D. (2002) *Securing our Future Health: Taking a Long-Term View. Final Report*. London: The Stationery Office

*Waste Strategy 2000 for England and Wales* (2000) London: The Stationery Office

Wolff, S.P. and Gilham, C.J. (1991) 'Public health versus public policy? An appraisal of British urban transport policy', *Public Health*, **105**, 3:217–28

# 9
# Meeting the Emotional Challenge in Organising Health for the Future

*Annabelle Mark*

## Introduction

'Medical practice is essentially an intellectual pursuit. Being ill is a highly emotional experience' (Kennedy, 2001:281). These words, taken from the Public Inquiry into children's heart surgery at the Bristol Royal Infirmary from 1984 to 1995, are indicative of a growing recognition of the themes of this chapter. First, the need to develop better understanding of the emotions of all participants in systems of healthcare. Secondly that health organisation systems themselves encapsulate inherent tensions between the rational and the emotional. Developing such understanding of emotions may not only improve the perceived effectiveness of healthcare delivery for patients as some doctors now recognise (Stewart Brown, 1998), but may also improve the experience of the workforce who provide this care. What do we need to understand about emotion and its role in the delivery of effective healthcare to patients in order to plan health futures more appropriately?

Emotional perspectives are often only present in discussions about healthcare through the metaphor of narrative (Cwarniawska, 1997; Greenhalgh and Hurwitz, 1999). Whereas the solutions to medical problems are usually approached and perceived intellectually by health professionals as a rational scientific pursuit, they may in fact be seen very differently by others (Stenmark, 2001), especially patients and carers. The rational scientific perspective is just one way of interpreting the world, but it is a world which is largely recognised by clinical scientists, health professionals, funders and planners, whereas the world of patients and carers is dominated by emotion.

The course of action determined by clinicians may in fact reflect just one of several competing interpretations of the 'facts' as presented. This chapter summarises approaches to emotion as a factor in understanding work and organisation and analyses and discusses the importance of emotion as a characteristic in, and of, organisational systems and individual clinicians and patients in the NHS. It provides a discussion of what we know, and what we may need to find out, about emotion and its place in the delivery of effective healthcare in the future.

## Defining and studying emotions at work and in organisations

The exploration of emotion at individual and organisational levels is of increasing interest to scholars of work and organisations as any review of current literatures shows (Fineman, 2000; Hassard, Holliday and Willmott, 2000; Payne and Cooper, 2001; Ashkanasy and Daus, 2002; Sturdy, 2003) and this interest is now extending into the world of healthcare (Mark, 2000; Hinshelwood and Skogstad, 2000; Ashforth and Humphrey, 1995). Ashforth and Humphrey (1995) for example argue that emotions in the workplace are integral to and inseparable from other aspects of organisational life; and that emergence of an historical focus on rationality occurred as a defence against the perceived dysfunction of emotions. Sturdy (2003) illustrates continued ambiguity and confusion, and a lack of adequate theory, about emotions in organisations. Ashkanasy, Hartel and Zerbe (2000) suggest the absence of commentary on emotion in work organisations is based on views that emotion is not a proper subject, accounting only for what might be described as the noise in the system. As a counterbalance, at the beginning of the 21st century, the importance of acknowledging everyday emotions is emphasised in many so-called new ways of working (Ashkanasy and Daus, 2002) and in new scientific understandings of the importance of emotion (Damasio, 1999) as an area of scientific study. Whilst then emotions give meaning to our actions and thoughts, they have only recently become a subject for systematic analysis in organisational theory and their definition in organisational contexts is proving challenging and the subject of continuing debate (Stanley and Burrows, 2001).

A distinction is often made between the 'corporeal' emotions which we share as a physiological response with others and the 'cultural' emotions (Burkitt, 1997), which we learn from and share within the social and cultural context in which we live. As (Ekman and Davidson, 1994) describe, 'corporeal' emotions are part of our physiological responses, for example fear with its attendant physiological manifestations such as a racing heart, shortened breaths and sweating. These primary 'corporeal' (Kempner, 1987) or basic emotions are multi-cultural in their shared interpretations (Ekman, 1992) and include joy, distress, anger, fear, surprise and disgust. These can be contrasted with the cultural manifestation of emotions that arise only in relation to learnt behaviours. These secondary 'cultural' emotions are, research suggests (Evans, 2001), specific to their context and interpretations and can include love, guilt, shame, embarrassment, pride, envy and jealousy.

An example of how both corporeal and cultural emotions may be important in healthcare, is the different manifestations of emotion in the doctor–patient encounter. For example two women from differing ethnic backgrounds may both fear the thought of an impending examination by a male doctor because of the pain involved and what it might reveal as illness. But for one of these women it could also include the addition of guilt and shame at having to violate religious or ethnic cultural norms in acceding to the request to expose her body to a strange man.

Another issue attracting attention is how organisations are themselves expressions of emotions, which are linked through what are described as the shifting complexes of organisational practices (Hassard, Holliday and Willmott, 2000). Within these practices emotion as opposed to technical, rational calculation is described as occupying the core of organisational reality, even though control is often the primary organisational purpose and it is, in the minds of many, predicated on what are assumed to be rational means. Control and emotion may not however be so separable. Fineman (2001) argues 'feeling and emotion are crucial to organisational functioning; they underpin the very essence of control. They also expose the myth of organisational dispassion and rationality.'

## Emotional labour and emotional intelligence

The concepts of emotional labour (Hochschild, 1983) and emotional intelligence (Goleman, 1996) provide the most prominent routes currently available for looking at emotions in organisations. Both rest on the capacity of individuals, rather than characteristics of the organisation. Hochschild's developments of the concept of emotional labour in *The Managed Heart: the commercialisation of feeling* (Hochschild, 1983) discuss role-play with emotions to achieve professional and organisational goals. Management of emotions for a wage (Grandey, 2000) incorporates the notion of what is termed 'surface' and 'deep' acting. In surface acting one regulates emotional *expression*; for example the doctor does not express views about a patient's injuries and how they may have been acquired. Whereas in deep acting one consciously modifies *feelings*, which are our individual internal experiences, in order convincingly to express the desired emotion; for example the nurse who shows sympathy and empathy for patients while on duty detaches herself when the shift is finished. Both surface and deep acting can be employed as strategies with a twofold purpose in healthcare: to maximise patient confidence and cooperation, and minimise staff stress. Role-play thus becomes a critical activity of healthcare provision, where engaging patient confidence is the goal. The pace and duration of patient-clinician engagements have over time both increased in speed, for example with the increased utilisation of day surgery (Hensher, Edwards, and Stokes, 1999) moving from under 18 per cent of all provision in 1985 to over 50 per cent by 2000. As circumstances and context change, so too may the balance between the rational and the emotional in decision processes. Gordon and Arian (2001) argue that emotions come to the fore in times of stress, at the expense of rationality. In the Bristol example, the high death rates in paediatric cardiology led the local medical community, who knew about the problem but felt unable to change it, to give emotional expression to their frustration and anxiety in their description of the services as 'the killing fields' (Hammond and Mosley, 2002:44). This description was also a means to provide distance from a horrific situation in which they would otherwise have been implicated.

Contexual changes reshape shared organisational 'feeling' rules (Hochschild, 1983) which create organisational and team cultures. Where the pace of organisational change means these rules are not fully developed or understood, the potential for failure increases as emotional understanding plays a crucial role in the successful management of change (Kotter and Cohen, 2002). It is readily acknowledged that there is much change in healthcare organisations. Services are being redesigned, new technologies and therapeutic interventions are being developed and executives are seeking to increase efficiency. When these trends are combined with increased diversity and mobility of populations, new and different expectations emerge and need to be managed (Department of Health, 2000a). We can thus speak of a move away from systems based on relationships in the NHS, for example the continuity of care provided by a family doctor, to one based on encounters (Gutek, 1997), where an individual will access a range of providers, often simultaneously. For example advice from NHS Direct through the telephone or Internet may be combined with advice in person from the local pharmacy and a reported encounter of a friend with a GP. In the example of the increasing move to day surgery, more transitory relationships between members of clinical and community teams and patients occur.

Inherent in these changes is a move away from contexts which foster emotional involvement between individuals to ones which require surface expression of emotions which may not be deeply felt by those engaged in what we now understand as emotional labour.

Insights provided by an understanding of the emotional labour process are often linked to the part played by emotional intelligence (Goleman, 1996), which is the individual capacity successfully to manage emotions for oneself and others. Emotional intelligence is beginning to play a prominent part in the training and development of many health professionals (Evans and Allen, 2002; Freshman, 2002).

## Organising emotions in healthcare

The development of theory and methods to describe and analyse emotional labour (Hochschild, 1983) and emotional intelligence (Goleman, 1996), describe the centrality of emotion in contemporary healthcare to everything from decision-making to managing change and workplace stress. While attention to the emotional work required of individual clinical professionals (Smith and Gray, 2001) now acknowledges changing circumstances, much less attention has been given to organisations and their systems. Healthcare organisations as Anton Obholzer from the Tavistock Clinic has suggested, act to contain the emotional and psychological well-being of those inhabiting them, especially where the primary task of the organisation is to provide what he describes as 'the keep death at bay service' (Stokes, 1994). Expressions of emotion occur in healthcare organisations when the patient encounters what they see as 'the system' rather than, or in addition to, individuals within it. An example of this is the fear and frustration generated by long waits in Accident and Emergency Departments where patients or their relatives become angry, not with individuals, but with the perceived ineffectiveness and lack of care within the system for them as people. The generation and management of emotional problems which are seen to be 'caused' by the organisation (Garnham, 2001) is indicative of the values and culture of the organisation. Organisational cultures as Beyer and Nino (2001) point out can provide a means to manage and either inflame or lessen the anxieties posed by uncertainty. Organisational cultures encourage or discourage the expression and experience of emotions, which may engender or diffuse identification and commitment.

Thus a positive culture sensitive to the emotions of anxious patients and carers in A & E will ensure that patients are kept well informed about why they are waiting and how long it will be before they are seen. Thereby emotional heat may be reduced and patients enabled to make more rational decisions about their actions and choices, providing of course that those waiting believe and trust the information given. Belief and trust are in themselves influenced by emotional state and cultural context.

A lack of attention to systemic aspects of emotions in healthcare organisations is related to attempts to neutralise their impact. Their presence may be seen to be dysfunctionally challenging to all involved and providers may therefore draw on a mask of rationality to hide their feelings (Mark, 2001). Such an approach is likely to be embedded in the organisational culture, as the experiences documented in Bristol reveal (Kennedy, 2001). This tragedy in paediatric cardiology was the result of both medical and managerial systemic failures compounded by the failure to acknowledge the growing concerns of families. Rapid changes in both organisations and roles in healthcare may allow such mistakes to occur again, if organisations do not maintain their shared memories as the Chief Medical Officer's Report 'An organisation with a memory' so aptly points out (Department of Health, 2000b). Further crises can also be prevented, or at least curtailed, if those involved in healthcare take steps to prevent their experience of constant changes, staff turnover and reorganisations 'orphaning' (Caddy, 2001) current knowledge and memories. Shared experiences can be the access points to organisational knowledge, as they embody the history of action and emotional effort (Reddy, 2001). As Korzybski (1959) says 'the map is not the territory' unless it incorporates, in the context or this chapter, the highs and lows of emotions. Collective feelings about healthcare shared by patients and other members of the public are also important in creating, in a national system such as the NHS, congruence over the nature of health as a public good. Such emotional collectivity also implies a joint commitment to the purposes of the organisation (Gilbert, 2002).

Healthcare organisations offer a unique opportunity to enhance our understanding of emotion because of their role in society. As Persaud has observed in a review of an Exhibition entitled The Museum of Emotions:

> General hospitals and clinics themselves could be considered as museums or repositories of feelings for they contain the extremes of emotion, from the joy of birth to the hopelessness of death ... The

Museum of Emotions suggests that privacy and concealment are vital in our culture for allowing emotional expression. Such privacy is rarely given to patients in hospital. (Persaud, 2000)

Emotions have a special significance in healthcare organisations because of the subject matter of sickness, health, well-being, life and death which are par excellence, the subject of clinical encounters. Consider for example the emotional dimensions in encounters where patients look to doctors for reassurance, or employees in NHS Direct provide information and support to anxious parents worried about a screaming child's health, or to a middle-aged man who fears he has the symptoms of a heart attack.

Consider also the scandal over the retention and storage of post mortem body parts in the UK NHS, which began at Alder Hey Hospital in Liverpool but was revealed as an issue in many hospitals (Redfern 200l). Strong emotions in relatives of the deceased were aroused by these revelations, even though from a rational scientific viewpoint these emotional responses failed to take account of the benefits to be gained from research. Such a conflict in perspectives is indicative of the emotional distance that can occur between the intellectual world of medicine and the emotional world of the patient or carer. Sensitising individuals in such circumstances is not enough; organisations must develop systematic responses and approaches which ensure issues which have high emotional potential are assessed as part of the organisation's duty to provide quality care. Patients and carers often feel as if they are placing their whole being at the mercy of the health system, and not just the individuals involved in treatment. Patients need to trust that they will be safe, and not fall victim to what Hammond and Mosley (2002) describe as a 'climate of fear' which, the enquiry into childrens' heart surgery in Bristol (Kennedy, 2001), showed can pervade some hospitals and result in a failure to act on evidence that things are going very wrong. The problems in Bristol, as the Public Inquiry revealed, following years of unusually high death rates among children receiving cardiac surgery, were not unknown. Individuals had attempted to raise the issue, but there was a systematic failure to hear claims which were seen as 'emotional'.

Emotions may also be important in healthcare because of links between emotional state and health status. Links have been made between emotional responses and physiology which throw new light for example on the placebo effect (Evans, 2003), demonstrating that it acts as a form of catalyst to the bodies' own defence systems, thus challenging assumptions of its benign role in scientific research to date. In addition, the work of the new medical discipline of psychoneuro-immunology is showing how the suppression of negative emotions can be one of the highest predictors of cancer (Kiecolt-Glaser, 2002), which may have implications for how employers handle workplace stress in the future.

Part of the founding principles of the NHS in the UK after World War II was a belief that removing the fear of ill health and infirmity was the mark of a civilised society. This was best expressed by Beveridge (1945) in his epoch making report through the metaphor of the five giants of want, disease, ignorance, squalor and idleness which were to be slain on the road to post-war reconstruction (Rivett, 1998). The premise was that self-interest for health was best served by a shared community interest in the provision of healthcare. Thus emotion was linked directly to the organisational purpose of the NHS. Like many such visions, a rational justification was soon found. For the NHS, it derived from economic analysis at both national and international levels and economics has remained the dominant analytical paradigm (Issel and Kahn, 1998) for NHS policy makers accountable to the tax paying public. Other paradigms, such as the sociological interpretations of healthcare and its role in society, including a reduction in fear for those who could not previously afford healthcare (Rivett, 1998) have been somewhat submerged in the search for the more usual and dominant purpose of technical and economic efficiency.

The need to redress this balance is emphasised by the insights of reviews which enquired into the Bristol (Kennedy, 2001) and Alderhey (Redfern, 2001; Department of Health, 2000a) scandals. Both emphasised the importance of increased sensitivity to emotional consequences of actions, the need to learn from past mistakes and the need for a more systemic and holistic approach to solving problems. This however may not be sufficient to realise an improved service in the future (Vince, 2001) because as insights from complexity theory suggest, in the increasingly complex nature of healthcare organisation, cause and effect are only coherent in retrospect and do not necessarily repeat themselves (Snowden, 2002). Solutions do not lie in analysing emotions in a 'cognitivist' way (Carr, 2002) with its assumptions that we can always know what will resolve the issues, and people will change their behaviour accordingly. Other strategies are required (Snowden, 2002) to supplement rather than replace assumptions. For example it may be advantageous to participants in healthcare to appreciate and practice creative thought and empathetic anticipation when making future plans at all levels of organisations.

## Emotion in patients' experience and expectations in the NHS

Having considered emotion in the NHS from an organisational perspective, the paper now moves to focus on the experience and expectations of patients. The concept of 'the patient's journey' is a way of understanding how people experience healthcare. It is used as a descriptor in official reports (Kennedy, 2001), and research (Kristjanson and Ashcroft, 1994), and furthermore is at the heart of the government's objective of putting the patient at the centre of health policy. Within their journey through the NHS the patient must negotiate both their individual choices about care and treatment, and their experience of a democratic involvement with the impact of society's choices about what is made available to them as individuals.

Healthcare in the UK at the beginning of the 21st century is no longer just about meeting unambiguous needs, if it ever was. It is increasingly required to contemplate how to navigate boundaries between what is 'required' and 'desired' in the provision of health and what is required or desired in the improvement of lifestyle for individuals and communities. Consider for example the debates over what are described as the new 'lifestyle' drugs such as Viagra, or the role of genetic screening, (Jones and Zimmern, 1999) or the place for cosmetic surgery, within the NHS. Identifying boundaries and how the health budget should be allocated between competing products and treatments, is a key challenge in priority setting at local, regional and national levels. It is also a central part of the new governance framework in which the National Institute for Clinical Excellence (NICE) assesses the efficacy of treatments using what is at root intended to be rational decision processes. However, much of the promotion of products and treatments is emotionally based, as the pharmaceutical industry acknowledges (Bashe, 2001) so rational solutions will not suffice in providing answers. Rationing and priority setting are themselves emotive words that express the inherent conundrum for politicians in allocating resources. The absence of the word 'rationing' in favour of the more positive 'priority setting' confirms a continuing desire to remove emotive issues from debates about resourcing as much as possible.

Current practice within healthcare policy continues to reinforce the dominance of the rational perspective, for example in the rise of Evidence Based Medicine (EBM) which seeks to determine the most appropriate treatments given the current vast quantities of research, both good and bad, which is available (Gray, 1996), even though one can argue that the implementation of EBM is itself a social construction (Fitzgerald et al., 1999). Studies of the development of clinical practice provide cogent arguments for acknowledging the need to incorporate the role of feelings and emotion as part of the implementation process in any practice development if one is to improve both professional and patient uptake of the conclusions of EBM applications. This is shown in studies of glue ear (Dopson et al., 1999), adult asthma (Dawson et al., 1999) and in the review article by Dopson et al. (2003).

Trust, itself a feeling or emotion (Lahno, 2002) through which vulnerability is revealed and exposed (Korczynski, 2000), is at the heart of healthcare where the patient is vulnerable in both interpersonal and organisational contexts (Kennedy, 2001). Lahno (Lahno, 2002) suggests that if we want to promote trustful interactions we must first form our institutions in ways that allow individuals to experience their interests and values as shared. Where organisational values are in doubt, as they are in relation to an NHS in the early 21st century rocked by scandals of clinical negligence and faced with the imposition of a new set of values which underpin the governments modernising agenda for public services in the UK, individual patients become sceptical about how much they can trust the organisation as well as the practitioners within it. Furthermore the success or failure of an intervention or innovation, either medical or managerial, may be marred by a lack of appropriate attention to emotional barriers to change (Gould, Stapley and Stein, 2001), which create dysfunctions in terms of both individual and organisational decision processes and thereby make outcomes from planned change less reliable.

Attempts to bolster trust in the system are now being supported by organisational initiatives for quality and control, for example through the development of clinical governance and the Commission for Health Audit and Inspection.

The place of trust as part of the emotional labour process for clinical staff has its own cost to clinical professions in terms of stress and burnout (Mayor, 2002), especially when the organisational pressures to increase activity are perceived to be under-resourced. Such pressure not only affects staff (Baruch and Winkelmann–Gleed, 2002) but may also increase risks to patients, as recent research on the positive effects on patient mortality of good human resource management has suggested (West et al., 2002). Control within healthcare organisations now extends to attempts to control the demands of patients (Mark, Pencheon and Elliott, 2000) which in turn are heavily influenced by emotions.

## Two contexts: the macro and the micro

Healthcare is unique in facing profound issues in both content and context which touch primary emotional responses such as joy, fear and distress (Roter et al., 1995) about both the beginning and end of life experiences, as well as culturally constructed secondary emotions, for example frustration when those involved fail to acknowledge their mistakes through shame and embarrassment (Davidoff, 2002). Two contexts are important in understanding the emotional journey for individuals through healthcare organisations. The journey through life is the *macro context* for patients and each encounter with healthcare provision will affect their responses to future encounters. Each individual journey through the system at specific times of particular needs, desires or public health requirements is *the micro context*, which will be experienced, at least in part, according to influences from the macro context. It is the micro context which has been the focus of healthcare organisation to date; but an understanding of the impact of the macro context, given the changing relationships already set out, also merits further discussion.

Each patient micro experience acts as a creator and carrier of meaning (Mark, Pencheon and Elliott, 2000) between multiple encounters. Increasingly, encounters in care and treatment processes are short and may indeed involve no face-to-face contact as technological substitutes such as NHS Direct are developed. The impact of changing care processes which allow less time and personal attention may be somewhat ameliorated by the caring role of the nurse, who uses professional skills to interpret the emotional context for the patients (Mark and Shepherd, 2001; Munro et al., 2000) but even so the ability to respond appropriately implied by these new forms of communication in care and treatment is further limited by a reduction in sensory information (Miller, 2003). Fear and frustration can also reduce patients' use of new systems. Such reactions may be behind the under-use of NHS Direct by the older age groups (Mark and Shepherd, 2001; Munro, Nicholl, O'Caithain and Knowles, 2000).

Evidence from increasing contemporary use of alternative practices (Kaptchuk, 2002) which usually promise a more personal relationship between patient and provider, may also be a reaction to the distances increasingly created between doctors and their patients. Reduction in emotional engagement may also delay recovery (Balint, 2000) and certainly is likely to increase dissatisfaction with the service.

## Organising health for the future

The hope implicit in the policy purpose of putting the patient at the centre of healthcare will be achieved only when there is acknowledgement that patients' involvement with the NHS is an emotional as well

as scientific clinical one. Such acknowledgements need to be incorporated into developments in professional education and training and in
healthcare provision and its organisation. The imperatives for changes
in approach lie in the following three observations, which derive from
the foregoing discussion on emotion in health and healthcare.

Firstly what appears as routine in the nature of their work for clinical
professionals is often alarming and exceptional for those who witness it
as lay 'subjects' (Mark and Shepherd, 2001). Secondly a policy to drive
up capacity to deliver efficiencies may distance and desensitise those
involved in healthcare from the emotional impact of their actions on
those witnessing or receiving service. Thirdly differing expectations and
outcomes may be sought between patients and healthcare professionals;
a patient's first priority is usually to feel better and only then to understand why.

Conflicts between what patients want and expect and what professionals give are rooted in part in disjunctions between a rational (professional) response to what is experienced as an emotional (patient)
problem. The bridge between such disparities is trust between the
patient and clinician, and the working assumption for many, that professionals will seek to move these disparate points closer together
(Tudor Hart, 1996). When trust is compromised, outcomes can be compromised, and this in turn can aggravate the problem by begetting alternative ways of managing with the particular emphasis of monitoring
and control. However such approaches fail to account for the fact that
the essence of the problem often lies out with such devices which in
themselves may exacerbate the problem. If trust is to be regained what
is required is not just a way of showing that the professionals and the
organisations which employ them are developing capacity for dealing
with an unknowable future created out of changes in science, technology, demographics, political economy and public expectations, but a
demonstration that the organisations will acknowledge and help to deal
with emotional detritus of a past experience shaped by public scandals
like Bristol (Kennedy, 2001), or perceived private scandals experienced
in particular individual encounters.

Micro encounters influence the macro perspective. An understanding
of the significance given to emotion at different stages of the life journey of individuals needs to be integrated into organisational learning
and development programmes. This would support the development
of Hochschild's 'feeling rules' which need to be shared as part of what
(Lahnos (Lahno, 2002) identifies as trust building communities. Such
activities are however context dependent and cannot be mapped across

from one organisation to another, although the mapping process employed may be transferable.

Three areas in particular offer opportunities to review organisational responses to an acknowledgement of the importance of emotion in healthcare: Firstly there are educational opportunities for incorporating a macro journey agenda, for example through the innovative approach to learning taken by the Peninsula Medical School based in South West England. Here students are learning medicine based on the patient life-cycle, starting training with prenatal work and proceeding through to medicine for old age. The objective is to move away from the reductionist approach to the body, where it is just a collection of itemised problems towards a more holistic perspective which incorporates awareness of a person's whole health and well-being including emotions as experienced by individuals and through their membership of social groups like families or small communities at different life stages. There is also a role for education and training in developing appropriate emotional understanding within and between professional groups. For example clinicians have only relatively recently developed methods of peer review and support, and even now some of these processes do not pay enough attention to the emotional content implicit in review, support and inevitably, monitoring and guidance. Neglecting the emotional impact places even the rational elements of this process in jeopardy, if they are construed so as to generate defence mechanisms against implied or explicit criticism. A greater ability to understand and characterise emotion explicitly within organisations will also have both ethical and legal benefits as patients in Bristol testified (Kennedy, 2001).

Secondly there are opportunities and challenges in the way policy is created and enacted within the wider social context. Consider the emotional impact of the re-organisations of the 1980s and 1990s which appeared to many involved in the service as providers, patients or carers, to cast aside attempts to provide a caring organisational context, in favour of a competitive approach. This set up emotive dissonance, that is a mismatch in feelings between expectations and delivery (Hochschild, 1983) for many of those giving and receiving healthcare.

In the wider social context of healthcare, peer group (Mestrovic, 1997) rather than political or organisational control is paramount; because organisational structures are more transitory and there is increasing cynicism (Fineman, 1997) about the manipulation of emotion to serve organisational purposes. Professional peers groups located through professional (Dent, 1998) rather than an organisational identity, may not be easy to challenge (Department of Health, 2000a) because they are rooted in emotional need to belong and are relatively impervious to external attempts to control them (Mark and Scott, 1992). Furthermore, attempts to manage emotions for organisational purpose may fall foul of the paradox that if emotion is more and more organisationally managed, the less it will feel truly emotional (Rafaeli and Worline, 2001).

Thirdly there are opportunities in patient perceptions and participation as one seeks to align expectation and utilisation with the system of healthcare. For example what makes people worry enough to seek advice, then get angry when there is a delay in receiving it? A number of interpretations for this area exist; some will be based on learnt behaviour as described through the social construction theory (Suttie, 1988), some will be based on physical responses and the use of past experience to understand the present as described through cognitive theory (Frijda, 1988). Much will also depend on the individual's attitude to risk; especially if, as Lupton (Lupton, 1999) suggests, risky behaviour increases in response to the intensification of control and predictability of modern life. Each individual response involves the interplay between rational and emotional process. Sorting these factors is complicated because the patient and organisational perspectives have also been disrupted by a wider corruption of emotions in society (Mestrovic, 1997), which inclines a breakdown of trust in general between the public and those seeking to persuade, influence and paradoxically, to serve them (Beck, 1992).

These broader concerns also include international and scientific contextual influences on healthcare organisations. Put simply, international comparisons influence expectations for provision, and scientific developments change expectations for intervention (Sykes, 2000; Appleby and Rosete, 2003). There is also need for the acceptance of the emotionally challenging aspects of risk and uncertainty by all the stakeholders, if we are to avoid a population divided between the chronically ill and the worried well (Brashers, 2001).

## Conclusions

The interplay between emotion and rationality provides a useful interpretation of how different participants from patient through to policy makers see what is happening in healthcare. It also helps to distinguish how the values of the organisation and its key players are changing and being operationalised, and how individuals reflect and enact these changes within organisations. A recognition of the emotional impact on the future of what appears to be almost continuous change in the organisation, and its effect on staff and patients, must be given greater consideration if the NHS is to retain its reputation as an institution for the public good. This is imperative not least because, as research has revealed, the effects of recent changes have led to emotional dysfunction of many of its key players (Williams, Michie and Parrani, 1998; Mayor, 2002) and the emotional health of the organisation itself is then jeopardised (Obholzer, 1994). Yet in healthcare perhaps more than any other context, patients must start from the assumption of a state of well-being in those people and organisations they entrust to provide healthcare.

Perhaps of most significance, for the claim that emotion should become part of the terrain of healthcare organisation and its systems, is an acceptance of the idea that knowledge based on reason is implicitly valued for its *emotional* role, and that this aknowledgement is essential to the maintenance of trust between patient and professional. Reason is, in this context, the third party agent used as a justifiable tool to persuade patients to set aside potentially negative emotional responses such as fear, to allow extraordinary interventions to occur.

Emotion represents a dynamic but fundamental process for both the individual and the organisation and its explicit incorporation is important to the future success of changing healthcare organisations and systems. Paradoxically, a full acknowledgement of the role of emotion may not only allow for emotional expression in personal encounters but also enable the more rational aspects of healthcare systems to operate to better effect (Mark, 2000). The challenges discussed in this chapter, if they elicit a positive response, can at best both enhance and enrich heathcare for all participants, and at worst prevent some of the systems failures of the sort which have occurred in recent times.

# References

Appleby, J. and Rosete, A.A. (2003) 'The NHS: keeping up with public expectations?', in eds Park, A., Curtice, J. and Thomson, K. et al., *British Social Attitudes: the 20th Report – Continuity and Change over Two Decades'*, Ch. 2. London: Sage

Ashforth, B.E. and Humphrey, R.H. (1995) 'Emotion in the workplace: a reappraisal', *Human Relations*, **48**, 2:97

Ashkanasy, N.M. and Daus, C.S. (2002) 'Emotion in the workplace: the new challenge for managers', *Academy of Management Executive*, **16**, 1:76–87

Ashkanasy, N.M., Hartel, C.E.J. and Zerbe, W.J. (2000) *Emotions in the Workplace: Research, Theory and Practice*. Westpoint, CT: Quorum Books

Balint, J. (2000) *The Doctor, His Patient and the Illness.* Edinburgh: Churchill Livingstone

Baruch, Y. and Winkelmann–Gleed, A. (2002) 'Multiple commitments: a conceptual framework and empirical investigation in a community health service trust', *British Journal of Management*, **13**, 4:337–58

Bashe, G. (2001) 'Emotion – the new brand integrator', *Pharmaceutical Executive*, **21**, 6:100–05

Beck, U. (1992) *Risk Society: Towards a New Modernity.* London: Sage

Beveridge, W. (1945) *Social Insurance and Allied Services.* HMSO, CMND 6404

Beyer, J. and Nino, D. (2001) 'Culture as a source, expression and re-inforcer of emotions in organisations', in *Emotions at Work, Theory, Research and Applications in Management*, R.L. Payne and C.L. Cooper, (eds), Chichester: John Wiley and Sons

Brashers, D.E. (2001) 'Communication and uncertainty management', *Journal of Communication*, **51**, 3:477–97

Buchan, J. (2000) 'Health sector reform and human resources: lessons from the United Kingdom', *Health Policy and Planning*, September, **15**, 3:319–25

Burkitt, I. (1997) 'Social relationships and emotions', *The Journal of the British Sociological Association*, **31**, 1:37–55

Caddy, I. (2001) 'Orphan knowledge: the new challenge for knowledge management', *Journal of Intellectual Capital*, **2**, 3:236–45

Carr, D. (2002) 'Feelings in moral conflict and the hazards of emotional intelligence', *Ethical Theory and Moral Practice*, **5**, 1:3–22

Czarniawska, B. (1997) 'A four times told tale: combining narrative and scientific knowledge in organisation studies', *Organisation*, **4**, 1

Damasio, A. (1999) *The Feeling of What Happens: Body, Emotion and the Making of Conciouseness.* London: Heinemann

Dawson, S., Sutherland, K., Dopson, S. and Miller, R. (1999) 'Changing clinical practice: view about the management of adult asthma', *Quality in Healthcare*, **8**:253–61

Davidoff, F. (2002) 'Shame: the elephant in the room', *British Medical Journal*, **324**:623–4

Dent, M. (1998) 'Hospitals and new ways of organising medical work in Europe: standardisation of medicine in the public sector and the future of medical autonomy,' in *Workplaces of the Future*, P. Thompson and C. Warhurst (eds), Basingstoke: Macmillan Business, 204–24

Department of Health (2000a) *The NHS Plan: a plan for investment a plan for reform*, London

Department of Health (2000b) 'An organisation with a memory: report of an expert group on learning from adverse events in the NHS', London: The Stationery Office

Dopson, S., Miller, R., Dawson, S. and Sutherland, K. (1999) 'Influences on clinical practice: the case of glue ear', *Quality in Healthcare*, **8**:108–18

Dopson, S., Locock, L. and Gabbay, J. et al. (2003) 'Evidence-based medicine and the implementation gap', *Health*, July, **7**, 3:311–30

Donnelly, L. (2003) 'Inquiring mind', *Health Service Journal*, **113**, 5841:22–3

Ekman, P. (1992) 'An argument for basic emotions', *Cognition and Emotion*, **6**:169–200

Ekman, P. and Davidson, R. J. (1994) *The Nature of Emotions: Fundamental Questions.* New York: Oxford University Press

Evans, D. (2001) *Emotion: the Science of Sentiment*. Oxford: Oxford University Press

Evans, D. (2003) *Placebo: the Belief Effect*. London: Harper Collins

Evans, D. and Allen, H. (2002) 'Emotional intelligence: its role in training', *Nursing Times*, **98**, 27:41–2

Expert Group on Learning from Adverse Events in the NHS (2000) *An Organisation with a Memory*. London: The Stationery Office

Fineman, S. (1997) 'Emotion and management learning', *Management Learning*, **28**, 1:13–26

Fineman, S. (2000) *Emotion in Organizations*, 2nd edn. London: Sage

Fineman, S. (2001) 'Emotions and organisational control', in *Emotions at Work, Theory Research and Applications in Management*, R. Payne and C. L. Cooper (eds) Chichester: John Wiley and Sons

Fitzgerald, L., Ferlie, E., Wood, M. and Hawkins, C. (1999) 'Evidence into practice? An exploratory analysis of the interpretation of evidence', in *Organisational Behaviour in Health Care: the research agenda*, Dopson, S. and Mark, A. (eds) Basingstoke: Macmillan, 189–206

Freshman, B.R.L. (2002) 'Emotional intelligence: a core competency for health-care administrators', *Health Care Management*, **20**, 4:1–9

Frijda, N.H. (1988) 'The laws of emotion', *American Psychologist*, **43**, 5:349–58

Garnham, P. (2001) 'Understanding and dealing with anger, aggression and violence', *Nursing Standard*, **16**, 6:37–42

Gilbert, M. (2002) 'Collective guilt and collective guilt feelings', *The Journal of Ethics*, **6**, 2:115–43

Goleman, D. (1996) *Emotional Intelligence*. London: Bloomsbury

Gordon, C. and Arian, A. (2001) 'Threat and decision making', *Journal of Conflict Resolution*, **45**, 2:196–215

Gould, L., Stapley, L.F. and Stein, M. (2001) *The Systems Psychodynamics Approach of Organisations: integrating the group relations appraoch, psychoanalytic and open systems perspectives*. New York: Other Press

Grandey, A.A. (2000) 'Emotional regulation in the workplace: a new way to con-ceptualize emotional labor', *Journal of Occupational Health Psychology*, **5**, 1:95–110

Gray, J.A.M. (1996) *Evidence Based Healthcare*. Edinburgh: Churchill Livingstone

Greenhalgh, T. and Hurwitz, B. (1999) 'Narrative based medicine', *British Medical Journal*, **318**:48–50

Gutek, B. (1997) 'Dyadic interactions in organisations', in *Creating Tomorrow's Organisations: a handbook for future research in organisational behaviour*, C. Cooper and S. Jackson (eds) Chichester: John Wiley, 139–56

Hammond, P. and Mosley, M. (2002) *Trust me I'm a Doctor: the guide to getting the best from your doctor*. London: Metro Publishing

Hassard, J., Holliday, R. and Willmott, H. (2000) *Body and Organization*. London: Sage

Hensher, M., Edwards, N. and Stokes, R. (1999) 'The hospital of the future: inter-national trends in the provision and utilisation of hospital care', *British Medical Journal*, **319**:845–18

Hinshelwood, R.D. and Skogstad, W. (2000) *Observing Organisations: Anxiety, Defence and Culture in Healthcare*. London: Routledge, an imprint of Taylor and Francis

Hochschild, A.R. (1983) *The Managed Heart: commercialisation of human feeling*. Berkeley: University of California Press

Issel, M.L. and Kahn, D. (1998) 'The economic value of caring', *Healthcare Management Review*, **23**, 4:43–53

Jones, J. and Zimmern, R.L. (1999) 'The impact of new technologies in medicine: mapping the human genome the genetics revolution', *British Medical Journal*, **319**:1282

Kaptchuk, T.J. (2002) 'The placebo effect in alternative medicine: can the performance of a healing ritual have clinical significance?', *Annals of Internal Medicine*, **136**, 11:817–25

Kempner, T. (1987) 'How many emotions are there? Wedding the social and autonomic components', *American Journal of Sociology*, **93**, 2:263–289

Kennedy, I. (2001) *Learning from Bristol: the report of the Public Inquiry into children's heart surgery at the Bristol Royal Infirmary 1984–95*. Norwich: The Stationery Office, CM5207(1)

Kiecolt-Glaser, J.K. (2002) 'Emotions, morbidity and mortality: New perspectives from Psychoneuroimmunology', *Annual Review of Psychology*, **53**:83–107

Korczynski, M. (2000) 'The political economy of trust', *Journal of Management Studies*, **37**, 1 January:1–21

Korzybski, A. (1959) *Science and Sanity: An Introduction to Non-Aristotelian Systems and General Semantics*. Chicago: Institute of General Semantics

Kotter, J.R. and Cohen, D.S. (2002) *The Heart of Change: real life stories of how people change their organisations*. Harvard: Harvard Business School Press

Kristjanson, L.J. and Ashcroft, T. (1994) 'The family's cancer journey: a literature review', *Cancer Nurse*, **17**, 1:1–17

Lahno, B. (2002) 'On the emotional character of trust', *Ethical Theory and Moral Practice*, **4**, 2:171–89

Lamb, M.C. and Cox, M.A.A. (1999) 'Implementing change in the National Health Service', *Journal of Management in Medicine*, 29 November 1999, **13**, 5:28–9

Lupton, D. (1999) *Risk*. New York: Routledge

Mark, A. (2001) 'Organising emotional health,' in *Organisational Behaviour and Organisational Studies in Healthcare*, L. Ashburner, (ed.) Basingstoke: Palgrave – now Palgrave Macmillan, 204–17

Mark, A., Pencheon, D. and Elliott, R. (2000) 'Demanding healthcare', *International Journal of Health Planning and Management*, **15**, 1:237–53

Mark, A. and Scott, H. (1992) 'General management in the NHS,' in *Rediscovering Public Services Management*, 1st edn., H.J. Willcocks Leslie (ed.) London: McGraw-Hill, 197–234

Mark, A.L. (2000) *Colouring the Kaleidoscope: Emotion in Healthcare Organisation*, Maureen Dixon Essay Series. London: Nuffield Trust

Mark, A.L. and Shepherd, I.D.H. (2001) *'Don't Shoot the Messenger': an evaluation of the transition from HARMONI to NHS Direct in West London*, Working Paper. London: Middlesex University

Maslow, A.H. (1954) *Motivation and Personality*. New York: Harper Row

Mayor, S. (2002) 'Emotional exhaustion and stress in doctors are linked', *British Medical Journal*, **324**:1475

Mestrovic, S.G. (1997) *Postemotional Society*. London: Sage

Miller, E.A. (2003) 'The technical and interpersonal aspects of telemedicine: effects on doctor–patient communication', *Journal of Telemedicine and Telecare*, **9**, 1:1–7

Munro, J., Nicholl, J., O'Caithain, A. and Knowles, E. (2000) *Evaluation of NHS Direct First Wave Sites: second interim report to the Department of Health*. Sheffield: ScHARR Medical Care Research Unit University of Sheffield

Obholzer, A. and R.V.Z. (1994) *The Unconscious at Work: Individual and Organizational Stress in the Human Services.* London: Routledge, an imprint of Taylor and Francis

Payne, R.L. and Cooper, C.L. (2001) *Emotions at Work: theory, research and applications for management.* Chichester: John Wiley

Persaud, R. (2000) 'The Museum of Emotions', *British Medical Journal,* **320,** 7246:1413

Rafaeli, A. and Worline, M. (2001) 'Individual emotion in work organizations', *Social Science Information,* **40,** 1:95–124

Reddy, W.M. (2001) 'The logic of action: indeterminacy, emotion and historical narrative', *History and Theory,* **40,** 4:10–33

Redfern, M. (2001) *Royal Liverpool Children's Inquiry Report.* London: The Stationary Office

Rivett, G. (1998) *From Cradle to Grave: fifty years of the NHS,* London: Kings Fund

Roter, D.L., Hall, J.A. and Kern, D.E. et al. (1995) 'Improving physicians' interviewing skills and reducing patients' emotional distress: a randomized clinical trial', *Archives of Internal Medicine,* **155**:1877–84

Smith, P. and Gray, B. (2001) 'Emotional labour of nursing revisited: caring and learning 2000', *Nurse Education in Practice,* **1**:42–9

Snowden, D. (2002) 'Complex acts of knowing: paradox and descriptive self awareness', *Journal of Knowledge Management,* **6,** 2:100–10

Stanley, R. and Burrows, G. (2001) 'Varieties and functions of basic emotions', in *Emotions at Work: theory, research and applications in management,* R. Payne and C. Cooper (eds) Chichester: John Wiley

Stenmark, M. (2001) *Scientism: Science, Ethics and Religion.* Aldershot: Ashgate Publishing Limited

Stewart Brown, S. 1998, 'Emotional well being and its relation to health', *British Medical Journal,* **317**:1608–9

Stokes, J. (1994) 'Institutional chaos and personal stress,' in *The Unconcious at Work: individual and organisational stress in the human services,* A. Obholzer and V. Zagier Roberts (eds) 121–8

Sturdy, A. (2003) 'Knowing the unknowable? A discussion of methodological and theoretical issues in emotion research and organizational studies', *Organization,* **10,** 1:81–106

Suttie, I.D. (1988) *The Origins of Love and Hate,* first published in 1935. London: Free Association Books

Sykes, R.B. (2000) *'New Medicines: the Practice of Medicine and Public Policy',* London: The Stationary Office

Tudor Hart, J. (1996) 'Caring effects', *The Lancet,* **347**:1606–8

Vince, R. (2001) 'Power and emotion in organisational learning', *Human Relations,* **54,** 10:1325–51

West, M.A., Borrill, C.S. and Dawson, J.F. et al. (2002) 'The link between the management of employees and patient mortality in acute hospitals', *International Journal of Human Resource Management,* **12,** 8:1299–310

Williams, S., Michie, S. and Pattani, S. (1998) *Improving the Health of the NHS Workforce: report of the partnership on the health of the NHS workforce.* London: Nuffield Trust

# Part 3

# People and Knowledge

# 10
# The Role of the Patient in Healthcare Reform: Customer, Consumer or Creator?

*Ian Greener*

## Introduction

Today, successful services thrive on their ability to respond to the individual needs of their customers. We live in a consumer age. Services have to be tailor-made not mass-produced, geared to the needs of users not the convenience of producers. The NHS has been too slow to change its ways of working to meet modern patient expectations for fast, convenient, 24 hour, personalised care.

Secretary of State for Health (2000), *The NHS Plan*, sec. 2.12,

Choice is very, very important, for two reasons. First, because it is absolutely in accord with the sort of society in which we live. People make choices in their lives continually. Second, because I think choice is the primary means by which you can drive the NHS to better focus on the needs of its individual patients.

Alan Milburn, Secretary of State for Health, interviewed by Nicholas Timmins (Timmins, 2002:132)

In post traditional contexts, we have no choice but to choose how to be able and how to act ... choice has become obligatory

(Giddens, 1994b:75–6)

This chapter examines the role of the patient in healthcare reform, the extent to which patients can transform themselves into health 'consumers', the reasons why the state appears to require this transformation, and the implications of attempts to reform health services along these lines. It concludes by presenting an argument that patients may well be able to meet the requirement of being health 'customers', but not, as the present reforms appear to require, health 'consumers'. First, we present a brief analysis of attempts by the UK government to introduce health consumerism, first through the 'internal market' of the 1990s, then New Labour's approach to 'patient choice' outlined in their policy documents the 'Extending Patient Choice', and 'Delivering the NHS Plan' (Department of Health, 2001a, 2001b; Secretary of State for Health, 2002). We consider how the role of the patient has changed, and how these changes are an attempt to change relationships between patients and doctors (especially general practitioners), and the extent to which this appears to rest upon an approach to human agency attributable to Giddens (1998, 2002). Empirical evidence based on general practitioner selection and patients' expectations of choice in Bristol is presented and the paper concludes with discussion of the difference between patients as 'customers' and patients as 'consumers'. It argues that, while the former may be possible, the latter is not. The implications of this analysis for attempts at health reform are then the subject of comment.

## The health consumer: a brief theoretical history

According to writers such as Marie Haug (Haug and Lavin, 1983; Haug and Sussman, 1969), public disaffection with vested interest professional groupings manifested itself in the 1960s and 1970s in resistance and opposition to providers of services that professed to know better than their clients, who 'revolted from below' in an attempt to reshape medicine. Theoretical studies of healthcare systems concluded that, if only health services could become more responsive to 'consumer' need, they would better serve the interests and needs of their patients (Segal, 1998). It is no coincidence that the rebellion against medical power occurred at the time of the collapse of Keynesian macroeconomic policy, with its associations of paternalism and patriarchy (Jessop, 1999), and its replacement with an approach which stressed enterprise and the virtues of individualism (Beardwood, Walters, Eyles and French, 1999; Irvine, 2002; Mishra, 1990).

The NHS managerial reforms of the early 1980s were made in the name of providing better 'customer service', with the vocabulary of private sector business enthusiastically imported to that end (Meerabeau, 1998). Patient 'choice' assumed centre stage in the 1989 White Paper, 'Working for Patients' (Secretary of State for Health, 1989) and was further embedded in the NHS with the publication of The Citizen's Charter in 1991 (Department of Health, 1991). This committed health workers to clear standards in public services, there-by introducing a 'mimic consumerism' into health services (Klein, 2000:179–80). This consumerism was 'mimic' in form because it was not driven by patient choice, but by the choices of patients' 'agents', either general practitioners or health authorities.

But any pretence of implementing a fully-blown quasi-market for health services in the 1990s appears to have quickly disappeared; the language of health policy moved from talk of competition to contestability, and from purchasing to commissioning (Sheldon, 1990). The reforms are now presented by Secretaries of State for Health of that time more in terms of the creation of market-like mechanisms as managerial additional tools rather than attempts to create a dynamic full market for health (Ham, 2000). There is also evidence that purchasing decisions were rather less radical than they might have been (West, 1998), and that, the reforms in retrospect, were a case of the 'bland leading the blind' (Klein, 1998).

Upon their electoral victory in 1997, New Labour characterised the internal market as a pariah; 'The market *forced* NHS organisations to compete against each other ... (Secretary of State for Health, 1997, sec. 2.14, italics added), 'Hospital clinicians ... have been deliberately pitted against each other' (2.12) in a 'system in which individual organisations were *forced* to work to their own *agendas* rather than the needs of individual patients' (2.10, italics added). The internal market fragmented health services (2.10), caused unfairness (2.12), distortion (2.14), inefficiency (2.16), bureaucracy (2.18) and instability (2.20). Labour, upon coming to power, claimed to have 'abolished' the internal market (1.3), but retained 'the separation between the planning of hospital care and its provision' (2.6), and thereby the essential separation between purchaser and provider introduced by the Conservatives. But it was not long before the health market began to assume centre stage once more in UK health policy. By 2000, a rather more obviously consumerist notion of the patient was once again apparent.

The 'vision' of the NHS plan (Secretary of State for Health, 2000) was to offer 'people fast and convenient care' (1.1) with services available 'when people require them, tailored to their individual needs' (1.1). In 2001, the government published a consultative document 'Extending Patient Choice' (Department of Health, 2001b) proposing that patients should not only be more active in choosing their primary care provider, but also, in consultation with a patient advisor, the type of treatment they should receive, where, and when. By this time, the notion of the 'Expert Patient' had also been mooted, suggesting that chronic care patients could become self-medicating managers of their own care (Department of Health, 2001a; Wilson, 2001). Finally, we have seen the return of an internal market of sorts in the NHS, apparently driven by consumer choice, but also with fixed prices for treatment (Secretary of State for Health, 2002). This is a remarkable turnaround in policy.

Part of the justification for the revival of the health consumer comes in the literature concerning the potential of 'self-help' groups to provide an alternative support mechanism beyond, or instead of, the medical profession. This revival has been given increased salience from the growth of the Internet, which has a number of implications for health consumerism. For example, the Internet can facilitate the formation of worldwide self-help groups, with heavy reliance on experiential knowledge, which can be seen as a challenge to medical knowledge and expertise (Hardey, 1999). The challenge is all the greater if linked to expressed dissatisfaction with conventional medical encounters; either because they are predicated upon a model of the passive patient subject to the decisions of an all-powerful doctor, or because of a loss of faith in medical expertise where it has been unable to 'cure' the problems put before it, or both.

Access to Internet self-help groups provides patients with the opportunity to challenge the treatment prescribed by their medical practitioner, and potentially puts the doctor in a position where he or she must now justify both diagnosis and treatment (Burrows, Nettleton, Pleace et al., 2000; Hardey, 1999, 2001). It also creates the problem of how those using self-help groups are meant to discriminate between the alternative prescriptions or lay advice offered them in relation to any problem for which they are looking for help and advice. Coexistence between 'unconventional' and 'conventional' medicine creates a 'new medical pluralism' (Cant and Sharma, 1999). Hardey (1999, 2001) argues that his examinations of self-help groups provide evidence that participants are able to discriminate between narratives that proposed alternative treatments, but another reading of his material, in which use of Internet self-help groups is 'not a problem any more than it is on TV or a magazine', (Hardey, 1999:828), could arguably be used to undermine the credibility of the lay expertise offered in such groups. The potential for anonymous access to self-help groups by commercial interests, and the lack of systematic medical knowledge on offer there, raises concerns about the quality of information on offer, and the ability of those using such groups to discriminate between information about practices which are more or less safe and harmful, especially where drugs are becoming more available on the Internet making it possible for consumers to by-pass the medical profession completely.

Much of the theoretical justification cited by authors considering the rise of health consumerism, especially in relation to the Internet, points to the work of Giddens as providing a theoretical basis for its analysis (Burrows and Nettleton, 2000; Burrows et al., 2000; Hardey, 1999). Giddens' work is hugely important to a discussion of the role of the patient in healthcare for two reasons. First, because it provides an intellectual justification for 'positive welfare', presenting a dynamic model of welfare recipients that casts them in the role of active participants in contrast to the often passive role in which patients have been placed in health services in the past. Giddens, in being central to the formulation and development of the 'Third Way' (Giddens, 1994a, 1998, 2002), has moved from presenting a sociological description of the state of welfare to a political prescription for the restructuring of the welfare state (Nettleton and Burrows, 2003). This prescription has been hugely influential; the term 'The Third Way' has been used prominently in health policy documents (Secretary of State for Health, 1997, 2000), and Giddens continues to be invited to contribute as an 'insider' to the publications of organisations such as 'Policy Network' (Giddens, 2003), where his work appears alongside that of Prime Minister Tony Blair and politician Peter Mandelson.

The second sense in which one can argue that Giddens' work is hugely important is that health policy in the transition from 20th to 21st century embodies many of his distinctive taken for granted assumptions about the reform of welfare. It is thus to Giddens' work we now turn in an effort to understand the theoretical underpinnings of New Labour's health consumerism.

## Theorising health consumerism

Giddens' work on the 'risk society' (see especially Giddens, 1994b), suggests that scientific (or 'traditional') knowledge is coming increasingly under question as it intrudes ever more into our lives. We are increasingly required to make lifestyle choices that involve us in assessing and making calculations about the potential risks that effect our lives, forcing a reflexivity of the self that is quite different from that which has been 'traditionally' been required of us. The construction of the self is an ongoing project in an effort to construct ontological security (Giddens, 1991) that requires a process of reflexively organising evidence and information in order to strengthen or undermine our emotional security (Burrows and Nettleton, 2000). The search for answers to health problems outside of conventional medical encounters is a manifestation of this process. In the context of our health, one supposes, we must analyse in detail our food and exercise regimes and assess their costs and benefits in terms of our well-being. This approach appears to be based on a model of behaviour and approach to assessment of risk and calculation deriving from Giddens' theories of human agency and structuration (see especially Giddens, 1984) which is designed to 'illuminate the duality and dialectical interplay of agency and structure' (Bernstein, 1989:23). Structuration is based on the analysis of human practices, which Giddens sees as recursive, so that activities are 'not brought into being by social actors but are continually recreated by them via the very means whereby they express themselves as actors. In and through their activities agents produced the conditions that make these activities possible' (Giddens, 1984:2). Agency and structure are bound by history in a processual and dynamic way (Rizter, 1996), making the theory appear at least a little market-like; the dynamism and reflexivity of structuration theory present an portrayal of humans as active participants in their interactions with others. This is largely because of the way in which Giddens treats structures.

Giddens's definition of structures are that they are effectively based around rules and resources (Giddens, 1984:17; Thompson, 1989:62), alongside a radical claim that structure only exists in and through the activities of human agents. Structure is in no way external to human action, it is what gives shape or form to human life but 'not *itself* that form and shape' (Giddens, 1989:256, italics in original). Structure is always both constraining and enabling. Structures, in turn, are reproduced through practice as social systems, they are 'instantiated' as such, but they are also manifest in the 'memory traces orienting the conduct of human agents' (Giddens, 1984:17). The structural properties of social systems are therefore the 'outcome of the practices they recursively organise' (Giddens, 1984:25). For Giddens, the social system is 'the product of a stable personality working routinely. Social order exists because we are creatures of habit' (Craib, 1992:158). This is a little contradictory; we appear to be creatures of habit, but of reflexively moving away from those habits should they prove to be ineffective. This requires a degree of calculative rationality that, as we noted above, appears to be rather over-stating the case in much human behaviour (Greener, 2002; Hoggett, 2001).

It is not clear from reading Giddens what he believes are the limits to the reflexivity with which he endows his actors (Craib, 1992:150; Hoggett, 2001:39). This reflexivity manifests itself in actors being able to understand and interact with their social world, and is clear in Giddens' concept of the 'autotelic self' (Giddens, 1994:192–4), which is at the heart of his 'positive welfare' prescriptions (see especially Giddens, 1998). Within this, we find subjects seeking to 'translate potential threats into rewarding challenges' (Giddens, 1994b:192), not acknowledging the structural restraints upon actors because they appear to exist primarily cognitively. We can all, then, 'awaken the giant within' (Robbins, 2001), and overcome the barriers to challenging doctors to secure we are empowered in our relationship with the medical profession.

All of this would be important in the agenda of sociologists only, had Giddens' work not become such an important influence on the development of the 'Third Way', and had it not assumed such a central role in the subsequent health policy of New Labour in the UK (Giddens, 1994a, 1998, 2002; Nettleton and Burrows, 2003; Westergaard, 1999). In a real sense, Giddens has assumed a position assumed by Keynes in the inter-war period; he has gone from being a policy commentator to providing the intellectual justification for a particular range of ideas that policy makers have adopted. The Third Way has gone from being a policy description to a policy prescription. But the problems we have identified as characterising structuration theory suggest that the health consumer model might be based on assumptions about human behaviour that are unsustainable, and possibly even dangerous. We will test the model in our empirical study below, after we have considered health consumerism from perspectives other than Giddens'.

Hugman (1994) differentiates between 'market consumerism', in which the consumer is purchaser and the state regulator, and 'democratic consumerism' in which the consumer is not the purchaser, but is involved in defining the service. Hugman argues that the internal market introduced by the Conservatives in 1991 contains elements of both models. As such the internal market of the 1990s was a clear example of a consumerist policy as patients were now meant to take responsibility for making provision to meet their own needs where possible. In the same text, Abercrombie (1994) appears to endorse this, noting that authority had shifted from the producers of public services to its consumers. The more radical model outlined in 2002 by the Secretary of State for Health (2002), based apparently around individual patient choice, is perhaps the clearest attempt at 'market consumerism' yet.

This positive view of health consumerism is a considerable distance from other sociologists, who note the mechanisms through which doctors 'control' their patients. Fox (1993), shows how doctors control conversations with patients, avoiding questions, and removing patients' individuality in the process. There appears to be little discursive space for patients to assert their individuality as consumers, a situation more akin to Foucault's (1977) description in which the patient is disciplined under the 'gaze' of the doctor. This is not the only line of attack on the reality of the health consumer. Stacey (1998) makes the crucial point that the patient's body is the work object for treatment, raising a series of underlying tensions concerning medical knowledge and power, and the ability of the patient to act as a consumer given such information asymmetries and potential for self-damage. Toth (1996) claims that many of the prerequisites in neo-classical theory for the functioning of a market do not exist in healthcare; we do not have a range of competing goods or high quality information. Lupton, Donaldson and Lloyd (1991) make similar points, noting that patients do not have the bargaining power, freedom of choice, knowledge or the motivation to choose, and also lack the power to challenge medical authority. Gabbott and Hogg (1994) question the extent to which patients are able to assess their doctor's ability to cure or to make evaluations about the type of treatment they are receiving. Shackley and Ryan (1994), whilst acknowledging that patients appear to want more information concerning their treatment, argue they do not necessarily want to make treatment choices and that this is representative of considerable barriers to consumer sovereignty in healthcare. Needham (2003) is perhaps most damning of all, arguing that the government is presenting an artificial 'straw man' comparison between the modern world of competition and consumerism, and the unresponsive public bureaucracies of the past, so falsely concluding that the former is the only solution to health reform when other options are available.

There is also some confusion over notions such as 'customer', 'consumer' and 'citizen' in relation to healthcare. This paper initially follows Mol (1999:85), in differentiating between 'market-based', and 'state-based' approaches. The first attempts to 'configure' the patient as a 'customer who represents his or her desires in the act of buying' (p. 85). There is an immediate problem in this conception, as patients do not purchase their own care in the NHS, having instead to rely upon an intermediary. This automatically moves consideration to 'State-based' approaches to health consumerism. Here the patient is configured into citizen, and consumerism is realised through achieving representation in organisational decision-making. This paper is concerned with 'market-based' consumerism because it appears to be the dominant paradigm of health consumerism in the policy documents discussed thus far. Readers should see Allsop, Baggott and Jones (2002; Needham, 2003) for the limited progress made so far on 'citizenship' and state-based consumerism in the NHS.

To further tidy up the confusion between and within the terms 'consumer' and 'customer', Mullen's (1990) distinction between Type I and II markets may be helpful. In Type I markets, individual users are purchasers, and we will call these 'consumer' markets. Type II markets, where an intermediary such as a doctor makes choices on behalf of the ultimate user, we will call 'customer' markets. There is a clear difference, articulated by Needham (2003:42); 'We can think of the customer as a sub-category of consumer; involved in a specific transaction with a particular supplier, and experienced only for the duration of the transaction.' The difference between consumer and customer is an important one for policy, and one to which we will return below.

Having considered the theoretical basis of health consumerism, we now turn to an empirical investigation of 'consumer choice' in practice.

## An empirical study into 'choice'

To investigate the process through which choices are made in the NHS, in the summer of 2002 I conducted an empirical investigation of parents of children about to attend primary schools in the predominantly middle-class areas of the Fishponds/Staple Hill and Frenchay in Bristol. In total 65 parents participated in focus groups and follow-up interviews about their experiences of choosing their GP, with follow-up questions concerned with their experiences of choosing health services. Ten focus groups were held, followed up by thirty interviews, some of which were conducted with two parents, others with one. The findings were remarkably straightforward. (Greener, 2003a).

When asked how they chose their GP, in excess of 80 per cent of parents answered that they had simply chosen the surgery closest to them (a very similar finding to Wearne, 1998). When asked if they then chose a specific GP within the surgery, around half of the parents stated that there were definitely GPs who they preferred to see (with more women than men expressing a preference for a particular GP), but that resource constraints made it very difficult to see that particular doctor, and so they felt they had little choice in practice. Equally, if they demanded to see a particular doctor, the interviewees were aware that this might lead to a prolonged wait, especially where that doctor was in demand from other patients as well. When asked if they felt they wanted to make more active choices over treatment when with a GP, most parents answered in the negative, often looking slightly puzzled. When further probed for the reasons for this puzzlement, answers such as 'Well you have to trust a doctor' or 'I don't have the expertise' were given. Finally, when asked if they had ever chosen where or when the treatment would be performed, no NHS patient answered in the affirmative (Greener, 2003a).

A small group (five interviews) of those questioned paid for private health insurance. These parents still visited their own NHS GP for an initial diagnosis, but then would, before receiving an NHS referral, contact their health insurance provider to find out to what extent they were covered for the treatment they required. The privately insured patient group did expect to be informed to a greater extent than the NHS group as to what treatment they would receive. They did not have higher expectations to be active participants in the decision-making process about the nature of the treatment, except where the condition was relatively minor, and where a range of possible therapies existed, for example, whether there were choices between physiotherapy, osteopathy or chiropractic.

Another manifestation of election to use private healthcare came from those who were usually NHS patients but who found they were scheduled for a considerable wait before they could receive the determined treatment. In such circumstances they were often happy to use their GP for advice about private sector providers so they could 'by-pass' the waiting list.

Patients did not appear actively to choose their GP, and considered it unlikely they would change practices unless they experienced a dramatic failure of care (a similar finding to Wearne, 1998). Patients did not report making active choices about their treatment unless the treatment they required was relatively minor, and had close substitutes. They did not appear to be especially eager to be a part of the decision-making process about the treatment they were to receive, even within the private sector (even though the group interviewed in this category was very small). No group expected to be consulted as to exactly where they would be treated, but they did expect their treatment to be local. Those parents that paid for private sector health expected to be consulted about the timing of treatment, and for it to involve a minimal wait.

In the context of community care, parents often found themselves in difficult positions with respect to 'choice'. A small group of the parents interviewed (four in total) suffered from chronic diseases of various types and degrees. They appeared torn between the demands made upon them to become more autonomous from the medical profession, and their feelings that they needed increased, rather than reduced support from doctors and community health specialists. Much of this confusion can be traced to the UK's chronic care policy, the 'Expert Patient' (Department of Health, 2001a). This policy suggests that chronic disease sufferers can become increasingly self-managing in their care, and consequently more empowered in the process. Once again this has much in common with the 'Third Way', and with Giddens' analysis of human behaviour. But it carries with it many of the attendant difficulties we discussed above; patients suffering from chronic diseases may well find themselves 'experts' in a particular condition, primarily in line with the expert patient model, through experiential knowledge of their condition. But such knowledge, even where supplemented by some medical knowledge, is incomplete and fragmentary. Equally, there is something rather Foucaultian in attempting to convert chronically ill patients into self-managing self-carers (Wilson, 2001); the shift in discourse has considerable elements of governmentality around it in attempting to persuade patients to make their care a management, rather than illness, problem. Perhaps the most damning criticism of all, however, is that the presentation of the 'Expert Patient' approach carries an explicit association with saving the NHS money by getting chronically ill patients to see their doctors less regularly. On page 29 of the policy document (Department of Health, 2001a), a table lists the 'impacts' of self-management programmes on care services, with every impact being a reduction in medical visits. If such a policy is being implemented to achieve savings, policy makers may well be disappointed. Chronic care patient groups appear to suggest their members want greater rather than less support from the health services, than they are currently experiencing (Multiple Sclerosis Society, 2003).

In terms of the use of the Internet, over 50 per cent of those interviewed said they often used it to find out about health issues. But in contrast to studies we noted above, they often presented the knowledge they had gained from the Internet as being unreliable, inconsistent and of little use. Only a small proportion of parents (two of the interviews) had spoken to their GP about information they had taken from an Internet self-help group, and then it had not helped inform their choice of treatment in a direct way. On this evidence material from the Internet is more likely to be used as a mechanism for getting GPs to justify their selection of treatment in more detail than has been the case in the past, rather than as a direct feed into the process of widening choice, although this remains a possibility.

Finally, those parents who had been admitted to hospital, even where the intervention was routine or minor, were clear that they found their experiences in hospital to be almost entirely choice-free. Even in areas where patients wanted choices (maternity services are a case in point), parents often found themselves unable to assert them because of resource deficiencies (for example, birthing pools not being available because of insufficient staff, or side-rooms being full where patients wanted to pay additional sums to secure them), or for medical reasons, for example the choices they wished to make were no longer available in cases of surgery where their consultants had ruled out alternatives to a given operation upon closer examination of the patient.

The results of this study into choices concerning health contrasted remarkably with those illustrated by the same parents when they discussed their choice of primary school for their children. In contrast to their expectations of health choice, their primary education choice was highly calculative (Callon, 1998), and appeared to demonstrate a highly developed 'feel for the game' (Bourdieu, 1998). They felt they knew how to maximise the chance of getting their child into a school that they had, through a deliberate and prolonged period of evidence-collection, decided was the best for them. Rationality appeared to be extremely contextual, with parents moving from almost passive recipients of healthcare to highly calculative, participative choosers of education within the space of a few sentences.

## A market in healthcare? Implications and conclusions

The empirical evidence and theory presented within this paper suggests that attempts to put in place a market in the NHS based on individual patient choice are likely to be problematic. The relationship many patients hold with health professionals is not one between equals, but a dependent one. Patients feel they need to trust doctors because they are unable to take decisions about the type and location of treatment for themselves, with a consequent reliance upon health professionals who are seen to have specialist knowledge that no amount of personal experiential expertise might be able to replicate.

Medical knowledge is too complex, and any experiential knowledge we hold about the conditions from which we suffer is too fragmentary, too local, to take account of the complexities within our own body, between our condition and the rest of our complex medical system, and between our location within the NHS and the rest of the health service. But trusting health professionals is not easy, and not helped by frequently reported poor communication skills and time pressures in the service (Coulter, 2002a). Self-help groups provide a challenge to medical knowledge based primarily around the experiences of others, but such information loses its context and so much of its legitimacy, when transferred to others. Most people in the UK would not (yet) accept a consultation via email, so assuming we can somehow do better than a personal medical interview, even a flawed one, seems fanciful.

There are also considerable doubts as to whether we can display the degree of reflexivity necessary to be active consumers in a health market (Greener, 2002). Far from the structuration model suggested by Giddens, we as patients do not appear to behave in a dynamic and reflexive manner in dealing with the medical profession. We do not possess systematic medical knowledge, or rely upon doctors simply to provide us with access to the resources the NHS is able to provide; we also depend upon the judgement of community nurses, physiotherapists and other health professionals in order to receive treatment. Even where we attempt to by-pass the NHS through the use of private care, the conventional access point for diagnosis at least is still within the NHS, and still relies upon medical expertise. We are dependent upon health professionals, and must learn to regard this dependency not with hostility, as if it offends our status as empowered individuals, but to remember that dependency is not, as we have been taught in the concept of 'welfare dependency', a negative idea (Hoggett, 2000). Instead, dependency, where we recognise its necessity and enter into it voluntarily, is perhaps amongst the most positive emotions in our repertoire. Doctors often represent an extreme case of information asymmetry, but one that is also apparent in our dealings with community nurses, physiotherapists and other clinicians. It seems odd that we often seem so keen to assume we know more about particular heath conditions than professionals trained in them.

That the relationship between doctor and patient is increasingly under strain is a symptom of several things including pressures on GPs to treat more and more patients, the problems senior consultants often appear to have in communicating with patients, an increased awareness of the limits of medical expertise, and a function of high-profile cases of medical abuse. Equally, as health services become more primary-care focused, we are learning to deal with health professionals in other fields more frequently, especially with nurses to whom many tasks traditionally associated with doctors are now being delegated. We need to put in place systems that attempt to insure against the abuse of the relationship between patient and health professional. We must learn to accept our position of dependency upon health professionals, but equally, there are changes we can make within health settings better to reflect the structural location of patients within it. One way of dealing this is to think of ourselves not as health *consumers*, active participants driving reform and making choices we cannot possibly calculate, but instead as health *customers* (Greener, 2003b). There are important differences.

Health customers, in line with the 'Type II' health market typology, would judge the level of service they believe they have received, and assess health services according to their own expectations of the service as well as to national standards. They recognise the dependencies they have on the medical profession and do not wish to enter into a health decision with medical knowledge as apparently required in the consumer model. As long as patients recognise the information asymmetries implicit in their relationships with health professionals, there is no reason to assume that this service assessment is unviable – it is certainly a far more workable assumption supposing that health consumers can drive the market process in an informed way (the 'Type I' market). Systems need to be more robust in dealing with the concerns patients have with regard to waiting, and also with regard to dealing with medical complaints. It is interesting that comparatively little research still exists that investigates the concerns and preferences of patients, while both the state and representatives of the medical professions appear to believe they are acting on behalf of these interests in healthcare systems.

The medical profession, in a relationship with the patient as customer, needs to improve its capacity to consult and explain (Coulter, 2002b; Elwyn, Edwards and Kinnersley, 1999), if it is to build trusting relationships with patients. In this model patients have to accept that they are reliant on clinicians to 'frame' the health decisions they face. Patients may be able to negotiate treatments once a diagnosis has been performed, but moving towards a model where patients have the possibility, through their use of the Internet, to diagnose and then even medicate themselves by importing medicine, appears simply dangerous. Doctors must learn to explain their decisions rather better, but must continue to take responsibility for the diagnosis, and for the framing of the health choice before the patient. Other health professionals often appear to have better skills in negotiating and discussing care where appropriate, and doctors may have much to learn from them. In cases where there are close substitutes in treatment and little is at stake from choosing between them, greater freedoms may be negotiated, but still the health professional has a substantial role to play in the presentation of that choice.

Health customers would assess the standard of the healthcare they receive. Instead of relying upon crude and unreliable non-clinical data (Audit Commission, 2003) to put together a performance measurement regime, a system based on actually asking health customers for their opinion of the level of service they have received, and their experience of the impact and efficacy of the treatment, might be far more reliable, and create more representative statistics than the present measures offered (Coulter, 2002a; Jenkinson, Coulter and Bruster et al., 2003). Many health professions, such as physiotherapists, work on a basis in which patient or customer goals and measurements are decided in consultation with their clinician. This is a form of patient 'empowerment' more viable and more practical than that of the health consumer model, and more likely to lead to a satisfactory assessment of care from the patient (Coulter, 2002a).

In the context of the UK, there appears to be an accumulation of evidence suggesting that the continuous process of health reform is making those working within the NHS cynical and fatigued (Greener and Powell, 2003), and resulting in diminishing returns; if any returns at all (Commission for Health Improvement, 2003; Smith, Walshe and Hunter, 2001). There are limits to areas where the state can construct quasi-markets, and the reasons for their reintroduction in the UK now in retrospect at least, appear unclear. The voice of those receiving health services in other ways may be incorporated in ways other than through the market – primarily by involving them in giving their views about the levels of service they have received and desired. Models of health reform based around health 'citizens' can, perhaps rightly be accused of being little more than 'window dressing' (Coulter, 2002a:103), and appear to fall into the same error as Giddens in assuming that active participation in local health policy decisions is what local people want, in a time when nearly all forms of public political participation are falling year-on-year. By continuing to assume over-reflexive models of human agency, attempting to create markets where none can exist, or assuming an eager decision-making polity is available to be transformed into health citizens, we persist in errors that appear unjustifiable empirically and theoretically.

# References

Abercrombie, N. (1994) 'Authority and consumer society' in Keat, R., Whiteley, N. and Abercrombie, N. (eds) *The Authority of the Consumer*, London: Routledge, 43–57

Allsop, J., Baggott, R. and Jones, K. (2002) 'Health consumer groups and the national policy process', in Henderson, S. and Peterson, A. (eds) *Consuming Health*, London: Routledge, 48–65

Audit Commission (2003) *Waiting List Accuracy: Assessing the accuracy of waiting list information in NHS hospitals in England*. London: Audit Commission

Beardwood, B., Walters, V., Eyles, J. and French, S. (1999) 'Complaints against nurses: a reflection of "the new managerialism" and consumerism in health-care?' *Social Science and Medicine*, **48**:363–74

Bernstein, R. (1989) 'Social theory as critique', in *Social Theory of Modern Societies: Anthony Giddens and His Critics*, ed. D. Held and J.B. Thompson. Cambridge: Cambridge University Press, 19–33

Bourdieu, P. (1998) *Practical Reason: On the Theory of Action*. Cambridge: Polity Press

Burrows, R. and Nettleton, S. (2000) 'Reflexive modernisation and the emergence of wired self-help', in Burrows, R. and Pleace, N. (eds) *Wired Welfare? Essays on the Rhetoric and Reality of e-Social Policy*, York: Centre For Housing Policy Discussion Paper, 9–22

Burrows, R., Nettleton, S., Pleace, N., Loader, B. and Muncer, S. (2000) 'Virtual Community care? Social policy and the emergence of computer mediated social support', *Information, Communication and Society*, **3**:95–121

Callon, M. (1998) 'Introduction: the embeddedness of economic markets in economies' in Callon, M. (ed.) *The Laws of the Markets*, Oxford: Blackwell, 1–57

Cant, S. and Sharma, U. (1999) *A New Medical Pluralism?* London: UCL Press

Commission for Health Improvement (2003) *Getting Better?* London: Commission for Health Improvement

Coulter, A. (2002a) *The Autonomous Patient: Ending paternalism in medical care*. London: Nuffield Trust/The Stationery Office

Coulter, A. (2002b) 'Patients' views of the good doctor', *British Medical Journal*, **325**:668–9

Craib, I. (1992) *Anthony Giddens*. London: Routledge

Department of Health (1991) *The Patient's Charter*. London: Department of Health

Department of Health (2001a) *The Expert Patient: a New Approach to Chronic Disease Management for the 21st Century*. London: Department of Health

Department of Health (2001b) *Extending Choice for Patients*. London: Department of Health

Elwyn, G., Edwards, A. and Kinnersley, P. (1999) 'Shared decision-making in primary care:the neglected second half of the consultation', *British Journal of General Practice*, **49**:477–82

Foucault, M. (1977) *Discipline and Punish: the Birth of the Prison*. London: Penguin

Fox, N. (1993) *Postmodernism, Sociology and Health*. Buckingham: Open University Press

Gabbott, M. and Hogg, G. (1994) 'Competing for patients: understanding consumer evaluation of primary care', *Journal of Management in Medicine*, 8:12–18

Giddens, A. (1984) *The Constitution of Society*. Cambridge: Polity Press

Giddens, A. (1991) *Modernity and Self-Identity*. Cambridge: Polity Press

Giddens, A. (1994a) *Beyond Left and Right: the Future of Radical Politics*. Cambridge: Polity Press

Giddens, A. (1994b) 'Living in a post-traditional society', in Beck, U., Giddens, A. and Lash, S. (eds) *Reflexive Modernisation*, Cambridge: Polity Press, 56–109

Giddens, A. (1998) *The Third Way: the Renewal of Social Democracy*. Cambridge: Polity Press

Giddens, A. (2002) *What Now for New Labour?* Cambridge: Polity Press

Giddens, A. (2003) 'Challenge of renewal', *Progressive Politics*, 1:36–9

Greener, I. (2002). 'Agency, social theory and social policy', *Critical Social Policy*, 22:688–706

Greener, I. (2003a) 'Patient choice in the NHS: the view from Economic Sociology', *Social Theory and Health*, 1:72–89

Greener, I. (2003b) 'Who choosing what? The evolution of "choice" in the NHS, and its implications for New Labour', *Social Policy Review 15*, Bristol: Policy Press

Greener, I. and Powell, J. (2003) 'Health authorities, priority-setting and resource allocation: a study in decision-making in New Labour's NHS', *Social Policy and Administration*, 37:35–48

Ham, C. (2000) *The Politics of NHS Reform 1988–97: Metaphor or Reality*. London: Kings Fund

Hardey, M. (1999) 'Doctor in the house: the Internet as a source of lay health knowledge and the challenge to expertise', *Sociology of Health and Illness*, 21:820–35

Hardey, M. (2001) ''E-health': the Internet and the transformation of patients into consumers and producers of health knowledge', *Information, Communication and Society*, 4:388–405

Haug, M. and Lavin, B. (1983) *Consumerism in Medicine: Challenging Physician Authority*. Beverley Hills: Sage

Haug, M. and Sussman, M. (1969) 'Professional autonomy and the revolt of the client', *Social Problems*, 17:153–161

Hoggett, P. (2000) *Emotional Life and the Politics of Welfare*. Basingstoke: Palgrave – now Palgrave Macmillan

Hoggett, P. (2001) 'Agency, rationality and social policy', *Journal of Social Policy*, 30:37–56

Hugman, R. (1994) 'Consuming health and welfare' in Keat, R., Whiteley, N. and Abercrombie, N. (eds) *The Authority of the Consumer*, London: Routledge, 207–27

Irvine, R. (2002) 'Fabricating "health consumers" into healthcare politics', in Henderson, S. and Peterson, A. (eds) *Consuming Health*, London: Routledge, 31–47

Jenkinson, C., Coulter, A. and Bruster, S. et al. (2003) 'Factors relating to patients' reports about hospital care for coronary heart disease in England', *Journal of Health Services Research and Policy*, 8:83–6

Jessop, B. (1999) 'The changing governance of welfare: recent trends in its primary functions, scale and modes of coordination', *Social Policy and Administration*, **33**:348–59

Klein, R. (1998) 'Why Britain is reorganizing its national health service – yet again', *Health Affairs*, **17**:111–25

Klein, R. (2000) *The New Politics of the NHS*. Harlow: Longman

Lupton, D., Donaldson, C. and Lloyd, P. (1991) 'Caveat emptor or blissful ignorance? Patients and the consumerist ethos', *Social Science and Medicine*, **33**:559–68

Meerabeau, L. (1998) 'Consumerism and healthcare: the example of fertility treatment', *Journal of Advanced Nursing*, **27**:721–9

Mishra, R. (1990) *The Welfare State in Crisis*. Brighton: Wheatsheaf Books

Mol, A. (1999) 'Ontological politics: a word and some questions', in Law, J. and Hassard, J. (eds) *Actor-Network Theory and After*, Oxford: Blackwell, 74–89

Mullen, P. (1990) 'Which internal market? The NHS White Paper and Internal Markets', *Financial Accountability and Management*, **6**:33–50

Multiple Sclerosis Society (2003) *Measuring Up: Experiences of people with MS of health services*. London: MORI/Multiple Sclerosis Society

Needham, C. (2003) *Citizen-consumers: New Labour's Marketplace Democracy*. London: Catalyst Forum

Nettleton, S. and Burrows, R. (2003) 'E-scaped medicine? Information, reflexivity and health', *Critical Social Policy*, **23**:173–93

Ritzer, G. (1996) *Sociological Theory*. London: McGraw-Hill

Robbins, A. (2001) *Awaken the Giant Within: How to take immediate control of your mental, emotional, physical and financial life*. London: Pocket Books

Secretary of State for Health (1989) *Working for Patients*. London: HMSO

Secretary of State for Health (1997) *The New NHS: Modern, Dependable*. London: HMSO

Secretary of State for Health (2000) *The NHS Plan: a Plan for Investment, A Plan for Reform*. London: HMSO

Secretary of State for Health (2002) *Delivering the NHS Plan: Next Steps on Investment and Reform*. London: HMSO

Segal, L. (1998) 'The importance of patient empowerment in health sector reform', *Health Policy*, **44**:31–44

Shackley, P. and Ryan, M. (1994) 'What is the role of the consumer in healthcare?', *Journal of Social Policy*, **23**:517–541

Sheldon, T. (1990) 'When it makes sense to mince your words', *Health Service Journal*, 16 August, 121

Smith, J., Walshe, K. and Hunter, D. (2001) 'The 'redisorganisation' of the NHS: another reorganisation leaving unhappy managers can only worsen the service', *British Medical Journal*, **323**:1262–3

Stacey, M. (1998) 'The health service consumer: a sociological misconception', in Mackay, L., Soothill, K. and Melia, K. (eds) *Classic Texts in Health Care*, Oxford: Butterworth-Heinemann, 54–9

Thompson, J. (1989) 'The theory of structuration', in *Social Theory of Modern Societies: Anthony Giddens and his Critics*, ed. D. Held and J. Thompson. Cambridge: Cambridge University Press, 56–76

Timmins, N. (2002) 'A time for change in the British NHS: an interview with Alan Milburn', *Health Affairs*, **21**:129–35

Toth, B. (1996) 'Public participation: an historical perspective', in Coast, J., Donovan, J. and Frankel, S. (eds) *Priority Setting: the Healthcare Debate*, Chichester: John Wiley, 169–202

Wearne, S. (1998) 'How do patients choose a GP and do patients use directories to inform their decision?', *Family Practice*, **15**:259–60

West, P. (1998) 'Market – what market? A review of Health Authority purchasing in the NHS internal market', *Health Policy*, **44**:167–83

Westergaard, J. (1999) 'Where does the Third Way Lead?' *New Political Economy*, **4**:429–36

Wilson, P. (2001) 'A policy analysis of the Expert Patient in the United Kingdom: self-care as an expression of pastoral power?', *Health and Social Care in the Community*, **9**:134–42

# 11
# The Social Epidemiology of Information Technologies

*Justin Keen* and *Jeremy Wyatt*

## Introduction

There is a striking contrast between the rate of diffusion of electronic networks within society at large and the rate within healthcare systems. Millions of us use email and the web at home and at work, yet many people who work in the NHS and in healthcare systems in many countries use them relatively infrequently, or do not have access to them at all. In 2001 in the NHS in England, estimates suggest that some 60 per cent of staff do not have access to a computer (Department of Health, 2001).

In the first of two chapters focusing on the role of IT in healthcare (the second, Chapter 12, by Rigby follows) this chapter asks, 'Why has diffusion been so slow in healthcare organisations over the last three decades? What will happen in the future?' One approach to answering questions about the future direction of change involves the development of scenarios as aids to thinking. Scenarios have been used to aid thinking about possible futures for information and communication technologies (ICTs) in health and healthcare (Botterman et al., 2003). This chapter argues that evidence about past and current patterns of diffusion offers important clues about the future. The past is not always a reliable guide, of course, but in the case of ICTs there are consistent patterns of diffusion, in some cases extending back thirty years.

We compare and contrast three contexts where ICTs are already used, and where policy makers foresee a major role for them in the future: in civil society, within heath care organisations, and between citizens and providers of health services and information. The patterns of diffusion of ICTs in these three contexts are described and analysed. It is argued that the use of ICTs in health and healthcare applications will continue to increase, but that the current fragmented and relatively slow rate of diffusion in organisational contexts will persist. This chapter focuses particularly on healthcare organisations, since we think that the greatest puzzle lies in explaining the current low uptake and diffusion of a number of ICTs at the organisational level.

In the next section we sketch out evidence about the patterns of diffusion of ICTs in the three contexts. In the sections that follow we set out a general framework for understanding and explaining what these patterns tell us. That is, we argue that the patterns of diffusion offer insights in the same way that the epidemiology of diseases offers clues to understanding them. If there is a difference, it lies in our relatively underdeveloped models of technology diffusion. We can predict the spread of key infectious diseases, and our understanding of the non-linear patterns of diffusion of HIV/Aids and other sexually transmitted diseases has developed substantially over the last few years. The same cannot be said for information technologies, though, and this chapter makes a start on teasing out the underlying patterns for a range of systems.

## Three contexts

The starting point for our argument is that there are marked differences between general use of the Internet across society and the state of affairs in healthcare organisations in many developed countries. Understanding the reasons for the differences provides a reasonable basis for the prediction of future patterns of use of ICTs. Our method is to gather together observational evidence about large-scale patterns of diffusion of ICTs in different contexts, and then to identify evidence and argument that help us to explain the observed patterns.

### The Internet in society

It is now a commonplace that the World Wide Web was first used widely in 1994, and many commentators take this to be the year that the Internet as a mass medium took off (Abbate, 1999). Email has a longer history and was first used between remote sites in 1971. AOL was founded in 1985 and the Internet service provider Demon was founded in the UK in 1992. Data suggest that both Web and email use have been rising rapidly ever since 1994, both in the home and in business settings (see www.stanford.edu/group/siqss, Cole et al., 2000).

Citizens are enthusiastic about electronically mediated sources of information on health and healthcare, including the Internet and health kiosks (Nicholas, Huntingdon, Gunter and Williams, 2003). Successive polls by Harris Interactive, Newsbytes and other firms suggest that many millions of people use the Internet as a source of health information across North America, Europe and Japan. Research on the value of these technologies is relatively scarce: studies by Nicholas and colleagues in the UK (Nicholas, Huntington and Williams, 2003a) and a review of web-based resources by Bessell et al. (2002) suggest both extensive use and a lack of robust empirical evidence that they change health behaviour. It seems reasonable, though, to say that the evidence of widespread use of health-related sites is a reasonable proxy measure for their value.

## ICTs in healthcare organisations

The situation with ICTs within healthcare organisations is rather different. We focus here on the work of health professionals, and use four examples – personal electronic records, telemedicine, email and doctors' use of the Web – to plot the patterns of diffusion of ICTs.

Papers setting out ideas for electronic patient records were published in the 1960s, and in the UK the Department of Health published a report – the Tunbridge Report – proposing electronic medical records as long ago as 1965. Since that time there have been dozens of initiatives supporting the design and implementation of electronic records technologies, and many thousands of papers have been published. Much of the literature discusses possibilities and progress with electronic records for patients' encounters with single organisations, usually hospitals. More recently, interest has grown in the possibility of integration of all of an individual's health information in a single record, which would require professionals and organisations to pool their information – often large volumes of it. In some plans, supported in different places by private companies and by governments, patients will have access to their records via secure Internet connections (e.g. Kohane et al., 1996; Department of Health, 2001; see http://www.healthdatamanagement.com/html/PortalStory.cfm?type=trendandDID=9663).

Today, this vision of integrated personal electronic records has been realised in a small number of places, typically with a few dozen users, although in a handful of places the numbers are larger. It is more usual, however, to find electronic records used in one part of a healthcare system, as in general practice in the UK. Almost all GPs in the UK now have desktop systems which contain patient details about their contacts with their practice GPs – the details included range from basic summaries to extensive clinical details, including hospital-conducted test results.

Similarly, some hospitals have hospital information support systems (HISS) or large-scale picture archiving and communication systems (PACS): summary hospital records are typically integrated within HISS, and patient details are recorded alongside images and radiologists' reports of those images in PACS. The pattern, then, is one where partial records are held within organisations (and, we should add, often sitting on proprietary technology, and thus not easily networked). Taking a broader view, it is important to note that the majority of medical records are still paper-based, seemingly in all developed countries. Electronic records are therefore exceptions to the general paper rule.

What is more, there is no single, agreed approach to the design and implementation of records: time has not led to convergence. Some advocate personally held and controlled records. A general practice in southern England has pursued a different approach and distributed copies on CD-ROM of the individual records it holds to each of its patients (see http://www.tawhillsurgery.com/). These contrast with the large-scale integration plans in the NHS and elsewhere, see http://www.dh.gov.uk/PolicyAndGuidance/InformationTechnology/National ITProgramme/fs/en. In practice, the term electronic record covers a range of approaches and designs, which is itself indicative of their immediate future: if an agreed approach is needed, then there is no early prospect of more extensive diffusion.

The second technology on our list is telemedicine. As with electronic records, the history is longer than most people realise: the first trials of recognisable telemedicine systems were reported in the 1970s (Moore et al., 1975; Dunn et al., 1977). There have been technological improvements in some aspects of these systems over the years: there has been a progression from 'near-laboratory' applications, through early commercial systems using proprietary technology to solutions which use cheap and reliable mass-market equipment over the Internet. In spite of this, the diffusion of telemedicine applications in clinical practice has been slow and take-up is still very patchy (Balas et al., 1997; Mair and Whitten, 2000).

The diffusion of the use of email presents a different picture (van der Kam et al., 2000). Clinicians, and doctors in particular, are now routinely linked to internal organisational networks and through them to the Internet. Observational evidence suggests that doctors use email to communicate with one another, for example using ISPs tailored to their interests (Borowitz and Wyatt, 1998). They do not, however, use email to the same extent to communicate with nurses or other clinicians, and seem to use it sparingly to communicate with administrators and managers (authors' unpublished data). That is, there appears to be a qualitative difference in the extent to which doctors use email to communicate with different groups.

The fourth example, doctors' use of the Internet, is different again. Tens of thousands of UK doctors have visited dedicated Internet service providers such as Medix and Doctors.net. Surveys show that doctors – in many countries – access clinical information on the Web and find it useful. On the basis of the available evidence, then, it appears that doctors are in general willing to use Web and email services as part of their clinical practice, though email use may be selective. This seems to reflect the patterns that were developing before the Internet era, with many hospital doctors willing and able to use PCs – often standing alone on a desktop, not connected to other hospital systems, for clinical audit and other local purposes. Other clinicians are less likely to use either, though in the UK at least this may be because they do not have access in the first place.

## Interfaces between civil society and healthcare organisations

The third context lies at the interface between civil society and organisations: in healthcare this is a form of 'mixed economy' for ICTs, where the funding can come wholly or partially from the state or commercial organisations, but can be used by anyone. There is a range of different applications, including Internet-based markets for health services (GP advice) and products (such as Viagra) available over the Internet, services available via interactive digital television (iDTV), and telephone-based services such as NHS Direct. Briefly, empirical evidence suggests that citizens value telephone access to health professionals and Web sites that they perceive to be reliable (Munro et al., 2000). Across a heterogeneous set of applications, the evidence points towards health-based information and advice sources being popular.

This thumbnail sketch suggests a heterogeneous state of affairs, with very different fates for different technologies, at least to date. The questions posed in this chapter are: what accounts for these differences, and what does it tell us about possible futures? Space does not allow a full treatment of this question here, but we can begin to discern some useful pointers. For example, ICTs have diffused successfully – at least among doctors – when they support what one might call clinical administration. They appear to have had less success when designed overtly to support clinical decision-making and communications, as in the cases of electronic personal records and telemedicine and are less likely to be used across functional or professional boundaries

At first sight this seems paradoxical. Commentaries on the use of high-tech devices in areas such as surgery and imaging might lead one to believe that doctors should be interested in similar-looking ICTs, reflecting the 'toys for boys' syndrome. But, *co-ordination* of clinical work, *mediated* via ICTs, appears to cause problems for doctors, the group for whom we have the best evidence. The penetration of computers in general practice in the UK helps to make this point: they are helpful to GPs working within a practice, but opportunities to link them on networks and share information have not been taken up. Localities such as Bradford, and the shared clinical network in the Boston area of the USA, are notable exceptions that perhaps prove the general rule.

We can also say that success and failure, as judged by the extent of diffusion, has occurred against a backdrop of falling prices. Successive generations of a given technology such as telemedicine have not changed that technology's fortunes. It is, therefore, possible to begin to tease out structural factors which are, or are not, plausible explanations for differences in diffusion patterns.

## Towards an explanatory and predictive framework

The evidence from this brief overview allows us to make two general observations about the patterns of diffusion of ICTs.

First, there are distinct patterns of diffusion:

- Extensive diffusion for networked activities, for example for accessing health information on the Internet, and within particular communities, as in the case of ISPs for doctors;
- Extensive diffusion within any one function. Every hospital in the UK, as in most developed countries, has a patient administration system (PAS). The same is true for financial management systems;
- 'Polynesian' patterns of diffusion for technologies used within healthcare systems; that is, usage is in small islands scattered at low density across a large organisational seascape. Examples here include electronic records, telemedicine, HISS and PACS. These technologies are implemented and used in a number of places within any one country, but the number of places is a small proportion of the potential total, and the islands are not linked by ferry services;
- No diffusion. Many ICTs have simply never progressed beyond the research and development phase: unused and now forgotten decision support systems litter the ocean bed.

Second, the patterns in civil society and inside healthcare systems are very different. ICTs seem to have diffused successfully in open markets (e.g. the PC market) or across the Internet – or have been abandoned where there was no market or no interest. Within healthcare systems there has been either limited success (such as email) or relatively low diffusion rates over long periods of time. This has led to a situation, in many organisations, where there are many isolated systems in place. The proprietary nature of the technologies in this latter case has not helped, but problems of technical standardisation have been solved for key technologies, to the extent that we can plug and play on the Internet within an hour of taking a new PC out of its box. Proprietary technology can be a problem, but markets can solve the co-ordination problems involved if the circumstances are right.

## Diffusion within healthcare systems

What might account for these different patterns? Standard explanations, at least in the health services research literature, focus on the barriers to implementation (following Rogers, 1995). This approach seems to us to be flawed, because it cannot explain why some technologies *do* diffuse successfully. The 'critical success factors' identified in the literature do not seem to be related to identified barriers. For example, lack of resources is often cited as a barrier to technology implementation, but accounts of successes often note low purchase and running costs. The academic point here is that our understanding of innovation in ICT design and in organisational change in healthcare is poor. If innovation is the acquisition of the technical knowledge required to reproduce a process or outcome (Elster, 1983), then that knowledge appears to be deeply embedded in some areas – such as UK GP computing – and more or less absent in others.

The standard approach also focuses on technologies, and tends to lead to technology-driven accounts of barriers (Rogers, 1995). Our observational evidence suggests instead that wider organisational factors are more important, and that explanations based on organisation processes and innovation are likely to be more useful. Accordingly, here we draw on the work of Van de Ven et al. (1999) and Poole et al. (2000) on organisational innovation. They studied innovation processes in a wide range of organisations, and identified features that are associated with innovation that appear to be independent of any one organisational context. Poole and colleagues argue that there are distinct metaphors for innovation within and between organisations, including:

- Life cycle – straightforward implementation and periodic upgrading, as for email;
- Evolutionary – a 'survival of the fittest' model of diffusion, where some technologies succeed while others fail;
- Political – the pattern of diffusion is the outcome of serial and inter-locked negotiations between key stakeholders.

Evidence to support each of these three diffusion models can be found in relation to ICTs in health and healthcare. Where technologies are now well established, the focus is on upgrading, as for example in the case in GP computing. We note, in passing, that there is still a wide-spread belief in the life cycle approach, most evident in national policy documents. Some policy makers still believe, in spite of the empirical evidence, that ICTs are technologies that can be successfully imple-mented in organisations without too much organisational fuss. The National Programme for IT in England offers tacit support that this view is changing: suppliers are deemed to have the necessary technical knowledge and are going to have to drive implementation, too.

The use of health resources on the Internet is a good example of an evolutionary diffusion pattern, one where we are still in the process of a 'population explosion'. Conversely, the Polynesian pattern observed in many ICTs in healthcare organisations is not obviously well explained as an evolutionary process. Indeed, we think that the best explanation for this pattern, and the overall pattern of ICT diffusion, lies in the political model. We draw here on Moran's (1999) technology policy framework. Moran argues that the state, clinicians (particularly doctors) and technology suppliers are locked into a long-term triangular relationship. Each party derives benefits from the relationship. For example the diffusion of pharmaceuticals reflects a sort of equilibrium in relationships which facilitates diffusion in that pharmaceutical sup-pliers guarantee markets for their products, and clinicians have access to products that they can use in diagnosis and treatment. The state is seen to provide a comprehensive health service with the latest pharmaceuti-cals available. On balance, patients benefit from this arrangement: the relationships tend to limit opportunistic behaviour by any one party that might otherwise damage the quality of care.

In the case of ICTs the state, clinicians and ICT suppliers have not been able to form stable, long-term relationships with one another. The interest of major suppliers has waxed and waned over the last twenty years. They and others have reported frustration at the difficulties – as they see them – of eliciting precise and realistic user requirements from the NHS and Department of Health. Equally, civil servants and NHS managers and clinicians express concern that many suppliers simply do not understand healthcare processes and offer inappropriate products. In short, this particular triangular relationship is an immature one. This view is supported by international evidence, where the role of the state is effectively replaced, as it is for example with larger HMOs and other providers in the USA. Here, too, there are accounts of major problems with ICT implementation. This resonates with the point made earlier about the lack of understanding of innovation processes for ICTs around the world.

Detailed observational studies (Berg, 1997), and considered reports (Royal Academy of Engineering and British Computer Society, 2004) help to make the point that this is a complex problem. It can be approached from a number of angles: ICT project failures can be understood as stemming from poor understanding of the underlying technologies, as problems of the all-too-human tendency to invest unrealistic expectations in a technology, or as a failure of political will to solve a problem. Here, we acknowledge that the problem is indeed multi-faceted, but point to the increasing importance of the political dimension. Governments around the world are explicitly placing great emphasis on the benefits that – they believe – ICTs can bring in health and other public services.

The politics of the relationships are played out principally at macro– national or major company policy – level. However, their effects are felt at meso and micro levels. In the case of most healthcare systems the meso level is where clinicians, managers, suppliers and others come together, typically to make purchasing decisions about ICTs – at Strategic Health Authority and Trust level in the NHS. The Polynesian patterns we observed earlier are found at micro level. In more mature industrial relationships there would be a reasonably clear separation of the activities at macro, meso and micro levels (even in an era of flattened hierarchies). But in the case of ICTs, we believe, the immaturity of the relationship means that the distinctions are less clear cut.

## Micro level

The focus of much ICT-related development in healthcare organisations is at the level of service delivery. At this level we observe both the cross-organisational and (to a lesser extent) cross-professional use of networks noted earlier, and the penetration of functional systems in administrative and finance functions. Many developments have taken place without significant input from higher up in a bureaucracy, save often for the provision of finance to purchase systems. Suppliers and enthusiastic clinicians have worked together, in a sort of medical-industrial complex, to develop electronic records, telemedicine and other systems.

## Meso level: competition for nodes

Following Dunleavy and Margetts (2000), we believe it is useful to think of healthcare systems as networks of 'political nodes': a node is a place that is occupied and controlled by a professional group. GPs substantially control what happens in their practices, consultants largely control the patterns of their outpatient clinics, and so on. The control of many of the nodes in healthcare systems is long established. Of course, the control is not absolute, and clinicians do respond to environmental influences, including some performance targets: but change will not occur unless the key people are persuaded.

ICTs lead to competition for nodes. The sales pitch of 'ICT in health believers' down the years has centred on change: ICTs equal fewer people needed to do the same work, or beneficial changes in the way that work is done, for clinicians or patients or both. The available empirical evidence suggests that such positive changes can be achieved in certain circumstances, but success is far from guaranteed. Some have argued that ICTs themselves can lead to changes in work practices, but the patchiness of current usage and other evidence suggests that this belief is misplaced in healthcare at present (Hammer, 1998).

At meso level, the competition is generally between clinicians and managers. There is, for example, a long-standing tension between them over ownership of electronic patient records. During the 1990s, policy documents from many countries fudged the issue of ownership of such records (which at the time existed in very few places): ownership lay somewhere between the managers who paid for them and the clinicians who used them. Advocacy for patients' rights to records were less in evidence. Currently, the competition for both ownership of medical records (in essence the legal right to say who has access to them) and the day-to-day control over them (which most commentators now believe should be shared between clinicians and patients) is ongoing. The advent of electronic personal medical records seems set to intensify the competition. Secular trends, which tend to emphasise consumer-led thinking, suggest that patients will over time come to own their records and exercise greater control over them, notably in patients giving consent to clinicians to access their records, rather than the present situation where consent is in effect given by doctors to patients to see their own records.

There is a related but distinct competition for the ownership and control of information, about patients and clinicians themselves. There is a promise/threat (depending on your point of view) that ICTs will be used to performance-manage clinical work. Not altogether surprisingly, doctors and other clinicians have not generally responded well to these suggestions. This does not seem to be related directly to the technologies involved. It is possible to point to different reasons why this is the case. One argument is empirical: positive empirical evidence of effectiveness is lacking, and there may be evidence that ICTs tend to increase the time costs of administrative activities undertaken by clinicians, such as writing referrals or discharge letters. The more general problem, for clinicians, is political. ICTs may lead clinicians to reorganise their work, but they also allow for the possibility of being monitored by general managers more closely than they are at present. Viewed in this light, it does not seem surprising that clinicians have either commandeered ICTs for their own use, or resisted attempts (as they see them) to impose them.

A different option for those who promote ICTs is to create new nodes. NHS Direct and other telephone-based services have effectively created new nodes, reflected in the creation of new organisations and staff working in new roles. Where these nodes have been created, it is noteworthy that they are funded by the state – or a purchasing organisation in places where the state is not a player, as in the case of Kaiser Permanente in the USA –and are in effect the physical manifestation of a contract between the state/purchaser and health service users. That is, some clinicians may support the creation of such services, but in general, nurses and other clinicians are simply employees rather than in control of the node.

## Meso and macro levels: the wrong technology?

While the concept of political nodes helps us, it leaves a question unanswered: why have proponents of the Polynesian technologies been so persistent in the face of mounting negative empirical evidence? The results of systematic reviews of efficiency of various ICTs are summarised in Table 11.1. The answer appears to be that there have been persistent sets of political relationships supporting particular technologies. Indeed, it seems that a sort of hierarchy has evolved, with different technologies attracting different levels of financial and political support. One model involves technologies that have been developed initially by small groups of people who are all interested in a particular technology. This is the model of ICT believers who tend to be interested in a technology for its own sake. These take one of three forms:

*Table 11.1*: The results of systematic reviews of efficiency of various ICTS

| Topic | Authors | Reference | Comments |
|---|---|---|---|
| Internet sources of information | Bessell et al. | Health Expectations 2002;5:28–37 | Almost no good evidence |
| Telemedicine | Currell et al. | Cochrane Library 4, 2000 | Few reliable reports of effects |
| Clinical decision support systems | Hunt et al. | *JAMA* 1998; 280:1339–46 | Some positive effects on clinical process indicators – but few good studies |
| Clinical information systems | Balas et al. 1997 | *Arch Fam Med* 1996;5:271–8 | Modest positive effects on clinical process indicators found |
| Hospital systems (UK) | Lock | *BMJ* 1996;312:1407–10 | Very few well-designed studies |
| General Practice systems | Mitchell & Sullivan | *BMJ* 2001;322:279–82. | Improved GP performance; dearth of evidence on outcomes |
| Decision support – abdominal pain | Liu et al. | HTA report | Very few good studies |
| Primary care data | Thiru et al. | *BMJ* 2003;326:1070–4 | Difficult to assess data quality, hence cannot assess contribution of ICTs to improving data quality |

1. Alliances between clinicians (usually doctors) and suppliers. Individual clinicians who believe in a technology work with suppliers who are (quite properly) interested in developing new markets. In the early days conferences allow those interested to find one another and to exchange ideas. In the case of telemedicine, it appears to have been difficult to obtain funding on a consistent basis for development, at least outside military applications (which is where PACS originated).
2. Alliances between clinicians, suppliers and civil servants. For example, GP computer systems have developed the way they have because

of the close involvement of GPs in system design – and with GPs employed directly by supplier companies. Arguably, GP systems would not have penetrated as far as they have – almost all GPs now have PCs in their practices – if civil servants had not supported them, notably in the subsidies offered to GPs to purchase practice systems in the early 1990s.

3. Alliance between clinicians, suppliers, civil servants and politicians. There is a group of technologies that have 'broken through' politically and been adopted as central planks of government ICT policies. In the UK and elsewhere this group includes network 'backbones' (with email and Web browsing) and electronic personal records.

In many developed countries technology-focused groups have captured substantial amounts of the available funds for ICTs, as in the first of these models. These seem to be holding a number of ICTs in a kind of Purgatory – never abandoned and never breaking through. In England, the National Programme for IT is seeking to formalise relationships between the three power blocks, with the aspiration that it will lead to more mature relationships. By awarding large contracts to supplier consortia for key ICTs such as (shared) personal electronic records and electronic booking of appointments, the National Programme may lead to the abandonment of Polynesian Island ICTs, in favour of more extensively networked solutions. It is of course a moot point how the National Programme will fare in practice: it may or may not succeed in challenging existing nodes or creating new ones. The point in the context of this analysis is that the programme makes sense politically. The contracts tie together the three key players – state, suppliers and clinicians – in a very public arrangement. They need each other in order to succeed, and will succeed or fail in the full glare of the media and, no doubt politicians and the Treasury as well.

## Where are the natural networks?

In order to look forward, a key issue is about network relationships. Generally speaking, ICT policies in healthcare do not dwell at all on the nature of the social or organisational networks that ICTs are either supposed to support or whose development is crucial for the efficacy of the proposed ICT use. Healthcare is characterised by strong professional groups, which can operate over considerable geographical distances and are stable over long periods of time (Abbott, 1988). In Abbott's attractive metaphor professional groups do change over time, both internally and in relation to one another, in the same way that tectonic plates rub against one another and change shape over millennia. The landscape alters when relationships between professional groups alter. Our interpretation of current patterns of use of networked ICTs is that electronic networks will tend to reinforce existing professional and organisational relationships. They will strengthen the 'loose ties' that bind professionals together across time and space, to use a phrase of Castells (2001). We can see little reason to suggest that ICTs will create new cross-professional relationships, at least in the near future.

## Looking to the future

Prediction is a risky business. Prediction of ICT futures looks, on the face of it, a riskier business than most. But some of the patterns of stability and change in ICT diffusion may offer a basis for cautious prediction. Across societies generally, the evolutionary model seems set to dominate. Similarly, wider changes such as reductions in out-of-hours cover by doctors will lead to greater reliance on nurse-staffed telephone and other ICT-based services at the interface between health services and society. Put in economic terms, market forces will continue to operate. On this model, 'new' technologies such as interactive digital TV may succeed or fail, and so interactive healthcare advice and support also succeed or fail, on the outcome of market forces, and on externalities such as the penetration of interactive set-top boxes. For example, in the UK, the innocent-looking Freeview box may in practice sound the death knell for such services, as it has no capacity for two-way communications. If this model prevails, there will be continued increases in the consumption of health information via the Internet and other media, in line with the general growth of the Internet. If there is a key point here it is that the range of providers of such services and information will grow, offering ever more alternatives to conventional medical services as sources of information.

Within organisations, electronic networks will become the norm, and tend to reinforce existing relationships, rather than support the creation of new relationships across organisational and professional boundaries. ICTs may, against the expectations of policy makers, tend to exaggerate rather than solve problems of fragmentation of service delivery. Much hinges on whether ICTs can foster information sharing, given time. Combined with broader organisational developments, such as the implementation of integrated care pathways, new natural communities of service provision may develop. The result will be a blurring of organisational and professional boundaries, and a reshaping of relationships.

This is the single most difficult issue to predict in this area. As we noted at the beginning of the chapter, the epidemiology of ICTs in health-care is not well understood. This chapter suggests that it should be possible to develop models that help us to understand and – with care – predict future patterns of diffusion for the dominant technologies, with a consequent benefit in understanding for future policy-making.

## References

Abbate, J. (1999) *Inventing the Internet*. Cambridge, MA: MIT Press

Abbott, A. (1998) *The System of Professions*. Chicago: University of Chicago Press

Audit Commission (1995) *For your Information: a Study of Information Management and Systems in the Acute Hospital*. London: HMSO

Balas, E., Jaffrey, F. and Kuperman, G.J. et al. (1997) 'Electronic communication with patients – evaluation of distance medicine technology', *JAMA*, **278**:152–9

Berg, M. (1997) *Rationalising Medical Work. Decision support techniques and medical practices*. Cambridge, MA: MIT Press

Bessell, T., Macdonald, S. and Silagy, C. et al. (2002) 'Do internet interventions for consumers cause more harm than good? A systematic review', *Health Expectations*, **5**:28–37

Borowitz, S. and Wyatt, J. (1998) 'The origin, content and workload of email consultations', *JAMA*, **280**:1321–4

Botterman, M., Anderson, R., van Binst, P. and Cave, J. et al. (2003) *Enabling the Information Society by Stimulating the Creation of a Broadband Environment in Europe: Analyses of Evolution Scenarios for Future Networking Technologies and Networks in Europe*, Rand Europe Report MR-1579-EC. Available at www.rand.org/randeurope/

Castells, M. (2001) *The Internet Galaxy*. Oxford: Oxford University Press

Cole, J. et al. (2000) 'Surveying the digital future', at www.ccp.ucla.edu/ucla-internet.pdf

Department of Health (2001) *NHS Plan: Building the Information Core*. London: Department of Health

Dunleavy, P. and Margetts, H. (2000) 'The advent of digital government: public bureaucracies and the state in the Internet age', Paper delivered at the *2000 Annual Meeting of the American Political Science Association*, Washington, DC, 31 August–3 September

Dunn, E., Conrath, D., Bloor, W. and Tranquada, B. (1977) 'An evaluation of four telemedicine systems for primary care', *Health Services Research*, **1**:19–29

Elster, J. (1983) *Explaining Technical Change*. Cambridge: Cambridge University Press

Hammer, M. (1998) *Beyond Reengineering: How the Process-centred Organization is Changing Our Work and Our Lives*. London: HarperCollins Business

Keen, J. (1998) 'Rethinking NHS networking', *BMJ*, April, **316**:1291–3

Kohane, I.S., Greenspun, P. and Fackler, J. et al. (1996) 'Building national electronic medical record systems via the World Wide Web', *Journal of the American Medical Informatics Association*, **3**, 3:191–207

Mair, F. and Whitten, P. (2000) 'Systematic review of studies of patient satisfaction with telemedicine', *BMJ*, **320**:1517–20

Moore, G., Willemain, T. and Bonnano, R. et al. (1975) 'Comparison of television and telephone for remote medical consultation', *New England Journal of Medicine*, **292**:729–32

Moran, M. (1999) *Governing the Health Care State*. Manchester: Manchester University Press

Munro, J., Nicholl, J., O'Cathain, A. and Knowles, E. (2000) *Evaluation of NHS Direct First Wave Sites: second interim report to the Department of Health*. Sheffield: ScHARR,

National Audit Office (2002) *NHS Direct*. London: The Stationery Office

Nicholas, D., Huntington, P. and Williams, P. (2003a) 'Delivering health information digitally: a comparison between the Web and Touch Screen Kiosk', *Journal of Medical Systems*, **27**,1:13–34

Nicholas, D., Huntington, P., Gunter, B. and Williams, P. (2003b) 'Comparing the use of health information and advice in Birmingham and Hull: a case study of digital health information delivered via the television', *Journal of Informatics in Primary Care*, **11**

Poole, M. et al. (2000) *Organisational Change and Innovation Processes*. Oxford: Oxford University Press

Rogers, E. (1995) *Diffusion of Innovations*, 4th edn. New York: Free Press

Royal Academy of Engineering and British Computer Society (2004) *The Challenges of Complex IT Projects*. London: Royal Academy of Engineering

Sullivan, F. and Mitchell, E. (1995) 'Has general practitioner computing made a difference to patient care? A systematic review of published reports', *BMJ*, **311**:848–52

Van de Ven, A. et al. (1999) *The Innovation Journey*. Oxford: Oxford University Press

van der Kam, W.J., Moorman, P.W. and Koppejan-Mulder, M.J. (2000) 'Effects of electronic communication in general practice', *International Journal Medical Informatics*, **60**:59–70

# 12

# Harnessing Innovation in Health IT: Effective Support and Evaluated Visions

*Michael Rigby*

## Introduction

At present, health IT and informatics services are poised for rapid rollout, but may well disappoint all interests. Currently they tend not to supply the level of support to ongoing healthcare delivery desired by operational services because they are inadequately resourced and lack necessary innovation. In each of the United Kingdom home countries there are positive plans for Electronic Patient Record (EPR) and other systems rollout, though customisation and ongoing maintenance may be under-recognised. Yet at the same time visionaries are frustrated because they have no effective informed and reflective outlet to commission and develop their visions of the new patterns of healthcare that should be possible with the advent of new health informatics concepts and services. This paper analyses the issues, and gives examples of ways in which the use of modern information management techniques could beneficially re-engineer the process of healthcare delivery but are frustrated by the lack of vehicle to bring together clinical and technical researchers in an innovative research and discussion setting. Communities of patients and clients are disadvantaged because there is no informed forum in which to discuss, develop and test these ideas in all respects, including ethics, organisational change, safety and quality control. Consequently the priority inappropriately continues to be automation of existing processes.

## The two roles of health ICT

In line with other modern service industries, there is clearly a major role for the application of Information and Communications Technologies

(ICT) in the health sector. The application areas range from the comparatively straightforward business processes such as maintaining human resource records, financial transactions, and administrative tasks such as issuing appointments, through to specialist health applications ranging from electronic patient records (EPRs) to diagnostic and therapeutic systems. However, it is not often appreciated that the Information Technology support function in health has two quite separate roles. As these roles are quite often in conflict, failure to recognise this point has the potential (not infrequently realised) of causing misunderstanding and dysfunction. The two roles are:

## The neutral agent

This role is to provide immediate support in all areas of healthcare delivery and management, as required by those responsible for delivering and managing the services and overall organisation. This is a client–supplier relationship. The emphasis is on stability and reliability.

In this role, the IT support function should have good understanding of clinicians' and other end users' work practices and thus information support requirements, but the need is for effective implementation of systems and delivery of support. Assessing how best to configure and deliver an application solution to meet user needs is important, but within the construct of making best use of given opportunities. Any further more detailed or repeated questioning of how things might be different or better, or identifying too rigorously weaknesses in systems or absence of functions which could be useful, are not helpful as they merely stimulate dissatisfaction and frustration. Even where a number of different but mutually incompatible alternative options exist it is important to establish stability through best use of the selected one. Given the large-scale nature of the health sector, the number of staff involved even in specific departments or functions, and the effects of staff rotation and twenty-four hour operation, it is important that the Neutral Agent and the IT support systems are a stabilising and unifying factor, and therefore constant modification is undesirable as it causes confusion and potential disempowerment of other users, and therefore itself extends the dissatisfaction potential.

Therefore acting as the Neutral Agent requires self-discipline and the ability to maintain sound use and to control potential professional dissatisfaction. The professional achievement is in obtaining a stable and well-used support function albeit one with modest limitations, rather than risking a maelstrom of dynamic fragmentation. The success and professional satisfaction of the Neutral Agent must come from the achievement of stability and satisfaction amongst end users.

## The active innovator

Modern means of managing information have rapidly transformed many other service and manufacturing sectors, ranging from finance and insurance services to travel and supply logistics. This role requires the information and IT experts to be active in the innovatory process, identifying potential new opportunities and at the same time the potential pitfalls in applying such new innovations. This is a leadership role, with the client responding to the ideas and initiatives put forward as well as putting forward their own ideas.

Too often, not only is the health IT function under-resourced, but there is also confusion between the supply and leadership roles. At the same time clinical and similar end users seek their own innovations with less than perfect ICT technical knowledge.

Being an Active Innovator requires very different skills and understanding, and equally importantly a very different work environment, to that of the Neutral Agent. The NHS, and most other health sectors, have a wealth of people with positive and dynamic ideas about development of information support in healthcare delivery. These include IT professionals, and health professionals who can envisage modernised ways of working. Periodically these are called upon, whether in local initiatives and pilots linked to national programmes, or by software developers entering developmental contracts. However, too often these opportunities are under resourced, and are short term. Equally significantly, the innovators involved are seldom adequately trained in the overall innovation process, not least in understanding the listening role with regard to the partner professions, and the seeking of common solutions rather than imposing personal visions. Additionally, with developmental or pilot programmes being time limited, the team is frequently only just reaching the peak of its creativity when the end point and disbandment loom into sight.

If healthcare informatics is to develop more positively and constructively, much better means of harnessing and empowering the Active Innovators need to be found. 'Think Tank' environments close to operational settings but not disruptive to these, and teams who can work in harmony developing and testing ideas through ongoing mutual understanding, should be very creative but seldom have opportunity to exist. And conversely, where there is no realistic outlet for detailed innovation, attempts at active innovation in constrained situations such as procured external systems will only waste resources and cause frustration.

# ICT's ambivalent position in healthcare

Given the conflict of these roles, and the resultant tensions between ICT support functions and the developing aspirations of end users, there is a deepening crisis of perception of the role and quality of ICT systems within the healthcare community. There is considerable risk that serious frustration by each party with the other will cause further tensions. This can be attributed to a large degree to the lack of distinction between the two roles of the ICT support function.

Firstly, the role of information systems as servants of professional healthcare deliverers does not necessarily square with the expectation that health informaticians will be innovative in devising new and progressive ways of supplying information to the health sector. In the support role, health informatics is usually subject to inadequate investment, often without a thought-through implementation strategy. This may extend from the narrow investment concepts of systems and technical support staff, through to inadequate investment in implementation and training of end users, inadequate provision of adequate data entry and output devices, and limited resources for post-implementation adjustment as users become more mature.

Secondly, as IT innovation raises new concepts, including possible opportunities for new models of care delivery, there is no forum for their analysis and exploration. Even new issues in the support function, such as those raised by computerisation of patient records, the assessment of relevance of external knowledge bases to local care (Rigby, 1999), or potential new support paradigms, are given scant consideration at the policy formulation and implementation levels.

## Visioning within the support role

In looking to the future, visioning is fundamentally important. In the neutral support role expectations are being placed upon the IT and informatics functions, through implementation of modern systems such as Electronic Patient Records, Electronic Health Records, Telemedicine and Decision Support Systems, without serious consideration of new issues generated, such as those summarised below:

- the realism and the feasibility of rapid universal rollout as hypothesised;
- the size of systems, and of the investment and implementation tasks required;

- the need for new operational policies for large-scale information systems and technologies, to ensure their ethical and safe operation (Draper and Rigby, 2000; Rigby, 1997; Roberts et al., 1977);
- the IT skills, including ongoing maintenance, required;
- the amount of health professional education and training needed, and the availability of adequate educational resources, including the locum costs of release from duty for learning;
- ensuring equity of healthcare delivery in a patchwork and piecemeal health IT environment;
- the relevance of external (and often international) knowledge bases in the local environment (Rigby, 1999);
- ethical and system security issues given increasing networking;
- the organisational stability needed for the specification, installation and operational running of large complex inter-organisational systems.

In any other major service or commercial sector that harnesses information technology, the need to address each of these issues would be seen as paramount. For instance, the complete new paradigm in supplying components to a manufacturing plant, or perishable products to supermarkets, has been redesigned round the information systems (Roberts et al., 2000). This starts with the manufacturing plant or supermarket electronic point of sale (EPOS) tills generating real-time data as a by product of their recording of local transactions, and supplying this to partners upstream in the supply chain. This itself is then not merely a question of putting orders to a computerised warehouse, but triggers the actual supply manufacturing functions. Moreover, new-style logistics companies are often at the heart of these developments, organising the transport and distribution from warehouse collection through to supply to the production line or retail shelves. Further, it is self-evident that in these domains, as well as in finance and insurance, system reliability and system integrity, and secure audit and monitoring processes, have to be built in. In the commercial world advanced integrated systems are not developed in environments where there may be inadequate technology, support or training, whereas in the health sector the installation architecture may well lag behind the implemented systems' demands (Hasselbring et al., 2000).

In other words, when identifying a manual or non-integrated process which might benefit from IT application, commercial sector organisations are in a position to put professional and IT technical staff to work together, with adequate time and resources, to think through, design and implement integrated solutions. By contrast, the health sector has given priority (in some ways understandably) to specific major projects such as Electronic Patient Records, without giving opportunity for 'blue skies' or integrated application research to focus on overall organisational processes and on implementation.

The position of formal bodies does not appear to aid the situation. This field of visionary support falls to some extent between the gaps of responsibilities of the Research Councils. The Engineering and Physical Sciences Research Council (EPSRC) is supportive of research to develop new ICT technologies, but not the domain application re-engineering necessary to maximise the benefits of the technical innovation. This falls more within Economic and Social Research Council (ESRC) remit for management research, whilst the Medical Research Council (MRC) supports research into healthcare itself, and into modalities of healthcare delivery, but not aspects of health computing per se. Thus research into envisioning the effects of using an ICT technology in a healthcare setting, or into how better to harness such opportunities using known technologies in new ways, appear to fall between the two. However other, primarily commercial, service and industry sectors recognise that innovation in core business process is as important in maximising the yield of ICT applications as the purely technical research.

These gaps in integration mean that the health sector is potentially and increasingly at risk of designing, commissioning and implementing new legacy systems, as particular models get developed and promoted through strong central directives by those (at the centre) who will not be responsible for running or using these systems. Moreover, though there has been some recent movement towards increasing the skills and resource levels in the health IT domain, central policy implementation still tends to run ahead of capacity and competence. It also conflicts directly with the claimed policy objective of increased decentralisation and devolution of health policy and management. This leads to the worrying conclusion that there are likely to be more Fears than Hopes realised.

This paper next focuses on to two sets of objectives. First to highlight the importance of increasing capacity and competence, further better understanding of the two different roles of support and visioning in the health IT function, and the implications of these two different roles for relationships between the IT function and client departments. Second, the paper seeks to encourage Visioning in a more open and active way, so that it is seen as a patient-orientated and developmental process rather than (as is currently often the case) a diversionary if not insurgent activity.

## Ensuring appropriate scale and function

Considering that the promotion of information technology support to healthcare in the UK is taken so seriously, it is the source of considerable surprise that there is no adequate modelling of the scale and format necessary to ensure sound systems. The seminal foundational document, the study by the Institute of Medicine of the United States' Academy of Sciences, set forward a vision for electronic patient records and their benefits, but cites no evidence of success on an endemic scale of application (Dick and Steen, 1996). This is a visionary study, but it contains neither costings nor modelling of anticipated record sizes or transaction volumes, and consequently it has no estimate of the size of infrastructure or the complexity of the implementation tasks. The same avoidance of evidence, costings, or modelling exists in many countries' strategy documents which often are replaced even before their implementation has got under way.

When it comes to the development of the human skills necessary for successful application of ICTs in health, a similar situation applies though there are now some examples of serious consideration of the issues. The NHS has developed a career structure of Professional Awards which seek to develop a cadre of ICT support staff with the necessary hierarchy of skills (Rigby et al., 2003; www.nhsia ... ). There has been published by the English NHS a strategy document on preparing the workforce for modernised ICT working, though this is still a top-level document rather than a resourced and funded implementation strategy (NHS Executive). There has been enthusiastic adoption of the European Computer Driving Licence (ECDL) as a technical competence vehicle, primarily because it is in existence and validated, rather than because it is highly adapted to the health environment, though more recently an initiative has been instigated to seek to develop and recognise health sector specific ICT literacy skills for health sector end users (Rigby, 2004).

## Visioning potential new models

Notwithstanding the institutional lack of concerned effort in seeking to move forward in a visionary integrated manner with information technology innovations, there are exciting new possibilities for new healthcare delivery paradigms. Unfortunately, these do not currently have a vehicle for being considered or researched, and are thus not being adequately explored. Examples of such issues and opportunities, which ought to be the subject of deeper open research, include new models of evidence and of healthcare delivery.

## New models of evidence

It should be possible to make available to the public, and to practitioners, collated evidence of the likely outcome of healthcare treatments in stated situations, so that the patient may exercise an informed choice concerning the statistical probability of alternative outcomes (adverse and favourable), of the related risks, and of the treatment patterns and duration which might be necessary for each alternative. The modest but important step forward in Performance Indicators is noted and welcomed, but already conflict and potential confusion between the official Department of Health approach (www.doh.gov. ... ) and the attempt at quality performance measures by the Dr Foster initiative (www.drfoster ... ) show the potential pitfalls. What is needed is more discussion and visioning of the means of assessing overall outcomes, in terms of the total patient experience of an illness and outcomes in terms of mobility, elimination of pain, etc. The work of the National Centre for Outcomes Development is important, but again under-resourced, under considerable pressure, and not necessarily seen as a priority within the health IT context (Lakhani, 2000, 2004).

## New models of healthcare delivery

It is a well-known adage that IT systems in any sector should not merely automate existing procedures. For example if that were the case in the financial sector, there would be no twenty-four hour ATM automated teller machines, merely improved accounting systems. At the same time, the effects created by new innovations also need identifying, and any adverse effects identified counteracted or compensated. For instance, ATM machines radically improved the availability of cash withdrawal facilities, but simultaneously lead to the demise of many rural bank branches and thereby reduced other services.

Three developments in healthcare delivery are now discussed as likely subjects for further visioning in terms of new generation IT in health.

### *Timetabled personal integrated care delivery*

The current supposed move from provider-based to patient-based healthcare delivery has only made a very small shift along a continuum, arguably moving from departmental-based to organisation-based integration. A more radical development would be to move to a truly patient-focused model of forward timetabled personal integrated care delivery that crossed organisational boundaries, based broadly on care planning techniques. Rather than simply being told of a sequence of events that ought to happen the patient would receive a complete personalised schedule (which of course would be amenable to alteration if the course of their treatment necessitated this). This scheduling of the programme of treatment would seem at least as important as the primary care e-booking of initial outpatient appointments which is receiving such a high political profile. It would be dependent upon the next point analysed below, which in turn would be a means of ensuring that care plans could not be set unless the resources were available to honour them.

### Resource booking and deployment

The NHS has severely undervalued computerised resource deployment and operational allocation methodologies; indeed, it barely uses them. It ought to be possible to view all healthcare delivery components as time resources, whether these are operating theatre slots, supported bed days, day hospital attendances, or the clinical time of health professionals. 'Orders' could then be placed for all therapeutic requirements within a planned programme of care, and the time slots allocated – is it far fetched to speculate that this has not been done because it would identify the chronic overloading of so many NHS healthcare delivery resources? These concepts are not new, having been postulated several years ago as part of the work of one of the Community Information Systems for Providers (CISP) projects (Rigby and Robins, 1996), but this led to little follow-up and no further resourcing.

### Electronic patient healthcare portfolio

If the above two new aspects of healthcare delivery were built into the next generation of health IT and informatics systems, it would be possible to develop an integrated electronic patient portfolio, amalgamating all planned healthcare events – preventive services, screening services, health maintenance services, and therapeutic activities addressing current health problems. This has already been envisaged as being part of the future healthcare informatics strategy in Malaysia, in that country's ambition to move rapidly to progress the country's development status with a modern informatics superhighway as one of its future assets (Government of Malaysia). In a UK setting this patient portfolio could be web-based or smart card based, and it would link the patient and the secondary and community care providers with primary care. It could be synchronised with any of these providers at any time, and the patient could opt for e-mail updates where appointments or treatments changed. Such a patient healthcare portfolio would by definition be synchronised with the resource management systems in the form of clinical appointment systems, community health professionals' diaries, and hospital planned therapy programmes.

There is currently within the UK health sector somewhat disorganised consideration of smart record cards or personal health summaries, when for most patients protection of planned action is at least as important. It is significant that countries with opportunity for a fresh start, not least in Malaysia with its concept of personal health plans on the information superhighway, have looked at this more fundamental approach.

## Beckoning horizons or cold reality?

### A new vision of IT-enabled care delivery ...

Based entirely on existing concepts and capabilities in informatics applications in other sectors than health, it is possible to envisage a totally new pattern of healthcare delivery management. In this scenario, when a patient presented to a clinician with a condition needing treatment (including preventive health management), the clinician would not only be able to call up a treatment protocol which would act as the framework for developing a personalised care plan, but they would also be able to call up the current resource availability for each of the components of care. This might include specialist therapeutic procedures, day hospital, and community services delivered to the home. The prescribing clinician would be able to choose the best options available, balancing theoretical optimum with practical availability, and would then be able to book the complete suite of treatment resources. A patient episode identifier, not unlike a commercial airline booking ticket locator, would automatically be entered into the electronic diaries of all these providers and thus provide a linkage. Individual resource managers would be able to plan staffing and skill mix for the confirmed workload, and billing systems could operate in accordance with the health sectors' current mode of resource management. The patient would have a copy of the total treatment plan, with the location and time of every appointment. Delivery facilities would need to structure their electronic diaries to reserve some appointment slots for late-rising urgent or emergency treatments, as has already been postulated.

As treatment progressed, changes in the patient's overall condition and concurrent activities might render variations necessary to the planned pattern of care, and this could be effected through adjustments to the overall future schedule. There would be issues of ensuring that there was overall clinical cohesion and organisation compatible with the autonomy of individually contributing professionals, but the important concepts of leadership and mandates have already been developed and simply need expanding and applying (Rigby, 1998; Consorti et al., 2000). Changes could also be necessitated through unavoidable variations in service availability, whether longer term issues such as changed demands on a facility, or in the short term through staff sickness or the impact of epidemics on case load, but the planned electronic diary system and the knowledge of every episode of care being treated would enable optimal adjustment and notification to all parties. This would be true person-based care, giving the patient the basic confidence and expectation of reliable delivery and the courtesy of notification of changes already commonplace in less important service industries.

### ... and a new health IT system paradigm

Considering alternatives to the increasingly vast and monolithic organisational systems with their highly structured messaging interface with partners, there is an increasingly attractive alternative broker solution whereby record keeping is within departmental systems with intelligent brokers exchanging information on a need to know basis to locally set specifications, and with the individual clinician being alerted to the need to become involved at critical stages. Such solutions are already being researched in the health working environment under the aegis of the Engineering and Physical Sciences Research Council (EPSRC) (Kotsiopoulos et al., 2003; Turner et al., 2004).

None of this is idle speculating – it is merely applying to the health sector concepts already in operation in other sectors. The cold reality may nevertheless be very different. Why? A number of factors contribute to keep the health sector a tortoise amongst hares.

## Impeding factors

First, it is understandably difficult to allocate adequate IT investment to the health sector when there are major competing demands for the same investment to purchase immediate therapeutic assets such as new hospital facilities or diagnostic equipment. Secondly, increased expenditure on information systems is frequently seen in populist and political circles as less attractive than an equivalent investment in professional staff or therapeutic activities, and politicians are scathing about any increase in 'non-clinical' staff or equipment even if they facilitate therapeutic quality or productivity. The establishment of applied developmental 'laboratories' to test new ideas in a working environment not only faces these challenges, but the further risk that it additionally creates an atypical environment where IT-enthusiastic clinicians develop solutions, or adopt working practices, not readily acceptable to their more traditional peers. Yet without such proven developments yielding the evidence of practicality, ethics, and cost-beneficial improvements in care delivery it will not be possible to get either the support of managers for the necessary investment, or of the clinical workforce for the necessary process changes to enable achievable vision to become reality. Indeed there are sound arguments for not investing in major changes unless there is firm evidence to demonstrate not just the practicality, but the benefits. The strength of an evidence-based approach, and the limits to the literature in terms of realistically evaluated visionary approaches, is shown by the Australian experience of developing an evidence-based strategy (National Health Information Management Advisory Council, 1999).

## Discussion: better hopes, allayed fears?

This paper was first developed for a conference on the theme of studying Health Futures, but with a focus on identifying Hopes and Fears. The Hopes of many existing stakeholders in health IT, not least politicians and central managers, are the rolling forward of electronic patient record systems in a way which is organisation-focused, and the development of Electronic Lifelong Records, even though there is neither a proven model nor a feasibility study for these in terms of the proposed lifelong records for a total catchment population. These Hopes are based primarily on using the increased capacity of new IT systems to automate existing health organisational processes. The Fears are that many of these concepts are not tried and tested, and that both the capacity to implement and maintain them, and the degree of both education and training provided for the hundreds of thousands of end users, will be inadequate for the purpose. Further, because these systems are untested, but when developed will be extremely large and thus somewhat monolithic, there is the potential danger of creating new legacy systems.

A new and more positive set of Hopes and Fears is possible. The Hopes would be that there could be scope for more radical reviewing of healthcare delivery processes utilising new IT so as to bring to healthcare the significant changes for the better which have been achieved by other sectors. Moreover, from the examples given above, this would be both patient-orientated and beneficial to practitioners. This would lead to a new and more exciting future with truly patient-centric activities, information and knowledge, but linked in very firmly and positively to organisational processes. The initial Fear is that this could lead to major pressures for change in these directions once working models had been demonstrated, and that capital and human resources would become yet again overstretched. However, the alternative and probably more realistic Fear is that these ideas will be discussed as luxurious flights of fantasy, and the health sector will continue to fall behind its counterparts in other sectors.

The missing component towards achieving the brighter vision is any means of the interests coming together, not only to debate, but also to sponsor innovation through an innovative research fund. At present there is no body that has the remit or the resources to encourage the creation of visions, and to follow these through with scientific exploration. Present research programmes are narrowly focused on either validating specific technologies, or on finding 'solutions' to 'problems' and blockages. This is significantly less than the visioning for innovative paradigms of support to better informed and managed healthcare delivery processes. The aspects of health informatics which determine the quality of the applications and the service have previously been delineated (Rigby, 2002), but the development of knowledge bases to address these is limited.

Similarly, there is no adequate funding for Evaluation, though the evaluation function is crucial both to learning from application issues in the real world of non-research sites, and to enable building up of the evidence base on which policy and planning can be established. Just as healthcare delivery and healthcare policy should themselves be seen as being evidence-based disciplines, surely the same can be argued for the underpinning information systems. Evaluation is a field that is almost always avoided as a 'waste' of resources, when in fact it can be valuable to ensuring future optimal use of resources and indeed design and implementation of healthcare delivery support systems (Rigby, 2001; Ammenworth et al., 2004).

Without the provision of an appropriate body which can act as an applied research council, as well as providing a meeting place for visionaries, practitioners and researchers and providing an 'open skies' if not totally 'blue skies' policy development environment, there will continue to be the serious risk – indeed likelihood – that the Fears for health ICT will materialise and that the Hopes will be sadly frustrated.

## Conclusion

As healthcare delivery moves forward, new technologically-based opportunities will affect supply and demand. Demand and supply will interact with each other and be related to and articulated by an increasingly electronically articulate public. In this context modestly increasing expectations and increasing investment in IT, especially if it lacks integration between the parts, may make little impact on progress. Centralist programmes based largely on policy direction devoid of cited evidence, pressure on organisations to achieve implementation milestones devoid of local ownership, and increasing pressure on all those engaged in health to 'modernise' without consideration of the changes to their professional functioning, will all add to these risks. The fact that health professionals and others have no forum to which to bring visions for development and evaluation, whilst the ICT support staff are caught in a dichotomy of role between straightforward support and maintenance and inadequately steered and funded development without any research context, are compounding factors. In order to harness innovation in health Information Technology, a new paradigm of openness, research and evidence-based policy and resourcing are needed. Service and manufacturing sectors show what can be achieved, but they do so using a developmental framework not existing in the current health sector, but perfectly capable of being implemented if the will and the resourcing were to be provided. This ought to be and should be possible given the importance of Information Management and Technology support to healthcare delivery, but it would be even more effective if there were to be established an independent health policy forum drawing upon information and evidence to reach objective policy recommendations, as recently advocated by Detmer (27).

## References

Ammenworth, E. et al. (2004) 'Visions and strategies to improve evaluation of health information systems – reflections and lessons based on the HIS-EVAL workshop in Innsbruck', *International Journal of Medical Informatics,* **73**(6):479–91

Consorti, F., Lalle, C, Ricci, F.L. and Rossi-Mori, A. (2000) 'Relevance of mandates, notifications and threads in the management of continuity of care', *Studies in Health Technology and Informatics,* **77**:1035–9

Detmer, D.E. (2004) 'Improving Great Britain's health system: an adaptive model to harness information and evidence', in Rigby, M. (ed.) *Vision and Value in Health Information*; Oxford: Radcliffe Medical Press

Dick, R.S. and Steen, E.D. (eds) (1996) *The Computer-Based Patient record: an Essential Technology for Healthcare.* Washington, DC: National Academy Press

Draper, R. and Rigby, M. (eds) (2000) *Electronic Records: Ethical Guidance: a Framework for the Ethical Use of Electronic Record Systems.* Stillorgan, Ireland: Hospitaller Order of St John of God

Government of Malaysia (1997) *Malaysia's Telemedicine Blueprint: Leading Healthcare into the Information Age.* Kuala Lumpur: Ministry of Health of Malaysia

Hasselbring, W., Peterson, R., Smits, M. and Spanjers, R. (2000) 'Strategic information management for a Dutch University Hospital', in Hasman, A., Blobel, B. and Dudeck, D. et al. (eds) *Medical Infobahn for Europe: Proceedings of MIE2000 and GMDS2000.* Amsterdam: IOS Press, 969–73

Kotsiopoulos, I., Keane, J. and Turner, M. et al. (2003) 'IBHIS: integration broker for heterogeneous information sources', in *Proceedings of COMPSAC 2003,* IEEE Computer Society Press, November, 378–84

Lakhani, A. (2000) 'Assessment of clinical and health outcomes within the National Health Service in England', in Leadbeter, D. (ed.) *Harnessing Official Statistics* (Harnessing Health Information Series No. 3), Abingdon: Radcliffe Medical Press

Lakhani, A. (2004) 'Information for the assessment of health outcomes', in Rigby, M. (ed.) *Vision and Value in Health Information.* Oxford: Radcliffe Medical Press

National Health Information Management Advisory Council (1999) *Health Online: a Health Information Action Plan for Australia.* Canberra: Department of Health and Aged Care

NHS Executive (1999) *Learning to Manage Health Information.* Bristol: NHS Executive South and West (ISBN 0 953 27190 8)

Rigby, M. (1997) 'Keeping confidence in confidentiality: linking ethics, efficiency, and opportunity in healthcare computing – a case study', in Anderson R. (ed.) *Personal Medical Information: Security, Engineering, and Ethics.* Personal Information Workshop, Cambridge, UK, June 21–22 1996 Proceedings, Berlin: Springer-Verlag, 129–50

Rigby, M. (1998) 'Reviewing and developing architectural and technological concepts to meet the needs of long-term holistic health services', in Moorman, P.W., van der Lei, J. and Musen, M.A. (eds) *Proceedings of IMIA Working Group 17, Rotterdam, 8–10 October 1998 – EPRiMP: The International Working Conference on Electronic Patients Records in Medical Practice.* Rotterdam: Department of Medical Records, Erasmus University, 338–43

Rigby, M. (1999) 'The management and policy challenges of the globalisation effect of informatics and telemedicine', *Health Policy,* **46**:97–103

Rigby, M. (2001) 'Evaluation: 16 powerful reasons why not to do it – and 6 overriding imperatives', in Patel, V., Rogers, R. and Haux, R. (eds) *Medinfo 2001: Proceedings of the 10th World Congress on Medical Informatics.* Amsterdam: IOS Press, 1198–202

Rigby, M. (2002) 'Determinants of quality in health informatics', *Irish Journal of Medical Science,* **171**, 3, Supplement 1, 15–18

Rigby, M. (2004) 'Protecting the patient by ensuring end-user competence in health informatics systems: moves towards a generic health computer user 'Driving Licence', *International Journal of Medical Informatics,* **73**:151–6

Rigby, M. and Robins, S. (1996) 'Practical success of an electronic patient record system in community care – a manifestation of the vision and discussion of the issues', *International Journal of Bio-Medical Computing*, 42:117–22

Rigby, M., Millen, D. and Benjamin, D. ( 2003) 'Creating a structured progressive qualifications path in applied health informatics', in Proceedings of *Teach Globally, Learn Locally: Innovations in Health and Biomedical Informatics Education in the 21st Century*. International Medical Informatics Association Working Group on Education Conference, Portland, Oregon USA, April 23–5, CD-ROM, Oregon Health and Science University, Portland, Oregon

Roberts, R., Rigby, M. and Birch, K. (2000) 'Telematics in healthcare: new paradigm, new issues', in Rigby, M., Roberts, R. and Thick, M. (eds) *Taking Health Telematics into the 21st Century*. Abingdon: Radcliffe Medical Press, 1–17

Roberts, R., Thomas, J., Rigby, M. and Williams, J. (1997) 'Practical protection of confidentiality in acute care', in Anderson R. (ed.) *Personal Medical Information: Security, Engineering, and Ethics*. Personal Information Workshop, Cambridge, UK, June 21–22, 1996, Proceedings; Berlin: Springer-Verlag, 67–8

Turner, M. et al. (2004) 'Using web service technologies to create an information broker: an experience report', Proceedings of 26th International Conference on Software Engineering, IEEE Computer Society Press, 552–61

www.doh.gov.uk/nhsperformanceindicators
www.drfoster.co.uk/hospitalguide/main/methodology.asp
www.nhsia.nhs.uk/nhid/pages/awards/default.asp

# 13
# Public Perceptions, Ambivalence and the Endogenous Regulation of Biotechnology in the UK

*Joan Costa-Font* and *Elias Mossialos*

## Introduction

The development in the 1970s of genetic engineering techniques and, specifically, the discovery of the recombinant DNA have led to the so-called third generation biotechnology now under scrutiny for risks amongst national and international risks policy makers. Recent biotechnology developments may be seen as key drivers of healthcare systems. However, scientific developments are only transformed into health policy innovation through a process that takes enormous time and resources. The association between science policy and health policy is rather non-linear and time dependent.

Biotech will impact on health status by giving rise to more efficient clinical technologies. However, how new biotechnology will be developed is highly determined by public acceptance. Thus, one of the basic challenges for health systems is to secure appropriate communication and knowledge transfer on both opportunities and risks, as well as to understand better how behavioural reactions to technological knowledge influence acceptance of potentially efficient technologies. Survey analysis of individuals' acceptance of biotech can enable a better understanding of the issues. At the same time public perceptions should be appropriately interpreted in their context, in the light of respondents' awareness as well as taking into account the amount and novelty of public information available. The importance of public perceptions is noticeable by the fact that industry leaders worry deeply about public acceptance in order to reassure the consumer that technologies such as xeno-transplantation techniques and transgenic food are safe. It is in their interest to demonstrate safety while those against biotech wish to demonstrate the opposite. However, industrial leaders, along with public policy makers frequently frame public questioning about science and safety as irrational challenges by scientifically illiterate consumers; whereas the opposition conjures up a 'scientific-political-industrial' complex unconcerned with long term issues of safety and sustainability. There is therefore unhelpful labelling on both sides which is not conductive to a reasoned and productive debate.

The accelerated development of new technologies precludes both individuals and policy makers from reaching a decision on the 'accepted perceived safety and the perceived benefits' that derive from the introduction of new technologies into the health system and the economy as a whole. There is, however, still considerable uncertainty over scientific research, which indicates the need for improved knowledge on the risks and benefits of new scientific developments, as in the case of new biotechnology applications. Decision-making on how to regulate the diffusion of new biotechnology is substantially constrained by the existence of incomplete information on both the potential consequences, as well as on the public's reasoning process in the presence of incomplete information. People do not know much about the scientific benefits of biotech but are intrigued by the benefits both for themselves and for society.

As a precondition for regulating biotechnology, significant knowledge might need to be communicated not only to regulatory bodies but to the public as well in order to allow them to form 'informed preferences' that would improve reasoning and lead arguably to a collective acceptance of certain technologies. Otherwise, if preferences over biotechnology applications remain uninformed by knowledge and taken by an exclusive group of experts alone, the public may boycott unaccepted regulation. In democratic societies, policy-making is to some extent limited by public acceptance and support, giving rise to what may be called 'endogenous regulation'. That is, regulation rather than being merely dictated by experts, needs to meet public acceptance, which in turn determines future regulation. Indeed, the Resolution of the Nice European Council[1] in 2000 established:

> that public authorities have a responsibility to ensure a high level of protection of human health and the environment and have to address increased public concern regarding the risks to which the public are potentially exposed.

Therefore, if science policy-making is undertaken in a setting where accountability is a major issue, then public perceptions are expected to inform as well as constrain science regulation. Probably one of the greatest limits to biotechnology regulation is that even when knowledge is provided to formulate judgements on the acceptability of certain technologies, such decisions on acceptability might largely result from some consistency with the associated value systems rather than being exclusively based on knowledge diffusion on the possible risks and benefits.

The aim of this paper is to examine perceptions of biotechnology applications in the United Kingdom. It focuses on the inconsistency between perceiving large risks and benefits and concerns on moral acceptability; the so-called 'ambivalence'. The research question we examine refers to the extent to which acceptance of biotechnology in the UK is affected by 'ambivalence'. In this way we hope to shed some light on the future risk communication policies for biotechnology.

The paper is structured as follows: the following section discusses some issues influencing public perceptions. From that we examine the role of ambivalence in influencing perceptions; then provide empirical evidence from the 1996 (46.1) and the 1999 (52.1) Eurobarometer surveys on the public perception of science and biotechnology. This facilitates a comparison of the UK with the rest of the European Union.[2] The role and determinants of ambivalence are investigated further using a sub-sample of the 1999 Eurobarometer survey (52.1).

## Endogenous regulation and risk communication

Risk analysts have largely advocated the development of cost-effective measures in order to examine whether the social benefits outweigh the risks of specific technologies. Theoretically, the acceptance of new technologies should follow the risk assessment golden rule whereby benefits are supposed to exceed the 'acceptable risks'.[3] However when the probability as well as expected consequences of certain technologies (damages or benefits) are unknown, then insurance and other market instruments cannot be employed to diversify risks. In areas of new technology it is often the case that the potential benefits and risks to society are not fully understood, partly because the information available is on hypothetical grounds.

Public risk communication agencies often have to compete with other agents in the economy that act as risks amplifiers (advocacy groups) or risks minimisers (interested corporations). However, risks amplifiers are typically preferred by newspaper editors. Therefore, information highlighting potential risks is normally reported which leads to the so called 'risk ratchet' (Jenkins and Silva, 1998).[4] In essence, individuals are hypothetically both ambiguity averse and risk averse. In their personal risk assessment evaluations they are more likely to exaggerate risks (even when hypothetical), whenever there is widespread publicity on the adverse consequences of a particular technology. Therefore, the acceptance of specific technology not only depends on the substantial benefits that new and unknown technologies may bring, but on the extent to which information channels publicise information on the potential risks and whether this information allows a precise risk estimation. In addition to the coverage by information channels, and even when some sort of formal risk assessment is undertaken, regulatory controversies and policy debates often arise around how *safe is safe enough*. At this point debates are driven to some extent by public acceptance, and who is expected to contribute in finding an answer to this question.

Critics of biotechnology point to the long-term health and environmental concerns. Indeed, the extension of biotechnology on to the market has been met with considerable opposition in the European Union. Groups opposing GM crops draw on environmental and human health concerns when challenging regulatory decisions. A clear example is HRH Prince Charles who stated the following in the *Daily Telegraph* (8 June 1998):

'I happen to believe that this kind of genetic manipulation takes mankind into realms that belong to God, and to God alone ...' and '... it is all right to use science to understand how nature works, but not to change what nature is, as we do when genetic manipulation seeks to transform a process of biological evolution into something altogether different'.

Furthermore, religious groups advocate that genetic manipulation of the human genome is 'playing God' and should be banned even when it provides benefits in terms of health improvements. This explains significant opposition exercised by Pope John Paul II. Speaking to an estimated 50,000 farmers from Italy and elsewhere at a special outdoor mass dedicated to farmers on 15 November 2000 the Pope told them and their colleagues worldwide to:

'resist the temptation of high productivity and profit that work to the detriment of the respect of nature'.

As some authors point out, science sometimes is judged and condemned by people who have no idea of what they are talking about (Audétat, 2000). Therefore, survey analysis should provide information on how people form their attitudes and which personal characteristics are explanatory of ambivalence and other inconsistencies in decision-making.

Elucidating the nature of people's perceptions is a topical and key policy-making research question. Biotechnology offers huge potential for improving the dynamic efficiency of our healthcare system. Furthermore, it brings up some possible risks that we still need to know more about. In order to help decision-making under scientific uncertainty, examining the determinants of people's acceptance is a vital issue.

## Acceptance of biotechnology applications

### Evidence from the European Union

The lack of consumer acceptance of biotechnology is a matter of widespread policy debate in most European Union countries. Recent data from the Eurobarometer surveys shows that public support for biotechnology is not strong. Compared to other technologies, comparatively few respondents believe it will improve their life in the next 20 years and support dropped between 1996 and 1999. (Figure 13.1). However,

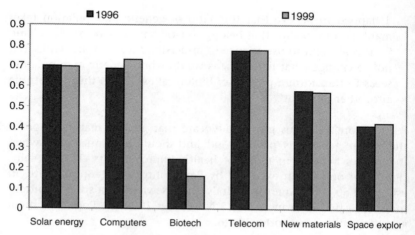

*Figure 13.1*: Attitudes towards several new technologies in the EU (measured using a scale from +1 (agree) to –1 (disagree). The higher the score the more likely individuals accept a technology.)

when looking at specific countries, significant heterogeneity was found. That is, the acceptance of biotechnology differed substantially across countries. Whereas the UK, France and Spain showed relatively high acceptance of biotechnology as improving the quality of life, Greece and Finland showed the opposite[5] (Sielgrist, 1999).

When thinking about biotechnology the European public associate and identify biotech mostly with cloning (43 per cent), scientific research (33 per cent) and genetically modified food (28 per cent). Interestingly, the highest percentage of 'don't know' answers were found in Portugal (64 per cent) and Greece (55 per cent), suggesting that there might be a potential positive correlation with income levels as well as differences resulting from cultural influences. However some studies show that risks perceptions were associated with income levels; that is, proportionately more people in poorer societies are more willing to accept risks than in richer ones. At the same time, due to the existence of ambivalence in perception and the role of the media, it might be that acceptance would increase with income.

## Product heterogeneity and resistance

When examining attitudes towards biotechnology applications, the evidence seems to show that *individuals are able to distinguish products from processes*. In a recent study we show that about 1.5 per cent of the UK population display an attitude of rejection towards all biotechnology applications (Costa and Mossialos, 2003). Nonetheless acceptance and perceptions of risk differ substantially across applications as well as across countries.

## Values and moral acceptability

A number of studies point out increasing European opposition to genetically modified foods (Gaskell et al., 1999) *which contrasts with supportive attitudes towards healthcare and environmental applications* (Worcester, 1999). This feature leads us to hypothesise that the way individuals *learn about biotechnology* might be constrained by the role moral beliefs play in determining attitudes. On the basis of existing literature, knowledge is not the unique explanatory determinant of acceptance. Moral beliefs do exert a key influence (Macer, 1994, 1996), as do protests from social reference groups (e.g., environmentalists on GMOs, or moral resistance from the Catholic Church to certain medical applications). Thus, a risk–benefit model alone might not fully explain how particular technologies are accepted (Gaskell et al., 2000) and thus an alternative model should be explored.

## The role of ambivalence in determining attitudes

The importance of moral beliefs as playing an influential role encompasses the emergence of 'ambivalence' in individual perceptions. Quantitative and qualitative research undertaken draws upon the concept of *ambivalence* in explaining attitudes. Ambivalence results from individuals expressing high positively associated judgements to contradictory dimensions (e.g., that cloning may be highly beneficial, incurring strong risks while being morally unacceptable). This phenomenon highlights that the influence of ambivalence may be one of the causes explaining scepticism in attitudes towards biotech. This feature has created strong debates on the demand-side limits to the extension of biotechnology applications. As a result, some point out the need for a more cautious evaluation of new technologies, while others question the role of the public in guiding scientific policy-making.

## The role of knowledge

Information is probably one of the main constraints to individuals when reaching a decision in the area of biotechnology. Experimental evidence exhibits that people prefer alternatives on which they feel more 'knowledgeable' (Heath and Tversky, 1991). Sheehy et al. (1998) finds that although consumers demand freedom of choice, this refers to the cases where they do have access to the information on which to make a choice. When it comes to biotechnology, individuals feel ill prepared to make 'informed decisions', and either they do not feel able to judge biotechnology applications,[6] or alternatively they draw upon core values instead of knowledge. Therefore, knowledge is an important factor in determining the influence of values on individuals' attitudes towards biotechnology (Costa and Mossialos, 2003). That is, values prevail as unique information determinants as a result of the individual's lack of information upon which to make 'informed decisions'.[7]

Arguably, the individuals' lack of information precludes that public perceptions of biotechnology are substantially influenced by ambivalence. Interestingly, the evidence suggests that in most procedures examined in the Eurobarometer surveys, the lay public perceives biotech procedures as being beneficial, but simultaneously identifies substantial potential human risks (Costa and Mossialos, 2003). An explanation of the connections between ambivalence towards biotechnology and a lack of knowledge is one of 'public mistrust in technology' resulting from the fear of the new and the uncertainty over unknown procedures. Accordingly, if ambivalence and sceptical attitudes are somehow the result of an individual's lack of knowledge, policy should focus on improving access to information in several ways, e.g., by improving science education.

## Trust in regulatory institutions

The lack of acceptance of biotechnology in the European Union has been regarded as being the result of the lack of individual trust in regulators. The European public displays by far the most trust in the medical profession, followed at some distance by trust in environmental and consumer organisations (Gaskell, 1997) This could be coupled with public mistrust of the motivations of regulatory institutions and innovating corporations.[8] One possible interpretation of the evidence on trust lies in the nature of the agency relationship between institutions and individuals. Although imperfect, the medical profession and consumer and environmental organisations are perceived by the public as working on the behalf of the public, unlike alternative institutions for example industrial organisations, national public bodies, the media and religious organisations. In order to reduce mistrust of some regulatory bodies decisions over the development of these technologies should be made more transparent.

## The trade-off between values and knowledge

We argue that ambivalence has to do with moral acceptance as being an expression of values conflicting with the standard risk–benefit decision-making rule. This phenomenon is what surveys dealing with valuing contingent goods identify as the 'embedding effect'. That is, when individuals are to express their attitudes and the costs of attitude provision are low, there is no incentive to express 'reasoned preferences' based on risks and benefits, and thus elicit values instead. Values might lead to the weighing of benefits and risks being relatively unstable irrespective of the individual's reasoning capacity. Moral attitudes might influence how people weigh risks and benefits, and thus intensify the difficulties in interpreting attitudes. From a policy perspective, the existence of 'ambivalence' might prevent us from trusting public opinion on science policy.[9] Alternatively, this might lead us to examine how attitudes are influenced by ambivalence.

Ambivalence is routinely the result of a lack of information combined with the simultaneous use of conflicting – positive and negative – dimensions in the information system when an individual is asked for attitudes towards biotechnology. Hence, ambivalence is acknowledged as a common decision-making limitation affecting attitudes as providing quantitative evidence in support for certain applications (Gaskell, 1997; Lujan and Todt, 2000; Heijis, Midden and Drabbe, 1993). It is common when evaluating the impact of new technologies that individuals display 'dual preferences'. If moral concerns, as we argue, are taken to express values and risk–benefit perceptions refer to individual reasoned attitudes, ambivalence might then be the result of a conflict between values and preferences. A lack of support for biotechnology in the face of the low real risks that the techniques entail leads us to sustain that lack of support might be the result of values prevailing over attitudes. Conversely, support for biotech applications would suggest that in this conflict attitudes prevail.

## Empirical evidence and methods

The empirical study has two clear parts. First, we examine perceptions of biotechnology in two years 1996 and 1999 using Eurobarometer surveys 46.4 and 52.1. This allows to examine how attitudes have varied as well as the role of ambivalence in the UK as compared to the EU. The second part of the study, employs exclusively The Eurobarometer Survey 52.1 to examine the attitudes and perceptions of biotechnology products. Eurobarometer surveys were developed by INRA (EUROPE) as a mandate from the European Commission, with around 16,000 people in the 15 EU member states. These surveys explore the acceptance of biotechnology and public knowledge on biotechnology at the EU level. From this survey we focus on the following four questions that show the same structure:

> 'To what extent do you agree or disagree that this application is ( (1) risky/ (2) useful/ (3) morally acceptable/ (4) should be encouraged)?'

This question was posed for each of the different biotech applications which were subjected to public scrutiny in the two surveys. The six applications can be divided into:

(a) *Food biotech*: the question referred to the 'use of modern biotechnology in the production of foods, for example to make them higher in protein, keep longer or to change the taste'.
(b) *Medical biotech*: the questions referred to 'introducing human genes into bacteria to produce medicines or vaccines, for example to produce insulin for diabetics'.

For each of the biotech applications considered, an individual was classified as ambivalent if *he/she perceived a specific application as being risky, useful and morally unacceptable*. Alternative combinations yielded the

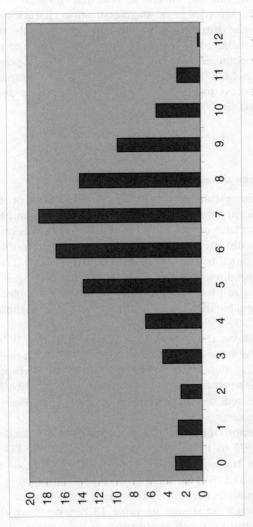

*Figure 13.2*: Knowledge of science in the UK computed as a response to 12 questions on science and biotechnology in Eurobarometer 52.1 (Gaskell, G. et al. 2000)

same results. Empirical analysis used multi-variate logistic regression analysis for qualitative data and the ordered logit model for ordered data. Multi-variate analysis was undertaken by sketching some variables contained in the Eurobarometer survey that proxied either information channels, knowledge or socio-economic characteristics. From these variables the interesting preliminary evidence is that knowledge of science seems to be normally distributed. The vast majority of UK respondents obtained between 5–8 points in a 0–12-point scale, as shown in Figure 13.2. The mean is slightly above 6 and is highly corrected with access to education and socio-economic determinants (Costa and Mossialos, 2003).

## Results

### Attitudes and their determinants

Table 13.1 displays estimated results on the acceptance of six biotechnology applications. Interestingly, when the UK was compared to the mean for EU countries, it was found that acceptance was much higher across all applications, although the UK has experienced a similar decline in acceptance to the rest of EU countries. Table 13.1 provides information of the dimensions of acceptance, that is the perceptions of usefulness, risks and moral acceptability for a set of six biotechnology applications. The table displays UK estimates as well as estimates for the EU average.

The evidence shows that perceptions of benefit in the UK were either higher than or the same as the EU average in 1996. With the exception of animal biotech where there has been a rise in the perceptions of its usefulness, *benefit perceptions have declined from 1996 to 1999.* That is, the British public has reduced its perception of utility for different applications of biotechnology.

With the exception of Plant GMO, perceptions of risks in the UK have declined from 1996 to 1999, which does not follow the EU pattern in general although there were some exceptions e.g. that of xenotransplants. Perceptions of risks for some biotech applications (e.g. GM food) are higher or equal in the UK as compared than the rest of the EU. Interestingly enough, as shown in Table 13.1, acceptance (labelled as 'Encouraged') of most biotech applications is on average higher in the UK.

The moral acceptability of biotechnology has declined from 1996 to 1999, with the exception of animal biotech, where it seems to have

*Table 13.1:* Public perceptions of modern technology in the production of foods UK versus EU (usefulness, risk perceptions, moral acceptability and acceptance)

Question: 'To what extent do you agree or disagree, that this application is useful/is risky/is morally acceptable/should be encouraged?'

| | 1996 | | | | 1999 | | | |
|---|---|---|---|---|---|---|---|---|
| | Useful | Risky | Morally acceptable | Encouraged | Useful | Risky | Morally acceptable | Encouraged |
| Food Production UK | 0.44 | 0.63 | 0.39 | 0.28 | -0.03 | 0.71 | 0.18 | -0.17 |
| Food Production EU | 0.24 | 0.55 | 0.12 | -0.08 | 0.03 | 0.72 | 0.31 | -0.40 |
| Plant GMO UK | 1.00 | 0.19 | 0.87 | 0.89 | 0.69 | 0.24 | 0.49 | 0.496 |
| Plant GMO EU | 0.76 | 0.18 | 0.53 | 0.41 | 0.53 | 0.43 | 0.32 | 0.06 |
| Pharmabiotech UK | 1.23 | 0.41 | 0.90 | 0.98 | 1.05 | 0.33 | 0.68 | 0.84 |
| Pharmabiotech EU | 1.25 | 0.05 | 0.89 | 0.95 | 1.13 | 0.31 | 0.65 | 0.75 |
| Animal biotech UK | 0.95 | 0.56 | 0.34 | 0.60 | 1.30 | 0.31 | 0.92 | 1.03 |
| Animal biotech EU | 0.43 | 0.30 | -0.19 | -0.05 | 0.92 | 0.51 | 0.38 | 0.50 |
| Xenotransplant UK | 0.55 | 0.88 | -0.12 | 0.20 | 0.16 | 0.64 | -0.21 | -0.08 |
| Xenotransplant EU | 0.22 | 0.57 | -0.38 | -0.23 | 0.25 | 0.61 | -0.20 | -0.18 |
| Genetic Testing UK | 1.38 | 0.26 | 1.06 | 1.20 | 1.32 | -0.04 | 1.02 | 1.18 |
| Genetic Testing EU | 1.32 | -0.18 | 0.97 | 1.04 | 1.29 | -0.04 | 0.90 | 0.99 |

Note: index estimated by giving a value of +2 to definitely agree answers, 1 to tends to agree, −1 to tends to disagree and −2 to definitely disagrees (Gaskell, G. et al., 2000).

*Table 13.2*: Partial correlation coefficients between benefit dimensions among EU countries

|  | Risky | Useful | Morally acceptable |
|---|---|---|---|
| **1996** | | | |
| Food production | −0.51* | −0.90** | 0.89** |
| Plant GMO | −0.61* | 0.83** | 0.97** |
| Medicine GMO | −0.27 | 0.80** | 0.94** |
| Animal research | 0.09 | 0.85** | 0.94** |
| Xenotransplant | −0.07 | 0.91** | 0.94** |
| Genetic tests | 0.40 | 0.92** | 0.97** |
| **1999** | | | |
| Food production | −0.83** | 0.91** | 0.89* |
| Plant GMO | −0.78** | 0.91** | 0.80** |
| Medicine GMO | −0.38 | 0.81** | 0.95** |
| Animal research | −0.26 | 0.87** | 0.95** |
| Xenotransplant | −0.64** | 0.84** | 0.94** |
| Genetic tests | −0.31 | 0.68** | 0.88** |

*Significant at a 5%
**Significant at a 1% level

increased. Interestingly, the moral acceptability of gene testing remains constant. Thus, a major source of the decline in acceptance in the UK over the three-year period considered is a reduction in moral acceptability.

## What drives attitudes?

Table 13. 2 displays the correlation coefficients between acceptance and its dimensions of risks perceptions, usefulness and moral acceptability for all EU countries. The evidence shows that whereas the association between moral acceptability and usefulness did not vary from 1996 to 1999, risks perception did significantly vary and as expected always displays a negative partial correlation coefficient. This result if examined in its context leads us to identify the rise in scientific uncertainty and the errors in science communication policy resulting from several foods scandals, such as the BSE, as being the major explanation for a decline in acceptance resulting from a rise in the role of risks perception in influencing attitudes.

## Non-attitudes

A traditional concern when ascertaining attitudes where there is a lack of knowledge is whether in these circumstances, it is valid to request, and even if offered, to examine, elicited attitudes. Table 13.3 highlights that there were significant differences in the response rate across different biotech applications. On average more than one-third of the population did not respond with an answer. Medical biotech was normally the area receiving the higher share of non-answers, with the exception of greater responses for gene testing and food GMO.

## Ambivalence estimates

Table 13.4 displays an estimate of ambivalence as obtained following the methods explained previously. In doing so we found considerable

*Table 13.3*: Non-respondents to several biotechnology applications in 1999 (UK)

| Application | % of respondents |
|---|---|
| Food production | 65.81 |
| Plant GMO | 59.33 |
| Medicine GMO | 58.02 |
| Animal research | 62.11 |
| Xenotransplant | 55.94 |
| Genetic tests | 61.18 |

*Table 13.4*: Share of ambivalent responses in 1999 (UK)

| Application | % Ambivalent | Mean attitude of ambivalent | Mean attitudes of non-ambivalent |
|---|---|---|---|
| Food production | 10.80 | 1.147 | 1.432 |
| Plant GMO | 8.26 | 1.0746 | 1.409 |
| Medicine GMO | 2.01 | 1.153 | 1.753 |
| Animal research | 3.16 | 1.243 | 1.757 |
| Xenotransplant | 7.41 | 1.062 | 1.338 |
| Genetic tests | 1.16 | 1.066 | 1.900 |

*Note*: Attitudes were computed by the following metric ranging from strongly agree equals 4 and strongly disagrees equals 1.

*Table 13.5:* Determinants of ambivalence in individuals' perceptions (UK)

|  | Definition | Food production | Plant GMO | Medicine GMO | Animal research | Xenotransplant | Genetic tests |
|---|---|---|---|---|---|---|---|
| Knowledge | Variable ranging from 1–12 | 0.027 (0.02) | 0.04 (0.02) | -0.04 (0.03) | -0.12 (0.02) | -0.001 (0.02) | -0.03 (0.04) |
| Gender | 1 = male | -0.19* (0.09) | -0.12 (0.99) | -0.07 (0.15) | -0.09 (0.13) | -0.15 (0.10) | 0.17 (0.19) |
| Household size | Number of members | -0.026 (-0.12) | -0.09 (0.14) | -0.012 (0.20) | -0.04 (0.17) | 0.007 (0.13) | 0.10 (0.22) |
| Cooperation | 1 = cooperates | 0.08 (0.06) | 0.26** (0.07) | -0.02 (0.09) | 0.02 (0.08) | 0.08 (0.06) | -0.13 (0.11) |
| News | 1 = reads press | -0.05 (0.91) | -0.08 (0.09) | -0.05 (0.15) | -0.36** (0.13) | -0.23** (0.10) | -0.56** (0.19) |
| Extreme political attitudes | Extreme right or left = 1 | 0.22** (0.10) | 0.21* (0.11) | 0.29* (0.15) | 0.16 (0.15) | 0.22* (0.11) | 0.39** (0.18) |
| Age | Years | 0.007** (0.002) | 0.007* (0.03) | 0.005 (0.005) | 0.006* (0.003) | 0.003 (0.003) | 0.002 (0.05) |
| Constant |  | -1.77** (0.23) | -2.23** (0.27) | -2.20** (0.38) | -1.83** (0.32) | -1.55** (0.25) | -1.74 (0.41) |
| Likelihood Ratio Test (Chi-square) |  | 19.82** | 29.58** | 20.56** | 17.49** | 16.77** | 15.34** |

*Note:* standard errors in parenthesis.
* Significant at a 5% level
** Significant at a 1% level

differences in the share of individuals that could be classified as providing ambivalent responses. *Whereas ambivalence was 10 per cent in the case of Food Biotech and 8.2 per cent in Plant GMO, it declined to 7.4 per cent for xenotransplant and it was about 1 per cent for gene testing.* Therefore, ambivalence seems to be affected by information channels and the role of pressure groups in presenting possible environmental and health concerns associated either with GM foods or xenotransplanation. Interestingly, *ambivalence significantly reduced support for all the biotechnology procedures.*

Table 13.5 provides some multi-variate analysis of the determinants of ambivalence. Ambivalence is found to affect attitudes towards all procedures regardless of knowledge of science. That is, unlike previous estimates made for other EU countries, in the UK ambivalence in attitudes is not explained by differences in knowledge. The influence of information channels is captured through age–gender variables. Gender was only significant for food biotech – suggesting that ambivalence is less likely to affect men in relation to such an application – but it was not significant for the rest. Age was positively associated with ambivalence in relation to those applications involving food or plant GMO and animal research, but was not significant for the rest. Household size, used to proxy the magnitude of people affected, did not display significance at the accepted 5–10 per cent level. With the exception of evaluating plan GMO, ambivalence was not affected by differences in cooperation with the interviewer. The role of the media reduced ambivalence towards animal research, xenotrasplantation and genetic testing, but was non-significant for the remaining applications. Finally, values played a considerable role in pushing up ambivalence levels due to the significance of extreme political attitudes, with the exception of animal research.

## Conclusions

The acceptance of biotechnology applications is a rather complex research area where simple risk–benefit rules do not apply in a linear manner, but rather are strongly constrained by individual core values and public knowledge and awareness. This study has sought to examine existing evidence on public attitudes towards several biotechnology applications in the UK as compared to the EU in general. We found that moral acceptability plays a key role in determining acceptance for biotechnology both in the UK and in the EU. Further, knowledge was found to influence the capacity of individuals to provide a judgement on the different biotechnology applications examined and non-respondents constituted at least one-third of the sample. Therefore, the provision of information is important; it increases knowledge and reduces non-respondents.

Alongside the prevalence of no-answers, attitudes were strongly influenced by ambivalence, which affected attitudes towards food-related biotech more than health biotech, with the exception of xenotransplants. Thus, ambivalence is a significant feature to take into consideration when examining attitudes even though it has a heterogeneous effect across different procedures. Nevertheless, reducing ambivalence would result in a significant increase in acceptance for all biotech applications. Rather than being specific to each application, ambivalence is a general phenomenon although it has a greater effect with regard to those applications of which the individuals have some experience and that information depends on individual choice combined with a lack of knowledge. Attitudes towards each application were affected by different information channels. Political values were key for most of the applications considered, while knowledge was not. This finding provides support for the hypothesis that values play a significant role in determining ambivalence, whereas access to information channels such as reading the press only reduced ambivalence towards certain medical-related procedures. This suggests that medical-biotech may be seen to be too technical for the lay public to understand and this might be a cause of ambivalence in forming attitudes.

This study indicates that the public might get involved in scientific issues whenever there is a moral antecedent or a means of value expression. From a policy perspective, this paper brings to the fore that reducing ambivalence might be a means of increasing support for all biotech procedures, although in a different intensity depending on the information channels that affect specific applications. Therefore, information plays a key role in determining acceptance of new health-related technologies. Furthermore, this feature suggests that within the conflict between 'values and attitudes' leading to ambivalent attitudes, a lack of support for certain biotech applications might imply that *values* prevail among reasoned *attitudes*. However, with the fast-changing nature of scientific discovery in biotech it is not a simple question of informing the public once, but raising the level of awareness and education so that new knowledge can be assimilated, and balancing the whole risks and opportunities as perceived as well as reducing ambivalence.

A sophisticated understanding of the formation and influence of lay attitudes to scientific advances which have huge potential for influencing health policy is fundamental to health planning for the future. This understanding needs to be placed in a context set by the interaction between scientific advances, technological developments, industrial advancement, clinical capacity and public expectations for the future of health policy.

## Notes

1. Council resolution on the precautionary principle, Presidency conclusions, Nice European Council Meeting 7, 8 and 9 December 2000.
2. The United Kingdom is the EU country with the highest national share in total number of publications on biotechnology and applied microbiology; it is equally represented in US national imports and exports in biotechnology and together with Germany is the EU country that allocates greatest public funding to biotechnology R&D. The UK biotechnology is concentrated in bio-pharmaceuticals (46 per cent), which is the largest revenue generating sector and the most R&D intensive (van Beuzekom, 2001).
3. The necessary balance between cost (treatment-induced risk) and benefit (therapeutic effect) underlies all healthcare decisions. A vaccination should be prescribed when its beneficial effect outweighs its inevitable risk. Mandatory vaccination, as in the case of the Hepatitis B virus, is a health policy requiring some courage because those who benefit will never be aware of its positive effect, while those who are victims of the risk could resort to litigation.
4. Jenkins-Smith, H. and Silva, C. (1998), 107–22.
5. Interestingly, acceptance declined from 1996 to 1999 for all countries except for Finland, Portugal and Germany.
6. A common feature is the abundance of non-attitudes ('don't know') answers. Twenty-five per cent of Europeans do not (or are unable to) reveal their attitudes towards specific biotechnology applications. Their responses are shown as DK and are answers associated with education and age as well as with the degree of interview cooperation (Costa and Mossialos, 2002).
7. Under conditions of lack of knowledge, decision-making is no longer rational, but rather based on so-called 'blissful ignorance'. Individuals only get involved in those issues upon which they do have previous knowledge (Costa and Mossialos, 2002).
8. However, it is hard to see trust with institutions as the main cause of ambivalence or sceptical attitudes when experience in regulating this area is limited. In addition, public knowledge on how the regulatory agencies work is normally scarce.

9. Although in this paper we undertake an explicit modelling of moral attitudes at the aggregate country level this is influential when perceptions are
modelled at the individual level.

# References

Audétat, M. (2000) 'Can risk management be democratic?', Paper presented at
the *3rd POSTI International Conference*, London, 1–3 December 2000
Bruhn, C.M. (1992) 'Consumer concerns and educational strategies: focus on
biotechnology', *Food Technology*, 46, 3:80–102
Cantley, M., Hoban, T. and Sasson, A. (1999) 'Regulations and consumer atti-
tudes toward biotechnology', *Nature Biotechnology*, 17:3738
Costa, J. and Mossialos, E. (2002) *Perceptions of Biotechnology Risks under an
Ambiguous Environment*, submitted for publication
Costa, J. and Mossialos, E. (2003) 'Knowledgeable attitudes to biotechnology in
the UK', *LSE discussion paper*
Couchaman, P.K. and Fink-Jensen, K. (1990) *Public Attitudes to Genetic Engineering
in New Zeland*, DSIR Crop Research Report 138 (Department of Scientific and
Industrial Research, Christchurch)
Doubleday, R. (2002) 'The transparent corporation as a legitimate regulator of
agricultural biotechnology', Workshop entitled *Organising Visions*, Cornell
University, 19–21 April 2002
Feldson, R.B. (1996) 'Mass media effects on violent behaviour', *Annual Review of
Sociology*, 22:103–28
Gaskell, G. (1997) 'Europe ambivalent on biotechnology', *Nature*, 387:845–7
Gaskell, G. et al. (2000) 'Biotechnology and the European public', *Nature
Biotechnology*, 18:935–42
Gaskell, G., Bauer, M., Durant, J. and Allum, N. (1999) 'Worlds apart? The recep-
tion of genetically modified foods in Europe and the US.' *Science*, 285:384–7
Gollier, C.H. (200 1) 'Should we beware of the precautionary principle?',
*Economic Policy*, 303–27
Gottlieb, S. (2000) 'In vitro fertilisation is preferable to fertility drugs', *BMJ*, 321:134
Heath, C. and Tversky, A. (1991) 'Preferences and beliefs: ambiguity and compe-
tence in choice under uncertainty', *Journal of Risk and Uncertainty*, 4:29–59
Heijis, W.J.M., Miden, C.J.H. and Drabbe, R.A.J. (1993) *Biotechnology: Attitudes
and Influencing Factors*, Eindhoven University of Technology
Hoban, J. (1996) 'Trends in consumer attitudes about biotechnology', *Journal of
Food Distribution Research*, 27:1–10
Hoban, J. (1997) 'Consumer acceptance of biotechnology: an international per-
spective', *Nature Biotechnology*, 15:232–4
Hoban T.J. and Kendall, P.A. (1993) *Consumer Attitudes About Food Biotechnology*,
Project Report 1993 (Raleigh, NC: North Carolina State University and
Colorado State University), 1–36
Jenkins-Smith, H. and Silva, C. (1998) 'The role of risks perception and technical
information in scientific debates over nuclear waste storage', *Reliability
Engineering and System Safety*, 59

Jonnson, E.J. and Tversky, A. (1983) 'Affect, generalisation and the perception of risk', *Journal of Personality and Social Psychology*, **45**:20–31

Kanheman, D. and Tversky, A. (1972) 'Subjective probability: a judgement of representativeness', *Cognitive Psychology*, **3**:430–54

Lujan, J.L. and Todt, O. (2000) 'Perceptions, attitudes and ethical valuations: the ambivalence of the public image of biotechnology in Spain', *Public Understanding of Science*, **9**:383–92

Macer, D. (1994) 'Perception of risks and benefits of in vitro fertilisation, genetic engineering and biotechnology', *Social Science and Medicine* **38**:23–33

Macer, D. (1996) 'Public acceptance and risks of biotechnology', in *Quality of Risk Assessment in Biotechnology* (International Centre for Human and Public Affairs, Tilburg, The Netherlands), 227–46

OCDE, Anonymous 'Biotechnology statistics in OECD member countries: compendium of existing national statistics', *STI Working Papers, 6*

Polkinghorne, J.C. (2000) 'Ethical issues in biotechnology', *Trends in Biotechnology*, Jan., **18**, 1:8–10

Sheehy, H., Legault, M. and Ireland, D. (1998) 'Consumers and biotechnology: a synopsis of survey and focus group research', *Journal of Consumer Policy*, **21**:359–86

Sielgrist, M. (1999) 'Poorer European countries are less concerned about biotechnology that richer ones', *Risk: Health, Safety and Environment*, **12**:29–39

Straughan, R. (2000) 'Moral and ethical issues in plant biotechnology', *Current Opinion on Plant Biology*, April, **3**, 2:163–5

van Beuzekom, B. (2001) 'Biotechnology statistics in OECD member countries: an inventory', OECD Working Paper 2000/6

Wahlberg, A. and Sjoberg, L. (2000) 'Risk perception and the media', *Journal of Risk Research*, **3**:31–50

Worcester, R.M. (1999) 'Science and democracy: public attitudes to science and scientists', *World Conference on Science*, 28 June 1999

# Conclusion

*Sandra Dawson, Zoë Morris, Linda Chang* and *Charlotte Sausman*

In this final chapter we attempt to pull together some of the common themes which emerge from previous chapters and consider their implications for future health policy. Many of the individual chapters have themselves given some view of the way UK health policy might (or should) develop in the future. The aim here is to draw some general conclusions in the context of challenges in the broader environment.

It is well recognised that health policy makers throughout the world face three sets of pressures. These are an ageing population, rising expectations and demands, and increasing costs associated with advances in our knowledge about what is possible and may be efficacious (Abel-Smith, 1994; Dargie, 2000). The issue of an ageing population is twofold. First, greater age is associated with increased morbidity (although it can also be argued that this relates to proximity to death rather than age per se), and, second, increasing proportions of retired older people relative to the number of younger people in the workforce from whom taxes are gathered. Whilst the significance of this trend is a contentious issue, the dominant view is that increasing 'dependency ratios' are deeply challenging for policy makers and society. Lister's chapter suggests that over the next 20 years healthcare costs will increase even up to 14 per cent in a twenty-year period; this despite greater use of information technology, new pay and conditions, and efficiency gains associated with work organisation and process design. The UK has the lowest drug costs in Europe but they are increasing, because of increasing research and development costs and increased scrutiny.

Although these are real pressures for health policy makers, they represent an over-simplified view of the social and technological changes which are likely to be relevant to future health policy and, therefore, current planning. This oversimplification arises in part from the seem-

298

ingly inevitable policy focus, highlighted by Yach, on illness and the healthcare system. In considering future health, more attention needs to be given to the wider determinants of health. After all, Bunker (2001) estimates that only one-sixth of health gain can be attributed to health systems. This should not be interpreted to mean that the health system is irrelevant and unimportant; rather that it must be understood as a part of an extremely complex whole.

Monaghan, Huws and Navarro (2003) provide an excellent overview of the wider determinants of health. Besides healthcare services, important factors contributing to health appear to be the environment, lifestyle and hereditary factors now understood through discoveries in genetics. Environmental factors include the pre-natal and subsequent social, psychological, economic and physical environments; for example, social inequality, exposure to hazards and housing quality. Lifestyle factors include diet, substance misuse (including smoking), exercise and so on. Genetic features and biological age are also relevant to health. These two factors are currently least amenable to policy intervention, but have potential significance in the future as genetic diagnostics and therapies evolve. However, as Costa-Font and Mossialos have argued in the preceding chapter, this is an area of considerable complexity where policy makers are required to reconcile divergent values. These concerns also relate to other areas of technological development likely to be of increasing importance for future healthcare; including advances in tissue engineering – potentially invaluable to organ replacement in the ageing population – advances in nanotechnology and so on.

The notion of the wider determinants of health is not, of course, new or under-rehearsed. Yet, it stands repetition because it continues to be largely sidestepped by policy makers, who focus instead on healthcare systems. There may be several reasons for this. Changing the distribution of the determinants of health is very difficult, making it an unattractive option of policy makers. Not only are the determinants of health comprehensive, complex, clustered and interactive, they are also politically sensitive (e.g. redistributive taxation policies) and necessarily longer term than one or even two electoral cycles. However, a brief review of the wider environment in which health policy exists suggests that if the responsibility of governments is health, this shift of focus is necessary.

The UK continues to compare unfavourably with other OECD (2004) countries on nearly all measures of morbidity and mortality. Consistent with most countries, the pattern of disease continues to shift from the young to the old; and from communicable to non-communicable;

lethal to chronic. But there are also some unwelcome anomalies: there has been an increase in communicable disease, such as TB and STD (including HIV infection), and the incidence of mental health problems, including in the young, continues to rise (BMA, 2003; DoH, 2003a; DoH, 2004; National Statistics, 2003). The single greatest cause of avoidable death in the UK, smoking, shows little change in uptake since the 1990s, and alcohol misuse is rising (DoH, 2003b; Strategy Unit, 2004). On the other hand, health gains have been made in accidental death. As the biggest killer of young people, the incidence of accidental death has been reduced by one-third since the early 1990s (National Statistics, 2004).

Health inequalities are widening, and it is likely that this can be explained by increasing inequalities in society generally. Household structures are also polarising with an increasing incidence of single-person households as well as an increase (although only small numbers overall) to three-generation households (Skipton Building Society, 2004). Single-person households are a potential worry, because many such people are older and therefore likely to be in need of care, and because single-person households may also indicate a decline in social capital. Strong social capital is associated with positive health outcomes.

Age and illness both demand higher levels of informal caring. Indeed, the demand for care (the focus of the sister volume, edited by Davies (2003), on workforce issues) seems unstoppable. Wanless estimates the need for a further 300,000 staff by 2022, and Carers UK (2002) estimate a potential shortfall of 2.1 million in informal (and unpaid) carers in 2037. One related trend is the increasing policy focus on 'self-care', 'co-production' (Halpern et al., 2004), 'expert patients', and 'fully engaged patients'. This reflects a new emphasis on the value of personal responsibility, at least on the part of policy makers. There has also been a shift in perceptions of service users, emphasising individualist consumerist values; reflected in the choice agenda discussed by Ian Greener in Chapter 12.

This emphasis on personal responsibilities is predicated on the assumption that health challenges reflect lifestyle choices. However, in order to maximise health, it will be important for governments to recognise that predictive factors lie outside lifestyle factors. Large environmental issues threaten health; for example, ozone depletion continues to contribute to higher rates of skin cancer, and there are increasing numbers of chemicals entering the UK environment (Health Protection Agency, 2004; WWF, 2004). Appropriate solutions are not always obvious. For instance, a switch to diesel fuel has reduced greenhouse gases, but increased particulates (Department for Transport, 2004). Despite some increase in renewable energy, UK governments have yet to show real enthusiasm for environmental measures, with most impetus for change coming from the EU. Thus a recent report from the Sustainable Development Commission (2003) noted that the UK was unlikely to meet its 2010 targets for carbon emissions, that government efforts towards climate change were 'disappointing', and waste management and traffic congestion were 'dreadful'. Recycling rates are the lowest in the pre-accession EU and commuting times the longest (ibid.). This serves to reinforce the general point made by Jochelson in her chapter on sustainability in the NHS, as well as raising a wider question concerning the appropriateness of policy reliance on increased personal responsibility.

In their introduction, Sausman and Dawson characterise the story of the UK health system as one of diversity and change. Such change is illustrated in the increasing divergence in process and outcome following devolution (Greer, 2004). The English health services, for example, have seen increasing complexity with 'plurality', greater use of markets, and the blurring of boundaries with implications for democratic accountability. Relationships are increasingly contract-based and managed through targets and inspection by statutory – as opposed to professional – self-regulating bodies. In 2002, the NHS in England was regulated by five organisations (Walshe, 2002). And there have been changes within changes. For example, inspection bodies include the erstwhile Commission for Health Improvement (CHI), which became the Commission for Healthcare Audit and Inspection (CHAI), and is now the Healthcare Commission. Both Paton and Greer have discussed some of the issues associated with these changes, including the erosion of relationships between the trio of the state, the health professions and the public; and the decline of professional morale and public trust. Furthermore, Greener (2003) has argued elsewhere that constant change makes the health system increasingly difficult for patients to 'calculate'.

Change has been consistently top-led, but often inconsistent. There is also considerable stability (or maybe inertia) within the system. It is still dominated by the NHS, a massive institution still popular with the public despite some decline in trust (Taylor-Gooby and Hastie, 2002), and thereby continuing to be a political hot potato. Politicians seem still not to have understood their role in the process, with each wave of reforms promising better outcomes for everybody. The system is still tax funded, still underfunded compared with other European countries despite significant increases in the recent period, and is still largely health-system focused. There is also inertia within the health system itself. This is most clearly brought out in Chapters 11 and 12 on information technology (IT) by Keen and Wyatt, and Rigby.

Nonetheless, for those engaged in the delivery and management of healthcare, the volume of change, and the tendency for successive initiatives to reflect an anxious Department of Health's desire to micro manage – is too great.

The purpose of this collection of papers was to examine some of the specific changes taking place in UK health organisations and systems, and to raise some new ideas which may be useful in thinking about future health policy. Together, they have raised a series of fundamental issues relating to UK health policy for the future. We identify five inter-related issues for further discussion: values, purpose, democracy and public engagement, relationships, and new opportunities.

The central importance of values in health policy emerges clearly from all chapters. Values influence whether policy makers are willing to refocus their efforts from a health system to a system of health, as advocated by Yach. In health promotion, the roles assigned to the individual, communities and the state are ultimately a question of values. Likewise, questions about the emphasis and style to be given to industrial, professional and technological regulation, social redistributive policies, and public participation, to name just three more hot policy issues also rest on values. Values also influence how the structures and dynamics of the health system are organised, and what care is provided, how and by whom. Thus, Rogers has argued for a more explicit and reflexive consideration of ethics within health policy and delivery. Mark has explored the role of values in modes of care (rational versus emotional), and Paton the role of ideology versus rational technical approaches to policy development. Costa-Font and Mossialos's chapter on public attitudes to biotechnology also reinforces the point, noting that the publics' values have the potential to delay or prevent developments in health technologies.

Owing to the subjective nature of values, smart policy recommendations do not automatically emerge. Yet one standard definition of policy describes it as consisting 'of a web of decisions and actions that allocate ... values' (Easton, 1953:130). It is important for policy makers to keep in mind that values are allocated whether they are explicit or not. Many policy choices are about 'conflicting goods', for example Rogers notes a conflict between harm reduction at the population level and personal autonomy. Pierre and Peters (2000) note that increasingly the state and society are more tightly bound through the process of governance (ibid:49), and this may have advantages for the state. Whilst ceding some power in policy formulation they gain more control over implementation having 'co-opted social interests that might otherwise oppose its actions' (ibid). There is the need for policy makers to engage with stakeholders to assess preferences and to legitimate political choices.

The purpose of the health system ultimately reflects values which are revealed rather than merely stated. At the highest level this is whether health policy is about health or sickness, but in order for parts of the system to maximise their efforts their participants must understand and appreciate their purpose within it. De Rond and Dash note how difficult it is for managers within the NHS to undertake their task because policy is emergent and messy. Paton argues for clearer definitions of the role of primary care, and Keen and Wyatt, and Rigby pick up the point indirectly in explaining why IT has received a lukewarm reception by the health workforce: partly because they do not understand how it can help them do their job more effectively. Mark's chapter, too, makes a strong case for emotional involvement to be given more emphasis within the health service. Part of her argument stems from the idea that the foundation of the NHS had an emotional base; namely to reduce fear of illness and death, and to enhance social cohesion. Given the constant change within the health service, more policy attention needs to be given to defining explicit and consistent purpose.

Emerging from nearly all the chapters is a concern about lack of democratic accountability and a plea for more public engagement in health. Greener addressed this issue directly, exploring patient choice, and concluded that whilst patients welcome more agency, they neither desire nor feel equipped to handle unmediated choice. This raises a whole range of issues for the current policy agenda designed to 'empower' patients. Notwithstanding, there are persuasive arguments for more lay involvement in health, both as public citizens and as patients. For example, Costa-Font and Mossialos note the need for better public understanding of biotechnology to make better policy.

More broadly, the idea of public participation is couched in terms of being the counterpoint to continuing, and detrimental, central government over influence and micro management. Thus, many argue that the health service would benefit from a more localist democratic configuration. Furthermore, this would have the potential to support policy in other arenas such as the rejuvenation of local democracy and civic engagement, the latter, incidentally, being associated with health gains. The problem for policy makers is finding the will to 'let go' and to accept difference, as well as designing effective mechanisms to engage any public,[1] even before ambitiously targeting a representative public rather than the 'usual participants'. In editorials for the *British Medical Journal*, Klein (2003; 2004) highlights the challenges to effective governance built into the *Guide to NHS Foundation Trusts*.[2] First, how will members of boards of governers be elected, so that they are representative? Here Klein asserts 'the first safe predication is that the membership will be unrepresentative ... skewed towards members with intense but possibly atypical views about the NHS'. The second is that 'apathy will rule'. Whilst then Foundation Trusts offer the 'promise of a devolved service' how is 'greater autonomy' for those actually doing the work to be achieved, and within that, what is the preferred model of regulation.

From other evidence we know that participants in any policy or monitoring process are typically older, more affluent and better educated (Beck and Jennings, 1982; Pattie et al., 2002; Whiteley, 2000).[3] According to the British Panel Survey 63 per cent of the poorest fifth in society did not take part in social, political and community organisations, including: trade unions and professional associations, parents' associations, pensioner groups, community and tenant groups, women's groups, religious groups, sports and social groups, and political parties. However, the fact that securing participation is difficult does not mean that it should not be attempted, and recent announcements in the press (HSJ, 2004) to abolish the Commission for Patient and Public Involvement in Health (CPPIH) is unlikely to send positive signals to the public on the value of their participation.

A fourth theme to emerge from many of the chapters is the importance of relationships. The health economy is huge and labour intensive, but also complicated and often conflicted. There is a pervasive view within this collection that both professions and patients are disempowered and tensions between the state and the professions in particular are not being adequately addressed in current arrangements; hence, arguments for greater localisation and more discussion of purpose as opposed to targets. Keen and Wyatt also draw attention to the importance of relationships in policy implementation. They explain the tardy progress in IT within the NHS partly in terms of immature relationships characterised by mistrust and misunderstanding. These issues, as well as conflicting values, are relevant to all relationships and, therefore, policy implementation and should be taken very seriously by policy makers seeking to achieve compliance. This also goes back to Pierre and Peter's point, that whilst engaging key stakeholders in policy formulation might not be welcome to formal policy makers, there are gains to be made in implementation.

The final theme discernible within this collection on future health policy is new (or missed) opportunities. Some of the chapters indicate potentially exciting developments with the potential for making a real difference to health – greater focus on the wider determinants of health and better use of resources – IT, human resources, public and patient engagement and waste management. Yet local initiative is continually challenged, sustainability has not been addressed, the implementation of the National Programme for IT has yet to be seen to realise its potential and policy continues to raise public expectations rather than manage them.

The challenge in going forward is in identifying and reconciling values that can underpin a national system of health. To do this, underpinning values have to be made explicit. Once explicit, they can be reflected in the purposes and structures of organisations. One fear for the future for those working in the health sector must be about still more change which on past experience will not be given sufficient time to become embedded and which will sit uncomfortably alongside other coincidental new developments. However, if key stakeholders are genuinely engaged in a more bottom-up process, if policy is purposive, understood and 'owned', it is less likely to be resisted. Policy makers need to adopt a more sophisticated understanding of policy implementation and change management. In the past, change has also been associated with rising expectations which have then not been meet. They can, and should be managed. Engaging the public can contribute to this process by increasing their understanding of the limits of government capacity.

The themes discussed in this last chapter are fundamental. Policy makers are often frustrated when analysis of policy results in critique of current policy without offering ways forward. However, many of the chapters contained in this volume have offered specific suggestions for the future. Their aim is to contribute to thinking about future UK health policy and patterns of organisation and performance in the context of change in the wider environment, and thereby to make a positive contribution to UK health.

## Notes

1. *The Times*, cited by LGA Information product – Daily Headlines provided by The Local Government Association, Local Government House, Smith Square, London SW1P 3HZ.

2. Department of Health, *A Guide to NHS Foundation Trusts*, DOS, September 2002
3. http://www.poverty.org.uk/41a/b.pdf.

# References

Abel-Smith, B. (1994) *An Introduction to Health: policy, planning and financing.* London: Longman

Beck, P. and Jennings, M. (1982) 'Pathways to participation', *American Political Science Review,* **76**:94–108

BMA 2003 *Adolescent Health.* London: British Medical Association Board of Science and Education, 56

Bunker, J. (2001) *Medicine Matters After All: measuring the benefits of medical care, a healthy lifestyle, and a just social environment.* London: The Nuffield Trust

Carers UK (2002) *Without Us ...? Calculating the value of carers' support.* London: Carers UK

Dargie, C. (2000) *2000 Report.* London: The Nuffield Trust

Department for Transport (2004) *Driving Force: four fifths of distance travelled is by car.* National Statistics

DoH (2003a) *Indicators of the Nation's Health: Female/male death rates by selected causes – 1996–2001.* London: Department of Health

DoH (2003b) *Statistical Bulletin.* London: Department of Health

DoH (2004) *Choosing Health? A Consultation On Action To Improve People's Health.* London: Department of Health

Easton, D. (1953) *The Political System.* New York: Knopf

Greener, I. (2003) 'Patient choice in the NHS: the view from economic sociology', *Social Theory and Health,* **1**:72–89

Greer, S. (2004) *Four Way Bet: How devolution has led to four different models for the NHS.* London: UCL

Halpern, D., Bates, C., Beales, G. and Healthfield, A. (2004*) Personal Responsibility and Changing Behaviour: the state of knowledge and its implications for public policy.* London: Strategy Unit

Health Protection Agency (2004) *Chemicals and Poisons*

HSJ (2004) 'HAD first to face axe in arm's-length review', 1 July: 3

Klein, R. (2003) 'Governance for NHS Foundation Trusts', *BMJ,* **326**, 25 January, 174–5

Klein, R. (2004) 'The first wave of NHS Foundation Trusts', *BMJ,* **328**, 1332

Monaghan, S., Huws, D. and Navarro, M. (2003) *The Case for a New UK Health of the People Act.* London: The Nuffield Trust

National Statistics (2003) *HIV and Aids*

National Statistics, (2004) *Accidental Deaths*

OECD (2004) *Health At A Glance. OECD Indicators 2004*

Pattie, C., Seyd, P. and Whiteley, P. (2002) 'Citizenship and civic engagement: attitudes and behaviour', Paper presented to the *Political Studies Association Annual Conference,* University of Aberdeen, 5–7 April 2002

Pierre, J. and Peters, B.G. (2000) *Governance, Politics and the State. Political Analysis.* Basingstoke: Macmillan – now Palgrave Macmillan

Skipton Building Society (2004) *Financing Your Future*. Skipton: Skipton Building Society

Strategy Unit (2004) *Alcohol Harm Reduction Strategy For England*. London: Cabinet Office, 100

Sustainable Development Commission (2003) *UK Climate Change Programme: a policy audit*. London: Sustainable Development Commission

Taylor-Gooby, P. and Hastie, C. (2002) 'Support for state spending: has New Labour got it right?' in *British and European Social Attitudes. How Britain Differs. 19th Report*. Aldershot: Ashgate

Walshe, K. (2002) 'The rise of regulation in the NHS', *BMJ*, **324**:967–70, 20 April

Whiteley, P. (2000), 'Economic growth and social capital', *Political Studies*. **48**, 3:551–4

WWF (2004) *Chemicals and Health Campaign*. London: World Wildlife Foundation

# Index